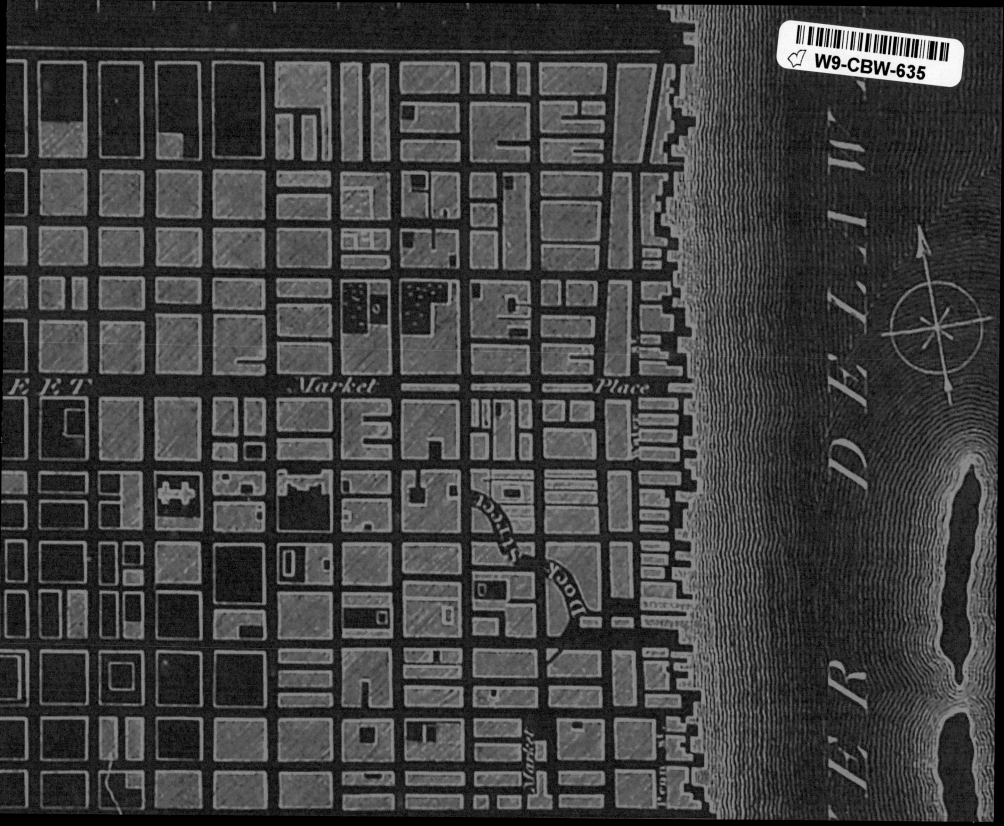

THE Vendue MASTERS

TALES FROM WITHIN THE WALLS
OF AMERICA'S OLDEST AUCTION HOUSE

Roland Arkell &

Catherine Saunders-Watson

ANTIQUE
COLLECTORS'
CLUB

ISBN 10: 1 85149 490 1

ISBN 13: 978 1 85149 490 3

British Library Cataloguing-in-Publication Data

A catalogue record for this book is available from the British Library

Design and layout by Graham Scott and Eddie Hams

Printed in the United States of America by Bentley Graphic Communications, Pottstown, Pennsylvania for the Antique Collectors' Club Ltd., Woodbridge, Suffolk

Thanks to:

Beau Freeman and his staff at Samuel T. Freeman & Co., especially Bill Cooper, for the many hours he spent at a microfilm viewer;

Pat Morfesis, for her thorough editing and proof checking; and

Stephanie Welch for holding it all together;

the staff at the Library Company of Philadelphia, particularly those in the Print Department where so many images were sourced;

the Newspaper and Database Center at the Free Library of Philadelphia;

the staff at the Historical Society of Pennsylvania;

Phil Weimerskirch at Providence Public Library, Rhode Island, for his information about Tristram Freeman's printing works;

Karie Diethorn, chief curator at Independence National Historical Park for her comments on the 'Franklin' desk;

Dr. Glenys Waldman, Librarian of the Masonic Library and Museum of Pennsylvania

Linda Reis and the staff of the State Archives in Harrisburg for help in the John Nicholson Papers and The Charter of Liberties;

Sue Wright for research pertaining to the Freeman family at Christ Church in Philadelphia;

Stephen Thomas at Achievements, Canterbury, Kent, for research pertaining to the Freeman family in London;

Sonnie Sussel for her insightful recollections of her late father-in-law, Arthur J. Sussel;

to the journalists, editors and diarists of the 18th, 19th and 20th centuries whose documentation of people and events in Philadelphia provided the essential groundwork for this book;

and to the photographers who have captured the images used in the production of this book:

Elizabeth Field,

Steve Sharp,

Brent Wahl,

Jason Hickey.

Contents

ONE HUNDRED AND NINETEEN YEARS AGO—

Auctions in the Old Coffee House

IN 1805, Tristram B. Freeman, soaring in the vital spirit of enterprise then abroad in the young Nation, applied for and obtained from the Governor of Pennsylvania a license to trade as an auctioneer in the city of Philadelphia. This step marked the inauguration of an enterprise which has survived without interruption for four generations from father to son, and has remained intimately associated with the civic and commercial life of Philadelphia for more than a century.

The first sales of T. B. Freeman were conducted in one of those picturesque institutions, now unhappily extinct—coffee houses. For a number of years his sales were cried under the kindly shelter of the London Coffee House, which stood on the southwest corner of Front and Market streets, then the busy center of the city's commercial life.

TODAY THIS BUILDING—

Specially Designed for Auctions—

ON JUNE 30, the auction business of Samuel T. Freeman & Company, lineal descendant of the auctions at the coffee house, will occupy its new building at 1808-10 Chestnut Street, a structure which crowns fittingly the achievement of more than a century of continuous activity in the interests of a greater Philadelphia.

The new structure is perfectly designed and equipped for its purpose. It incorporates every improvement that the experience of 119 years could suggest in Auction Service. Among its features an art gallery, dignified, tasteful, splendidly furnished and lighted; a salesroom for furniture, beautifully proportioned and decorated; and other salesrooms devoted exclusively to transactions in real estate, special sales of merchandise, etc. Nothing has been left undone to make it the most complete, practical and luxurious Auction Store in the country.

Samuel T. Freeman & Co.

ESTABLISHED NOVEMBER 12, 1805

After July 1st located at

1808-1810 Chestnut Street

*Facsimile of
First Circular*

*Tristram B. Freeman
Founder*

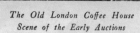

*The Old London Coffee House
Scene of the Early Auctions*

The New Home of
Samuel T. Freeman & Co.

Where, with more space and added facilities at its command, the firm of Samuel T. Freeman & Company, will be in a position more appropriately to carry on the traditions of forward-looking enterprise which have characterized its activities for over a century.

"One Hundred and Nineteen Years Ago." By the 1920s Samuel T. Freeman & Co., was beginning to use longevity to its advantage. This promotional handbill produced shortly after the move to 1808 Chestnut Street in 1924, includes reproductions of a T.B. Freeman circular and the founder's portrait. The text suggests that Freeman's early sales in 1805 were "cried under the kindly shelter of the Old London Coffee House" although in fact few auctions had been conducted there after the 1790s and the construction of the City Tavern.

I was delighted when asked by the publishers to contribute to this book, not simply because a bicentenary is cause for reflection and congratulation but because those of us who earn a living within the art and antiques trade all owe more than a small debt to the auction business.

On one level the essence of the auction process has changed little over two centuries. The term "vendue master" may no longer be with us but the following pages remind us that the successful 21st century auctioneer shares so many of the same qualities with the men such as Tristram Bampfylde Freeman who plied the trade of "sale by public outcry" in the early 19th century. Great auctioneers are some of the great networkers in society. They are keenly aware of the community and the age in which they live, and their places of work remain as important to the day-to-day running of towns and cities as church and school. Popularity has not always been forthcoming but the auction process appeals now for the same reasons it did then. Addison B. Freeman, Tristram B. Freeman's great grandson and the wordsmith in the family lineage, would sum it up best: "Auction sales," he said, "appeal to two deep-seated human failings – the desire to get something at a bargain price and the competitive instinct."

And yet, as Roland Arkell and Catherine Saunders-Watson chronicle the many ages of the auction business in Philadelphia, seismic change is clear. So many companies failed to make it through the upheavals of three major wars, economic depressions, industrial and technological change, competition, tragedy and the uncertain mix that is family blood and family business. What Freeman's has consistently demonstrated across seven long-lived generations is its ability to adapt, morph and sometimes reinvent itself, to face the challenges and take the opportunities 200 years have provided. It has taken the firm from the mercantile city docks and naval yards of Philadelphia to the cotton mills of Depression-hit Massachusetts, the fading mansions of West Palm Beach and now into the global marketplace. It is surely not fanciful to say that Freeman's, born within a few years of the Revolution, has grown up with America.

I am reminded of a quotation made by H.G. Wells in 1932. "History," he wrote, "is like a kipper with all the guts cleaned out ... We get all the Gladstones and Lincolns and Ramsay MacDonalds and such, and nothing about the booms and slumps and Krupps and Zaharoffs and suchlike realities." Well among the extraordinary events that stud the 200-year history of Samuel T. Freeman & Co., we catch a glimpse of the true character of the region, learn how the small man reacted to the bigger picture and mark the ebb and flow of the assets of a community. I am left wondering is there a better repository of social and economic history than the auction room?

On a personal note I was struck by how often the following pages highlight the continuing links between America and Britain that are so redolent in the art and antique world.

As the second city of the empire, Philadelphia took its artistic, philosophical and economic inspiration from London and it was from the Old World capital that T.B. Freeman and his family journeyed in 1795. Today, the transatlantic ties are as strong as ever and particularly so at Freeman's. The company has an English president and, as someone who is very proud of her Scottish heritage, I can only applaud the success of an international alliance with the Edinburgh saleroom Lyon and Turnbull, and the two companies' rapidly developing reputations as a significant force in the international marketplace.

JUDITH MILLER, SEPTEMBER 2005

The boardroom at 1808 Chestnut Street, home of America's oldest auction house. President Paul Roberts, who first visited Samuel T, Freeman & Co., in 1996, describes this room with its portraits of seven generations of the Freeman family, as the home of American auctioneering and Philadelphia's least-lauded historical site.

A six-story building on the eighteenth block of Chestnut Street is not a place you will find listed in any visitor's guidebook to Philadelphia. In Franklin's Town, where so many of the nation's most venerable and most worthy institutions are celebrated, it frequently goes unnoticed that here resides America's longest established firm of auctioneers.

And yet behind this handsome 1920's Beaux Arts façade lies something quite unique. Because if we really want to experience the life-cycle of a community, then the auction house – or the vendue store as it would have also been known in the late 18th century – is the place to be. It is here, buried among the archives of bought and sold merchandise, that we encounter the true character of a community: the estranged relationships, the waxing and waning of economic fortune, the debtors, the creditors, the personalities and the changing faces of taste and fashion. And at Samuel T. Freeman & Co. of Philadelphia, America's oldest auction house, those archives now date back two full centuries.

Paul Roberts first visited 1808-10 Chestnut Street in 1996. It had been 192 years since another Englishman, a failed printseller from London by the name of Tristram

Bampfylde Freeman, had first been appointed to the office of auctioneer in Philadelphia. Roberts had read his name in the company literature and liked the title "America's oldest auctioneer."

However, he had also learned Freeman's was in the final throes of an unhappy ten-year partnership with a previous competitor. A merger with Fine Arts of Philadelphia in 1988 had been designed to assure the venerable company's future in a rapidly changing auction market. In fact, conflicting ideas and clashing personalities had seemingly come quite close to achieving the opposite result. As an executive of the world's third-largest auction company, it was his business to know these things.

The red flag of auction day was flying outside. Making his way through the massive iron gates at 1808-10 Chestnut Street, his first sight had been a gentleman holding forth in a ground floor gallery of decaying grandeur. Gavel in hand, wearing a polka-dot bow tie, he was selling a rough and tumble sale of typical estate merchandise from a traveling rostrum. Roberts casually inquired at the reception desk as to the name of the auctioneer. "That's Beau Freeman – a direct descendant

of the founder of this company." They didn't know it at the time, but the two men were to see a lot of each other in the succeeding eight years.

Roberts was ushered into the elevator, the type with two sliding gates that requires an attendant, and then into a small room situated on the fifth floor of the building. "The Freeman's boardroom," gestured the company chairman. His guest was captivated. To one side of the room, a handsome chimneypiece carved from white marble mined in nearby King of Prussia, to the other a wall hung with framed letters in 18th century handwriting and fragments of early Philadelphia newspapers.

But perhaps what most captured his imagination, the most tangible reminder of America's long auction history, were the imposing oil portraits of redoubtable gentlemen, each of them representing a different epoch in the history of this firm but all sharing the same name and profession. Who were these men? For Roberts, this surely was Philadelphia's least-lauded historical site.

Vendue (vahn-doo)

A PUBLIC SALE OF ANYTHING, BY OUTCRY, TO THE HIGHEST BIDDER, AN AUCTION

Vendue master

ONE WHO IS AUTHORIZED TO SELL ANY PROPERTY BY VENDUE, AN AUCTIONEER

SOURCE: **WEBSTER'S REVISED UNABRIDGED DICTIONARY,** 1913

Early Days

CHAPTER ONE

Covent Garden Market Looking Eastward, an anonymous engraving of
Covent Garden's Italian-style piazza, circa 1786.

"At a crisis so interesting as the present, when Europe convulsed with intestine
commotions can no longer attend to the blandishments of taste, an attempt to
cherish [the arts] in the new world, cannot but merit a general approbation; for this
purpose has the manufactory been established, and although it may not offer at the
present moment, more than the production of European eminence and skill, yet it
contemplates, at no distant period bringing forward artists in this country, that will
convince the rest of mankind that America is their equal in elegance and taste, as
much so, as she has been found their equal in liberality and public spirit."

FREEMAN & CO., FEDERAL GAZETTE, MARCH 11, 1796

T.B. Freeman (1767-1842). This copy of a portrait by Jacob Eichholtz is one of several portraits of the founder of the company painted during his Masonic career. The commission was recorded by William Dunlap in his *History of the Rise and Progress of the Arts of Design in the United States*, first published in 1834. "Mr. T. B. Freeman informs me that in 1821 he saw at Harrisburgh a portrait by Eichholtz, which excited his curiosity; and going to Lancaster, he called upon him, and invited him to Philadelphia, where the first portrait he painted was Freeman's, and soon afterwards Commodore Gale's."

Morning, an engraving after William Hogarth showing the rich tapestry of life outside Tom King's Coffee House in Covent Garden. The austere classical building to the right is the 17th century St. Paul's Church designed by Inigo Jones that, although ravaged by fire in 1795, was restored and still stands today. Tristram Bampfylde Freeman and his wife Sarah Sophia Gibbard were married there on March 29, 1788.

"Although [the manufactory] may not offer at the present moment, more than the production of European eminence and skill ... it contemplates ... bringing forward artists in this country, that will convince the rest of mankind that America is their equal in elegance and taste, as much so, as she has been found their equal in liberality and public spirit."

It was with these words that Tristram Bampfylde Freeman launched his first solo business activities in Philadelphia. But it was not as an auctioneer; it was as a pioneering printer. And it was not as an American, but as an Englishman.

The founder of the Philadelphia auction business that now enters its third century was born into a good Georgian family in London in 1767 – his grandfather the scion of an old Devonshire noble family, his father a man of the cloth, his brother an officer in the British army. He had been raised in the Anglican faith and educated for the pulpit but, rejecting the life his father had planned for him, printing became T.B. Freeman's trade.

In 1787 – the year the Constitution was cast in the city that would become his home – we find one Tristram Bampfylde Freeman trading alone as a printseller and engraver, close to the market square in central London's Covent Garden. In among the lodging houses, the Turkish baths and the brothels – magistrate Sir John Fielding dubbed this quarter of London "The Great Square of Venus" – the Freeman print shop at 22 Henrietta Street was one of many small-time printing firms strategically positioned to provide the broadsides, woodcuts, engravings and pamphlets for the nearby auditoria of the theater district. By coincidence, his neighbors on York Street included a book auctioneer established in 1744, Messrs. Leigh and Sotheby.

It was as a printer in the new medium of aquatints that Freeman had sought to carve a niche. The process – its earliest practitioners were the French – had been refined in England at the time of the American Revolutionary War by the artist Paul Sandby, who had coined the term that ably described the medium's pleasing capacity to recreate the tonal complexities of watercolor and ink. The survival of topographical aquatints by T.B. Freeman from the late 1780s put him among the pioneers of the process, although he was not "the original inventor of picturesque printing" he would claim during his early days on the other side of the Atlantic.

The first Freeman business venture in London was to be short-lived, and its memory survives only in a bankruptcy

St. Martin-in-the-Fields, the Westminster church where Tristram and Sarah Freeman's first child Henry Gibbard was baptized on May 7, 1789. The famous church, now situated on the edge of Trafalgar Square, was designed by James Gibbs, and consecrated in 1726.

Federal Gazette, June 6, 1795. In a newspaper bristling with references to the political issues of the time – Hamilton's excise tax on whiskey, Jay's Treaty with the British, the unfolding drama of the French Revolution – is this small notice from Freeman, Annesley & Co. It announces the imminent opening of a store at the corner of Vine and Second Streets for the sale of recently imported prints and locally-made looking glasses and composition architectural ornaments.

record filed on June 28, 1788, just months after he had married Sarah Sophia Gibbard. Masonic biographies of the man whose portrait hangs among the Grand Masters at Masonic Temple on North Broad Street would refer to her as a second wife he had met while in Philadelphia, but marriage records at the Church of St. Pauls, Covent Garden confirm the union took place on March 29, 1788. Both blessed with extraordinary longevity, they would remain together until Tristram Freeman died, exactly 44 years to the day they had wed.

Their first child was Henry Gibbard, baptized at the church of St. Martins-in-the-Fields in nearby Westminster on May 7, 1789. The second, another son, Tristram William Lockyer Freeman, was born sometime in 1792 and was baptized at St. Clement Danes, Westminster on May 7, 1793. By then the T.B. Freeman printing operation had moved to the southern edge of Covent Garden and was trading at 95 Strand. Then, as now, the thoroughfare was dominated by the sumptuous neo-classical office block Somerset House, but at the end of the 18th century, it stood cheek by jowl with slum dwellings that were the notorious haunts of prostitutes and pickpockets. At its Fleet Street end, Strand teamed with engravers, printers and bookbinders, including Freeman and Co., whose innovative experiments in

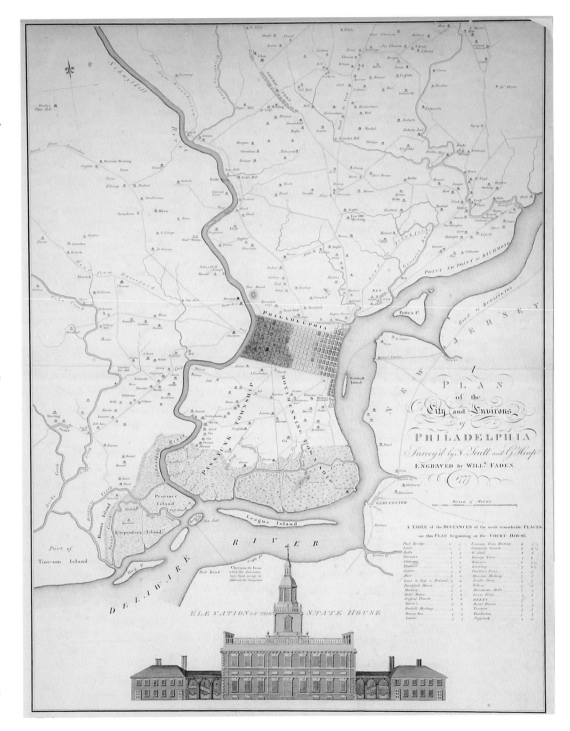

A Plan of the City and Environs of Philadelphia Survey'd by N. Scull and G. Heap, engraved by William Faden, 1777. Inset is an elevation of the State House.

"picturesque printing" had recently earned the patronage of the royal household of King George III and led to contacts in Germany and the United States. However, the boast "printsellers to King George III" – it was one he would repeat when T.B. Freeman moved to America – did not occasion great longevity for Freeman and Co. of London. By January 20, 1795, Tristram Bampfylde Freeman, age 32, was heavily in debt with two failed businesses behind him. Sarah had given him a daughter, Sarah Oldnixon Freeman, and was expecting the child they would name James Phillips Freeman. For a better future they would join the tide of European migrants making a new life in America.

*   *   *

It appears the Freeman family completed the uncomfortable eight-week voyage from Liverpool to Philadelphia sometime in the spring of 1795. The city they encountered was at the very peak of its eminence. It had been born out of the ideals envisioned by William Penn in his Charter of Liberties – the very document that Tristram's descendents would sell in 1924 – but the utopia most of its 60,000 citizens sought was economic rather than religious. Looking out across a splendid natural harbor were the vehicles of trade, and outside the city limits were the fertile soils that had been the

"Good workmen who will meet with constant employment and good wages." The first published reference to Tristram Freeman in Philadelphia appears in this small ad in the *Federal Gazette* dated May 25, 1795.

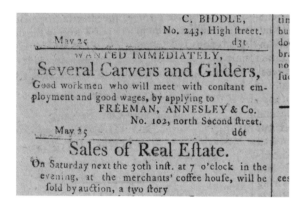

breadbasket of the colonies. The urban infrastructure itself, its curious rectilinear design and poplar-lined streets provided a stark contrast to the winding streets of medieval Europe. The city had earned the praise of many a foreign visitor who admired the sidewalks of cobbles, bricks or flagstones illuminated by lamps of whale oil, the set pieces of neoclassical architecture by a promising architect named William Thornton and rows of tidy, red brick houses trimmed by blue-toned Schuylkill marble. There was also disease, poverty, filth and class-consciousness. But with so many new faces in town, there was social mobility way beyond anything in Europe.

The earliest published reference to T.B. Freeman in America appears in the May 25, 1795 edition of the *Federal Gazette*. It suggests he wasted little time before completing the transition from English bankrupt to American entrepreneur.

Following a meeting with a group of Philadelphia worthies, T.B. Freeman entered into a business arrangement with William Moulder Jr., the son of a Philadelphia tea commissioner; and John Nicholson, the former Comptroller General turned land speculator whose widely spread business interests included investments in a number of early American manufacturing ventures. Nicholson had corresponded

with Freeman, discussing business ideas, before his emigration. Together with a group of other investors, they agreed to establish perhaps the first color printing works in Philadelphia and to plow money into the ailing firm of Annesley & Co., a manufactory of composition chimney pieces, architectural moldings and picture frames located at 47 Walnut Street.

Appealing in the press for carvers and gilders, the shop of Freeman, Annesley & Co., opened on the corner of Vine and Second in June 1795. It would offer "an elegant assortment of the newest London prints of recent importation" and "a variety of elegant-looking glasses and girandoles of all patterns," with the note: "The above firm will be conducted by a partner who has long been a publisher in London ... who is the original inventor of picturesque printing."

By November 1795, Annesley had been been bought out of the partnership and the first American incarnation of Freeman & Co. was brought into being. The new firm was selling "looking glasses, gerandoles [sic], chimney pieces and various composition ornaments" from a retail store at the south end of the city "next door below the custom house." The enterprise was also wholesaling prints from a workshop at 68 North Third Street. At the time, engravers were in short supply in Philadelphia, but the

A half-length portrait of John Nicholson, by Charles Willson Peale, circa 1790.

Born in Wales, John Nicholson emigrated to Philadelphia prior to the American Revolution and engaged in a variety of business enterprises, including button, iron, and glass manufacturing, and real estate development. His first government position was as clerk to the Board of Treasury of the Continental Congress in 1778, but in 1781 he opted to enter the service of the Commonwealth as one of the auditors for settling the accounts of the Pennsylvania Line. A year later, the new position Office of Comptroller General gave him broad powers to manage the financial affairs of the state. In 1785 he was authorized to collect and receive taxes and, in 1787, he was also made Escheator General with the power to liquidate the estates of those found guilty of treason. The brilliant Welshman had proved a mercurial money man at a time when his state needed a firm hand on the tiller, but – demonstrating a propensity for testing the boundaries of the proper and the possible – he had left the State House of Representatives under the cloud of impeachment and the small matter of $60,000 in federal securities that he allegedly diverted. He was acquitted after a protracted trial at the State Senate and, in 1794, resigned all his public offices to pursue a career in business.

An early example of the wares of Freeman & Co., the figure of
Meekness from a series based on The Three Graces, published in
August 1796.

proprietors were "in daily expectation of the arrival of one of the finest artists in Europe" and were "putting up presses for the printing of 18 new plates ... printed in colours as plain, by a partner in the concern whose abilities procured him the appointment of picturesque printer to the King of Great-Britain."

The manufacture of a new press had presented considerable difficulties. "Had I known you could not get [color] presses in America, I would have brought one for you and sent parts by different vessels," Freeman had written to Nicholson shortly after his arrival. The doors were not opened for inspection until March 11, 1796, when Tristram Freeman took his large advertisement in the *Federal Gazette* to issue his impassioned plea to buy American.

Bringing his technological advancements to a growing market for sophisticated popular prints, Freeman seems to have been the first American firm to make a specialty of printing in color. He certainly published some of the earliest aquatints printed on American soil.

Among those in his employ were George Isham Parkyns (circa 1749-1820), a Nottingham-born painter and engraver for whom aquatints were a specialty. Working in London from 1791-95, he had created 26 plates to accompany John Soane's *Sketches in Architecture* (it is among the earliest English architectural books to feature aquatint engravings), and in America he would produce the first topographical engraving of a small settlement on the mosquito-infested banks of the Potomac, titled *Washington, D.C.*

He was working with Freeman & Co. during the production of "a series of Interesting American Characters" and "Four Views in America" titled: *Philadelphia from Kensington, New York from Brooklin* (sic.), *Baltimore from Fell's Point* and *The Federal City from George-Town*. Some of these prints were sold locally at retail or wholesale, while others were sent to neighboring cities to be sold at auction. "The impressions came out better than ever and with less trouble to the boys," Freeman wrote to Nicholson in 1797. "I could print off a quantity and sell them at vendues in Baltimore, New York and other cities on the continent where they have not been seen and would bring a better price."

However, Freeman's most celebrated charge was the portrait engraver David Edwin (1776-1841), who solicited work from Freeman & Co. upon his arrival from England in December 1797.

During his celebrated career, Edwin – dubbed "the first good engraver of the human countenance, that appeared

Thespian Oracle or *Monthly Mirror consisting of original pieces and selections from performances of merit, relating chiefly to the most admired dramatic compositions and interspersed with theatrical anecdotes.*

Despite its roots in Quaker doctrine, Philadelphia enjoyed the constant coming and going of London stage companies to its Chestnut Street Theatre in the late 18th century.

Another product Freeman would bring with him from London was the theatrical review. Drawing upon his experiences of the theater and theatrical periodicals gleaned in Covent Garden, London, T.B. Freeman edited and published the January 1798 *Thespian Oracle* or *Monthly Mirror*, for which David Edwin was to supply a series of theatrical portraits of leading tragic and comedic actors and actresses. Apparently, only one edition of the monthly was published, and it is considered the first theatrical review produced in America.

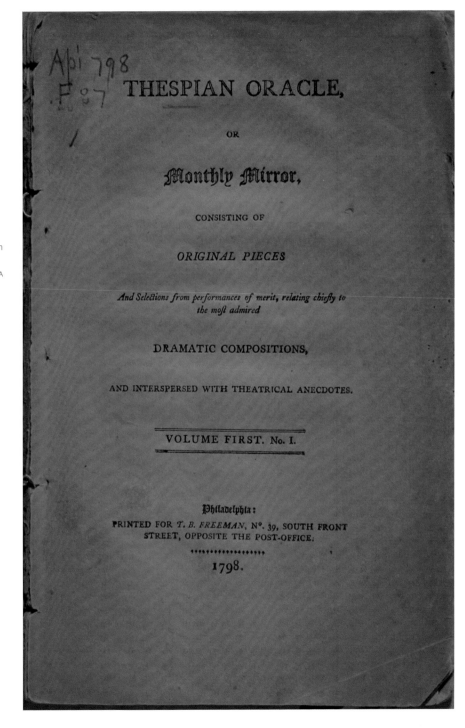

THESPIAN ORACLE,

OR

Monthly Mirror,

CONSISTING OF

ORIGINAL PIECES

And Selections from performances of merit, relating chiefly to the most admired

DRAMATIC COMPOSITIONS,

AND INTERSPERSED WITH THEATRICAL ANECDOTES.

VOLUME FIRST. No. I.

Philadelphia:

PRINTED FOR *T. B. FREEMAN*, N°. 39, SOUTH FRONT STREET, OPPOSITE THE POST-OFFICE.

1798.

A Freeman & Co. notice from the front page of Benjamin Franklin's
Aurora, dated June 7, 1796 announces the publication of a print of
General Anthony Wayne, the first in "a series of Interesting
American Characters." The print was priced at $2.50 in black and
$5 in color.

in this country" – would work with the best-known
painters and immortalize the great and the good of his
day. However, born in Bath, England, and apprenticed
from a young age to the Dutch engraver Christian Josi in
both London and Amsterdam, his first engravings
executed on American soil were for the print shop of
Tristram B. Freeman.

Remarkably, via William Dunlap's *History of the Rise and
Progress of the Arts of Design in the United States*, colorful
first-hand accounts of Edwin's stay at No. 40 South
Water Street have survived. Dunlap describes "facilities
so rude that, having just come from the professional
centres of London and Amsterdam, [Edwin] must have
felt that he had quite reached the frontiers of civilization."
New tools had to be fashioned, plates "finished rough
from the hammer" and, worst of all, the printing work had
to be conducted in cold weather on a crude press, in a
workshop that "was little better than a shell, and open to
the winds." A stark contrast, indeed, to the vistas of an
attractive and prosperous Philadelphia we know from the
engravings of William Birch.

But Edwin did overcome these obstacles. He first set to
work on the title page of a collection of Scottish airs by
Benjamin Carr titled *In fancy of the Scottish Muse*, and had
completed a new print of George Washington in his

trademark stipple technique by February 1798, in good
time for the observance of the ex-President's birthday. It
was sold together with the likeness of John Adams
"elegantly framed in best burnish gold frames, with
enamel glasses at six dollars the pair; printed in colours
on white satin at eight dollars." Edwin would
subsequently produce for his patron a series of portraits
for a publication now recognized as the first American
theatrical review in 1798.

As they went their separate ways, the two men would
remain in contact. In the early 1830s, as the artist's
health failed, Freeman would briefly employ Edwin as a
clerk in his auction house.

However, despite its importance to the history of
American printing, the enterprise did not turn a profit.
Letters from Tristram Freeman to John Nicholson
chronicle a tale of woe: a business unable to pay its
workforce, a family without money for firewood and a
man living in fear of debtor's prison.

T.B. Freeman wrote to Nicholson at his temporary
residence in the new Federal City in November 1796: "My
situation is deplorable (expecting very imminent arrest)
and the continual application of those friends to return
what they so kindly lent ... induce me to part with my

More than eight years before his appointment to the position of auctioneer in Philadelphia, T.B. Freeman was well acquainted with the culture of selling at auction. This 1797 broadside promotes an auction of "a large and valuable collection of prints and paintings" plus items of furniture to be conducted at the store of Freeman & Co., at 68 North Third Street on April 22. The auctioneer was William Shannon. The line in small print "Seats and accommodations in the room will be rendered more convenient for ladies and gentleman than on the last evening's sale" confirms that this was not the first auction conducted on the premises.

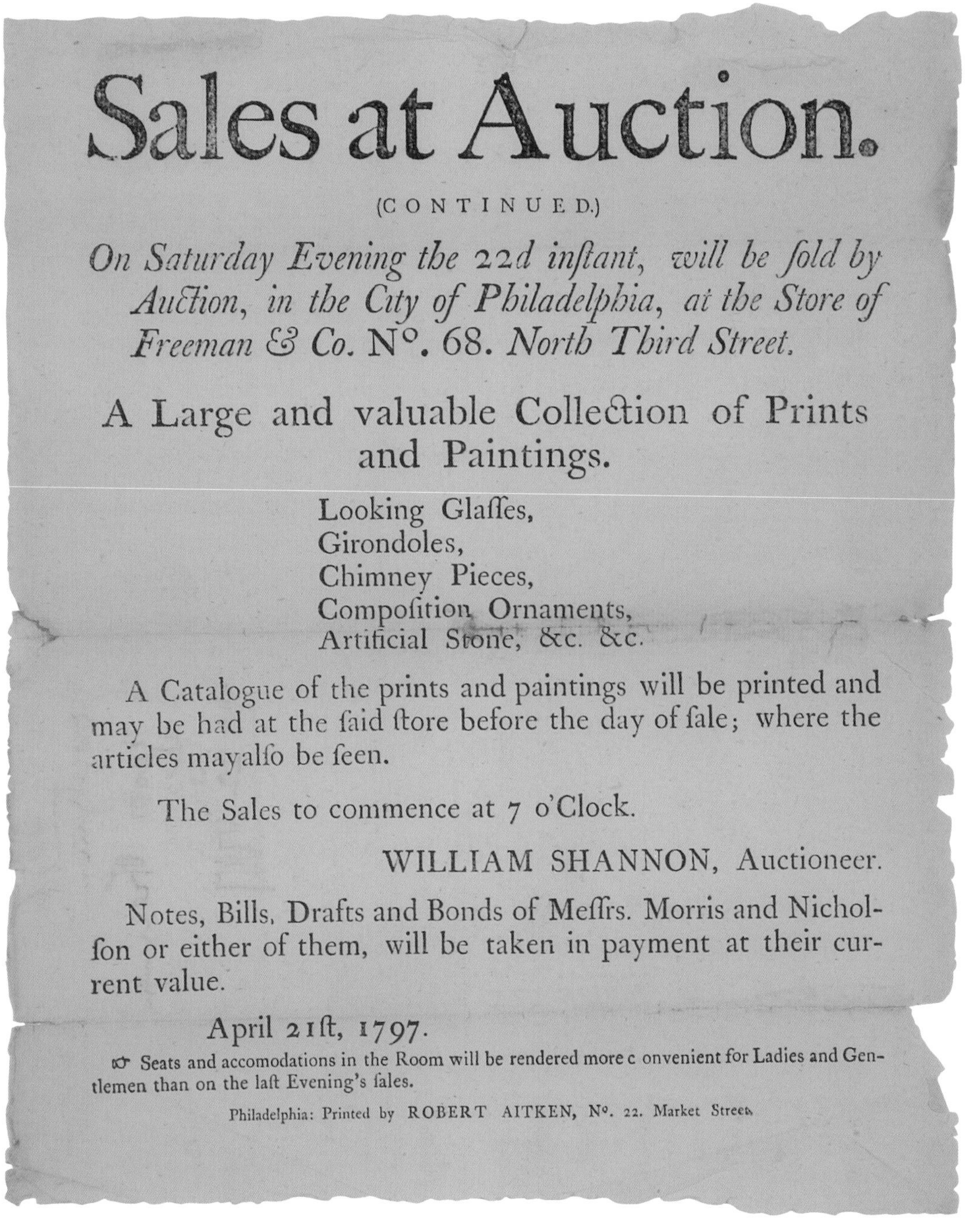

Sales at Auction.

(CONTINUED.)

On Saturday Evening the 22d instant, will be sold by Auction, in the City of Philadelphia, at the Store of Freeman & Co. Nº. 68. North Third Street.

A Large and valuable Collection of Prints and Paintings.

Looking Glasses,
Girondoles,
Chimney Pieces,
Composition Ornaments,
Artificial Stone, &c. &c.

A Catalogue of the prints and paintings will be printed and may be had at the said store before the day of sale; where the articles may also be seen.

The Sales to commence at 7 o'Clock.

WILLIAM SHANNON, Auctioneer.

Notes, Bills, Drafts and Bonds of Messrs. Morris and Nicholson or either of them, will be taken in payment at their current value.

April 21st, 1797.

☞ Seats and accomodations in the Room will be rendered more c onvenient for Ladies and Gentlemen than on the last Evening's sales.

Philadelphia: Printed by ROBERT AITKEN, Nº. 22. Market Street.

TREASURY DEPARTMENT, *August* 8, 1796.

PUBLIC NOTICE is HEREBY GIVEN,

IN purfuance of an Act of Congrefs paffed on the 18th day of May, 1796, entitled "An Act providing "for the Sale of the Lands of the United States, in the Territory north weft of the river, Ohio, and above "the Mouth of Kentucky river," that the Quarter Townfhips of Land defcribed in the annexed Schedule lying in the feven ranges of Townfhips, which were furveyed in purfuance of an ordinance of Congrefs paffed on the twentieth day of May, in the year one thoufand feven hundred and eighty five, will be expofed for fale at PUBLIC VENDUE, at the Merchants' Coffee-Houfe in Philadelphia, on the 4th day of January next, and thenceforward from day to day, until the tenth day of February enfuing, unlefs the faid quarter townfhips fhall be fooner fold, in the manner and on the terms and conditions hereinafter mentioned :

1ft. The faid quarter townfhips fhall be fold to the higheft bidder, but no fale can be made for lefs than two dollars per acre of the quantity of Land contained in fuch quarter townfhip.

2d. The higheft bidder as before mentioned, muft depofit at the time of fale, one twentieth part of the purchafe money, in the hands of the Treafurer of the United States, which will be forfeited if a moiety of the fum bid, including the faid twentieth part, fhall not be paid within thirty days from the time of fale.

3d. Upon payment of a moiety of the purchafe money in the manner before mentioned, the purchafer will be entitled to one year's credit for the remaining moiety ; and fhall receive a certificate defcribing the quarter townfhip purchafed, and declaring the fum paid on account, the balance remaining due, the time when fuch balance becomes payable, and that the whole Land therein mentioned, will be forfeited, if the faid balance is not then paid ; but if the faid balance fhall be duly difcharged, by paying the fame to the Treafurer of the United States, the purchafer or his affignee or other legal reprefentative fhall be entitled to a patent for the faid Lands, on his producing to the Secretary of State a receipt for fuch balance endorfed upon the certificate. But if any purchafer fhall make payment of the whole of the purchafe money at the time when the payment of the firft moiety is directed to be made, he will be entitled to a deduction of ten per centum on the part for which a credit is authorized to be given ; and his patent fhall be immediately iffued.

GIVEN under my hand at Philadelphia the day and year abovementioned.

OLIVER WOLCOTT,
Secretary of the Treafury.

interest – about 1,000 dollars would in some measure enable me to pay engagements of the most solemn nature as well as to provide for my family."

To generate funds, Freeman & Co. turned to William Shannon to dispose of its mounting unsold stock. He was one of the city's best-known auctioneers. During the spring of 1797, Shannon would conduct a series of sales from the Third Street store to offload "a large and valuable collection of prints and paintings and a valuable collection of American Manufactures, at whatever prices may be offered." The bankruptcy sale, Freeman & Co., would learn firsthand, is the auction process at its most utilitarian, and T.B. Freeman was unhappy with the lowly prices realized. "I have taken many of the prints myself," he wrote on August 7, 1797. "I think it would be a pity to sacrifice them by public sale, as they would bring little more than the value of the case."

As Freeman & Co. had folded in July, Tristram Freeman was saddled with substantial debts: "As of this moment it is impossible for me to describe the miserable situation into which I have plunged. I can no longer show my face in this city and … have in mind to leave Philadelphia for New York." As he defaulted on repayments, his possessions were seized and sold at marshal's sales (auctions conducted by the sheriff), while his pleas for

An announcement in the *Gazette of the United States* on December 22, 1797 for the sale of "2 copper plates of Shakespeare seized and taken in execution as the property of Tristram Bampfylde Freeman and John Nicholson, merchants trading under the name of Freeman & Company."

City auctioneer William Shannon announces the sale of stock from the store of Freeman & Co., in the *Aurora* dated May 20, 1797. "Notes, Bills, Drafts and Bonds of Messrs [John] Nicholson and [Robert] Morris will be taken in payment at their current value."

money from his friend and business partner grew ever more desperate. His wife wrote a touching note to Nicholson on November 21, 1797: "Mr. Freeman having represented his situation to me in which he states his necessity of going to prison for relief of my self and family … will you permit me to solicit of you … as the only person that can prevent it. I cannot drive from him the real situation of his affairs … which I flattered my self by industry and application he would have surmounted any difficulty he laboured under." Nicholson, who was not everyone's idea of the perfect business partner, came through.

Freeman's financial difficulties would continue into the new century but they would prove minor when compared to the travails of his partner. Nicholson had embarked upon a higher-risk venture with Robert Morris that was destined to bring them both down. Morris – as the hero/profiteer who brought Pennsylvania through the Revolution on an even fiscal keel, he scarcely needs an introduction – had retired from public service, attracted by the fortunes being made from vast swathes of new territory sold at auction up and down the country. The Morris-Nicholson vision was a grandiose scheme to virtually control the settlement and land prices of western New York, Pennsylvania, Maryland, Virginia, the

By 1804, the business of T.B. Freeman had become a substantial concern. According to advertisements in the *Philadelphia Gazette and Daily Advertiser* dated Friday, May 4, 1804, Freeman was selling not just the 120 baskets of London beer bottles, the 300 boxes of pipes, the 60 crates of earthenware and other sundries that had arrived from Bristol on the "fine sailing ship *Lewis William*," but also the 95-ton vessel itself, "now lying at Clifford's wharf."

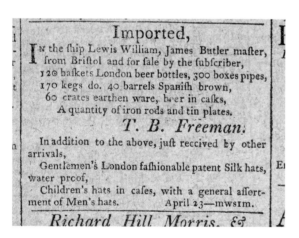

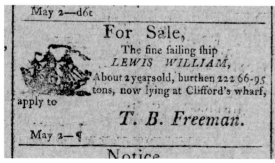

Carolinas and Georgia. Initially accompanied by the speculator James Greenleaf, the two men chose to gamble all on a series of companies whose vast expenditures at land auctions were to be offset by share sales and profits from the sale of lots, and house building, in the new capital city.

By 1797, close to 6 million acres of land appeared on the books of The North American Land Company, but there were insufficient revenues to meet the loan deadlines and pay the taxes. It was the greatest financial scandal of the era. In 1798, Morris was in debtor's prison, accepting visits from his ailing old friend George Washington. Early in the winter of 1799-1800, Nicholson would follow Morris to prison, and by December 5, 1800, he had left the world, leaving behind a wife, eight children, and, incredibly, debts of more than $4 million.

★   ★   ★

It was the attempt to settle Nicholson's estate through the sequestering of all his private and business papers – papers that still survive in the Pennsylvania state capital of Harrisburg – that shine such a bright light on the early moments of the Freeman's empire. The last surviving letter between the two men was dated July 23, 1800.

By then Freeman, at least, had begun to put financial troubles behind him. In newspapers reporting the scenes as Washington's funeral parade came through the city on December 26, 1799, we again pick up the trail of T.B. Freeman in the small ads. As a checkered business career took its first steps down the path towards the auction business, he was drumming up interest in his latest acquisitions as a trader in imported haberdashery goods from number 136 Market Street. In 1800, as the enterprise grew, Tristram and Sarah had their two youngest children, five-year-old James (1795-1814) and the sickly Isabella Dewees Freeman (1799-1805) baptized at Christ Church. In 1801 T.B. Freeman would become a naturalized citizen of the United States.

Freeman's days as a pioneering manufacturer were behind him. Instead the former printer chose to embrace Philadelphia's *raison d'etre*, and adopted a role that was well known to the mercantile economies of the early republic. As a commission merchant, T.B. Freeman learned to broker deals for others on the principle of commission or percentage, acting as the middleman between ship owners and the city's merchants and its auctioneers. Commission merchant was a title he would keep into the 1820s and one he would share with Joshua

A hand-colored engraving titled *South East Corner of Third and Market Streets* from William Russell Birch's *Views of Philadelphia*. To the far left is the famed Indian King tavern on Market Street, an upscale establishment catering to the mercantile crowd. It was also among the earliest Masonic meeting places in Philadelphia.

William Birch, an English immigrant who arrived in Philadelphia the year prior to T.B. Freeman, was perhaps the first artist to chronicle the expansion of the Federal city and record both its architectural set pieces and its commercial activity. Four different editions of his 28 or 29 print set were issued between 1800 and 1820 in both hand-colored and uncolored state.

On April 17, 1999, Freeman's sold a 29-print set of hand-colored plates for $87,360. It had belonged to William Sansom, one of the original 157 subscribers to this work.

THE LIBRARY COMPANY OF PHILADELPHIA

Ballinger Lippincott, founder of the Lippincott publishing house in 1785.

For a man with contacts but without the financial means to conduct larger and more formal assemblies the better of the city's 200 or more watering holes or the genteel surrounds of a coffee shop became his favored domain. It was here, over a bowl of coffee, chocolate, tea or perhaps something stronger, that members of the business and maritime communities and strangers from different stations in life gathered together to chew the fat of current affairs, read the Press and cut deals. They might also try their luck at the auction sales they called vendues. But any thoughts that the 38-year-old T.B. Freeman might himself become an auctioneer to the environs of Philadelphia will have been tempered by the knowledge that this was not a profession open to one and all. Indeed the six auctioneers of early 19th century Philadelphia were already proud of a long and jealously guarded heritage.

The London Coffee House was the public center for social and commercial activity during the third quarter of the 18th century. This engraving, one of 26 plates of some of Philadelphia's oldest buildings completed by W.L. Breton for John Fanning Watson's *Annals of Philadelphia*, shows slaves assembled for auction.

THE LIBRARY COMPANY OF PHILADELPHIA

Auction History

"Here you are all got together at this vendue of fineries and knicknacks. You call them goods, but if you do not take care, they will prove evils to some of you. You expect they will be sold cheap, and perhaps they may sell for less than they cost; but if you have no occasion for them, they must be dear to you. Remember what Poor Richard says, buy what thou hast no need of, and ere long thou shalt sell thy necessaries.

"... What madness must it be to run in debt for these superfluities! We are offered, by the terms of this vendue, six months credit; and that perhaps has induced some of us to attend it, because we cannot spare the ready money, and hope now to be fine without it".

BENJAMIN FRANKLIN, THE WAY TO WEALTH, 1758

They say auction is the second oldest profession. The institution of sale "by public cant" or "by public outcry" was likely more than two millennia old when Franklin's characters Father Abraham and Poor Richard visited a "vendue" in 1758.

First observed by the ancient Greek historian Herodotus in Babylonia in 450 BC, its enduring principles of utility had come down through the ages practically unchanged. Auction was embraced as the accepted method of liquidating property and estate goods by Europeans from the time of the Roman Empire though to the Stuart kings of England. By the late 17th century, notices of sales by auction of rare books and artworks at the coffee houses and taverns of London would pepper the pages of the *London Gazette*. This was this world into which James Christie, Walter Bonham, Harry Phillips, Samuel Baker, his nephew John Sotheby and T.B. Freeman were born and from which the great British auction houses would grow.

Typically there were two methods of conducting a sale. The system set out in the earliest known English book auction catalog dated 1676 is the descending or "Dutch" auction. Here the "price" would start artificially high and fall incrementally until it reached such a level that a bidder wished to claim the merchandise. At the ascending auction the process was reversed. The opening "price" was low and would rise by agreed increments until the "lot" was won by the highest bidder.

The basic principle was the same – whoever bids most is the buyer. But in Britain and its colonies it was the ascending method, occasionally conducted within a time limit set by the flame of a burning candle, that had gained favor by the early 18th century. And with it had developed much of the nomenclature and most of the subtle rules and practices still observed at auctions today.

Indeed, then as now, sale by public cant was just that – an audible experience, complete with the familiar cry of "once, twice, going, gone" and the crack of the hammer or cane that signifies the end of a bidding contest. By the 18th century, the term "lot" was understood to describe not just a parcel of land but any item offered for sale. Surviving from the sales of ancient Rome, was the concept of *caveat emptor* (buyer beware). This is the understanding that, at auction, the winning bidder takes full responsibility for inspecting the goods prior to their purchase.

Taking the place of the spear that, if stuck into the ground, was used by the Romans as the sign of an auction sale – *auctio sub hasta* (auction under the spear) it was called – flying the red flag came to indicate an imminent sale by public auction. At a time when there was very little difference in the design of residential and commercial properties, signs helped to indicate purpose and were of great help to the illiterate and those unfamiliar with the town. All professions had their signs: a druggist the mortar and pestle, a barber his pole, and the auctioneer his red flag. It's a tradition that Freeman's uphold at 1808 Chestnut Street to this day.

As the fastest way of converting assets into hard cash, sales by public outcry were as important to the mechanics of early Colonial America as the Bible and the beaver pelt. Here auctions became more commonly known as vendues, a word derived from the French meaning sold. Vendue described a method of sale that had proved an effective means by which to sell animal skins to European merchants, to disperse large tracts of land and to redistribute the assets of the dead, the dying and the destitute. The vendues also drove the labor economy and – just as in Babylon 23 centuries earlier when the merchandise was female flesh – the assets to be realized were human lives. It was from these makeshift and murky beginnings that the first American fortunes were made.

★   ★   ★

Slaves, sold like livestock at public auction in Philadelphia, were less likely to be newly arrived Africans than "secondhand merchandise" the owners had failed to sell privately. This *Pennsylvania Gazette* advertisement for an auction at the London Coffee House on July 27, 1765, publicizes an unusually large offering of up to "Fourteen valuable Negroes ... (who) have all had the Small-Pox, can talk English, and are seasoned to the Country."

John Leech and Joseph Antrobus, appointed by Pennsylvania Governor Colonel Charles Goodkin who held office from 1709 to 1716, were probably the first recognized "vendue masters" in Philadelphia. Given the sole power of conducting public sales in the city, and providing a considerable source of public revenue through taxation, theirs represented a position of some standing. They conducted their business from the Town Hall situated at Second and High Streets.

The powerful oral histories collected by the annalist John Fanning Watson also recall a Colonel John Patton who, assisted by two clerks, operated as a vendue master from a one-story brick house on South Front Street. The sales – typically of the dry goods that arrived during the spring, summer and fall from England or the "parcels of likely Negroes" from local slave owners – were held under the northwest corner of the courthouse on Second Street. Patton employed a Mr. Mitchell as the "crier," a celebrated orator and salesman who would summon purchasers to the door with several minutes of bell ringing and the cry, "We are just about to begin." The auction bellman and his untiring lungs would be a familiar sound echoing the streets of Philadelphia well into the 19th century.

According to J.F. Watson, on Colonel Patton's vacation of

in the Heart of the Country. Any Person inclining to purchase the same, on paying Part of the Money down, may have a confiderable Term of Years to pay the reft, giving Security, if required. For Terms apply to JOHN HOLTON, in Front-ftreet, in the Diftrict of Southwark. The Title is indifputable, and the Place may be entered on immediately.   &

T O   B E   S O L D,
On Saturday the 27th Inftant, at the London Coffee-Houfe, TWELVE or Fourteen valuable NEGROES, confifting of young Men, Women, Boys and Girls; they have all had the Small-Pox, can talk Englifh, and are feafoned to the Country. The Sale to begin at Twelve o'Clock.   &

S I X   D O L L A R S   Reward.
RUN away, on the 19th Day of June laft, from the Subfcriber, an Apprentice Lad, named William Siddons, about 17 Years of Age, by Trade a Shoemaker, about 5 Feet 5 Inches

A hangover from British rule when the Colonies were forbidden from manufacturing finished goods, America was still dependant on the Old World for finished goods well into the 19th century. This invoice from June 27, 1806 – the earliest bill of sale from a Freeman's auction extant – lists purchases made by Charles Bird including one cask of iron spikes, a bale of fish hooks, 12 shoemaker's knives and two dozen knives and forks.

THE HISTORICAL SOCIETY OF PENNSYLVANIA

the office in 1742, John Clifton offered £100 and Reese Meredith £110 per annum to the Corporation of Philadelphia for the privilege of conducting sales in the town.

From 1754, Philadelphia had its own auction exchange in the Old London Coffee House, conveniently situated near the city's docks at the corner of Front and High Street. Erected on land bought from Laetitia Penn in 1702 and established as a coffee house by the publisher of the *Philadelphia Journal* William Bradford, the site was a public center for social and commercial activity for almost half a century.

As familiar a sight to colonial Philadelphians as the Liberty Bell or the State House from which it swung, the Old London Coffee House was the popular location for all kinds of auctions. Sales of slaves were conducted here until taxation (a duty of £10 per head in 1771, bumped to £20 in 1773) saw the trade migrate to neighboring states by the mid 1770s. Famously, it was while staying in a building overlooking a slave auction at the Old London Coffee House in 1774 that Thomas Paine began one of his first essays attacking the institution of slavery.

By 1780, aided by pressure from the world's first antislavery society (the Pennsylvania Abolition Society

The Merchant's Coffee House or City Tavern pictured next to the
Bank of the United States in William Birch's *Views of Philadelphia.*
Situated on Second Street below Market, the City Tavern had
replaced the London Coffee House as the hub of American
commerce from the 1770s. Philadelphia auctioneers conducted
important real estate sales from this building before it was
demolished in 1852. A replica was rebuilt for the Bicentennial.

THE LIBRARY COMPANY OF PHILADELPHIA

had established just five years earlier) sales of "Negroes
and Mulatto slaves" had been struck from the list of
permissible items a Philadelphia auctioneer could sell.
Thereafter, as in the other port cities of New York,
Boston and Baltimore, the public vendues were focused
on real estate, estate sales and the remarkable panoply
of goods surplus to retail requirements that arrived at
the docks from the Indies, Continental Europe and Great
Britain. Kegs of raisins, plain and ornamented ostrich
feathers, silk taffetas and fringes, linens from Ireland,
rum and molasses from Barbados, ladies' gloves just
received from Leghorn, knives, forks and fish hooks of
Sheffield steel; blue-and-white porcelain and silks from
Canton. Far removed from the valuable works of art that
Tristram B. Freeman's descendents would begin to sell a
century or so later, it was these finished goods that
American industry – its growth stunted by the
restrictions of colonial rule – failed to provide in the
volume or at a cost that the new nation demanded.

The recollections of Jacob Mordecai of Richmond,
Virginia, bring colorful first-hand accounts of these early
sales. Mordecai, who visited Philadelphia in 1834 after
an absence of half a century, provided unused material
for J.F. Watson's *Annals* project including this description
of the city's vendue store on Front Street.

We, the Shopkeepers of Philadelphia ... A broadside printed by Henry Miller in 1770 proposing a boycott of the city's less reputable auctions.

WE, the Shopkeepers of PHILADELPHIA, and Places adjacent, whose Names are hereunto subscribed, labouring under many and great Difficulties in the present languishing Condition of TRADE in this City, partly owing to the unreftrained Liberties of VENDUES, have found it neceffary and expedient to come into an Agreement not to purchafe any Goods fo expofed to publick Sale, but under the following Regulations, which we think moft conducive to the General Good.

1. We will not purchafe a Lot of Goods expofed to publick Sale, that fhall be ftruck off for lefs than Five Pounds,——fuch Articles only excepted as fhall be hereafter fpecified.

2. We will not buy any Goods at Vendue, if the Vendue-Mafter is convicted of felling at private Sale to any Perfon or Perfons whofe Occupation is different to that of the Subfcribers.

3. We will not purchafe lefs than one Pound Silk, 3 Pounds Mohair, 6 Pounds coloured Threads, 6 Bags or 6s Grofs Buttons.

4. All new Wearing Apparel fhall be included in the Lots of Five Pounds.

5. All Woollen Cloths fhall be fold by the Piece as imported from Europe.

6. Sheriffs Sales and Goods fold at the Houfes of Perfons deceafed or broke, excepted.

7. Ironmongery fhall be fold by the Dozen and Grofs as imported from England.

8. If at any Time the Mafter of a Vendue fhall deviate from this our Agreement, we the Subfcribers do bind ourfelves to rife and quit his Vendue-Houfe; they that do not fhall be deemed Enemies to our Commercial Intereft, and their Names expofed accordingly.

N. B. The above Agreement to take place April 9th, 1770.

Philadelphia, Printed by Henry Miller, in Second-ftreet.

"It was a general custom for wives and widows to attend at auction stores, then called vendues, and purchase goods for their shop supplies. Benches were placed in rows in front of the vendue shelves. There a preference was always given to female purchasers to occupy the front seats. Goods were passed along, every body being seated."

Women, who are conspicuous by their absence in the Freeman's story, were clearly of great importance to the evolution of the auction process in America.

Built when Philadelphia was in its infancy, the London Coffee House (demolished for its prime real estate in 1883) no longer met the business demands of a swelling city by the third quarter of the 18th century. In the 1770s, recognizing the need for larger quarters, members of the social and mercantile aristocracy sought the erection of a newer, larger and purpose-built temple for commerce that would cater to the needs of the business community over the next half-century. The Merchant's Coffee House, or City Tavern, situated on Second Street below Market next to the Bank of the United States, was a stellar example of late colonial architecture with its two large elegant meeting rooms and a stuccoed dining room that was a fitting venue for the hub of American commerce. John Adams, one of the members of the First

Continental Congress who occasionally gathered here for refreshment, called it "the most genteel tavern in the country." Philadelphia's appointed auctioneers, including T.B. Freeman, conducted important real estate sales from this building and, from the 1820s until demolition in 1852, it would be wholly occupied by a prominent 19th century auction firm, Thomas Birch & Son.

As in London, where the guilds of that sprawling city had strictly controlled the sale of goods by auction, the system of public vendue in Philadelphia was subject to a surprising degree of regulation. Auctions in the city proper and its two largest incorporated districts – the Northern Liberties and Southwark – represented one of the early monopolies of the city corporation. The potentially lucrative positions of general or specialist auctioneer were appointed by the governor and numbers were strictly limited. The tally of white Protestant males considered for the role of vendue master operating "within two miles of the State House of the city, the Northern Liberties or the district of Southwark" would number only three in the days before the Revolution. Despite the city's remarkable population growth, at the close of the 18th century that number stood at just six.

However, from the beginning the system had been divisive, unpopular, abused and occasionally flouted. As

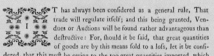

A
FEW REASONS
IN FAVOUR OF
VENDUES.

IT has always been considered as a general rule, That trade will regulate itself; and this being granted, Vendues or Auctions will be found rather advantageous than destructive: For, should it be said, that great quantities of goods are by this means sold to a lofs, let it be confidered, that this must be owing to the too great quantities imported, which must either be kept on hand a long time, or be difposed of in this manner.

By there being Vendues, or places of public sale of goods in and about this city, many strangers, (Captains of veffels and others) are encouraged to import quantities of goods, who, from their fituation, are prevented from felling them upon equal terms with our fettled merchants, not knowing the people, or who to truft, and perhaps obliged to return in a fhort time, they are of courfe led to this mode of fale, by which they are immediately in cafh for their goods, and enabled to purchafe our produce.

Particularly the traders to and from Ireland, who, it is well known, import large quantities of linens and other goods into this place annually, and depend in a great meafure on the Vendues to turn them into cafh, which they ufually lay out in the purchafe of flax-feed, flour or lumber.

But it has been objected, that encouraging ftrangers to fell their goods among us, who are here but a fhort time, and bear no part of the burdens occafioned by taxes, &c. is injurious to our merchants.

This muft appear to have little weight, when we confider that the prefent flourifhing ftate of this province and city, is in a great meafure owing to the encouragement given to ftrangers, (if the merchants and traders from Great Britain and Ireland may be called fo) who, by being permitted to bring their goods and wares to our market, have kept the country well fupplied; and in return, have taken off large quantities of our produce.

And to this, that where ever the greateft quantities of goods are, there of courfe will the people refort, both with their cafh and produce, not only from being fure of obtaining what they may want, but from a profpect of obtaining their goods on better terms.

If it be granted, that the importation of Britifh manufactures are neceffary, and of advantage to the country, then thofe perfons that introduce and difpofe of them on the loweft terms, muft be confeffed the beft friends to the community, and deferve their countenance and encouragement.

But ftrangers, from their fituation and circumftances, generally difpofe of their goods at a much lower rate than the ftated merchant; therefore, it is the intereft of the community to encourage their trade with us. By this means, we get thofe goods that we want for our own confumption (and for which we are beholden to other countries) at the loweft rates; and thofe people in return, generally give the higheft price for our produce.

We might here quote the New-England trade, by which large quantities of fifh, oil, &c. are imported into our province, and in return, they purchafe our flour, pork, iron, &c. which certainly keeps up the price of thofe commodities, and muft be of advantage to our country: They alfo fupply us with a great fum in bills of exchange, which prevents the merchants from fending off the fpecie in remittance. Put all thofe confiderations together, and they do certainly prove, that it is the intereft of the community to give the greateft encouragement to ftrangers trading among us; and therefore, the fuppreffing the Vendues, or laying any tax or duty upon the goods fold by them, which for the greateft part belong to ftrangers, muft be a difcouragement to their trade with us, and in its confequences injurious to the country in general.

Those perfons who are defirous to have the Vendues fuppreffed, or laid under a heavy duty or fine, have mentioned the conduct of the New-York Affembly, as a pattern for ours to follow (which, by the bye, is the firft inftance of the kind in America). In anfwer, it may be obferved, that the New-Yorkers once, by an order of their corporation, fixed the price of meat, butter, eggs, &c. that the country brought in for their daily provi-

fion; but this has not yet been copied by our corporation, as, no doubt, they muft have feen the abfurdity of it; for the event proved, they had like to have been ftarved, the country juftly refenting fuch a regulation, and with-holding their produce until the ordinance was repealed. In like manner, we find they have already been obliged to amend the firft law made againft Vendues, and have now reduced their duty from five to two *per cent.* and it is not to be doubted, but in a little time they will be obliged to take it entirely off.

The fuppreffion or taxing of Vendues will probably introduce Pawn-Brokers, as in London, when thofe who are in great want of cafh, and under the neceffity of raifing it in a fhort time, will be obliged to pledge their goods at, perhaps, quarter their value, and allow the Broker a large premium befide for the ufe of the money; and if thofe goods are not redeemed at the limited time, they become the property of the Broker, at the price they were pawned or pledged at. This evil muft be confeffed to be much greater than the moft extravagant defcription given of Vendues.

But, if it fhould be faid by any perfon, that the defign of the petition carried to the Honourable Houfe of Affembly, is not to fupprefs, but to regulate Vendues, then the queftion might be afked, In what manner the regulation is propofed? Whether, by fubjecting the goods fold at them to a certain fine or duty, or by only regulating the mode in which their public fales fhall be conducted?

If the firft fhould be attempted, it certainly will be injurious, and operate as a great difcouragement to ftrangers, and a tax upon the inhabitants, as it is confeffed, that goods, as they are at prefent fold at Vendue, will not bear an additional charge.

Should the latter be all that is intended, it is prefumed, that the Vendue-Mafters themfelves would have no objection, as feveral of them have frequently expreffed a defire that fuch a meafure fhould take place.

And in this, perhaps, we could not follow better examples, than fome of the great trading cities in Europe. In Amfterdam, the numbers of Brokers are limited to 395, who are obliged to take out licences, give fecurity, and be upon oath. In London, the number of Brokers are unlimited, but they are alfo obliged to take out licences, give fecurity, and be upon oath.

This is mentioned, as it appears from the face of the petition, that the fubfcribers only requeft a regulation; and, it is beyond all doubt, that a very great majority of them look on Vendues both ufeful and neceffary, and would not have figned the petition, had they imagined any thing more than regulation was intended.

It has been hinted, to fupprefs all Vendues in the Northern Liberties and Southwark, by which all bufinefs in that way will fall into the hands of one only. The partiality and injuftice of fuch a meafure, is too great to fuppofe it would meet with the leaft encouragement by fo refpectable and impartial a body as our Reprefentatives.

There are at prefent a number of gentlemen employed in that bufinefs, of unexceptionable characters, who have done the bufinefs of their employers with the greateft honour and punctuality, notwithftanding the many illiberal reflections thrown out by fome perfons: And muft thefe perfons at once be deprived of their livelihood? fhall a bufinefs that can give bread to fo many be monopolifed by one? will the public be better ferved by this means? or, will it put a ftop to the pretended evil? Certainly, No.

Upon the whole, therefore, as this matter is now laid before the Honourable Houfe of Affembly, it is not to be doubted, that, fhould they be of opinion, that a regulation of Vendues are become neceffary, they will endeavour to do it in fuch a manner as will tend to promote the beft intereft of the community in general. At the fame time, that they will be tender of the intereft of thofe individuals who are employed therein; by not giving an undue preference to one to the great injury of the reft.

Sales at Auction of
Horfes & Carriages.

THE Subfcribers ~~incorporated into~~ Office for the fale of HORSES, CARRIAGES, CATTLE, &c. at Public Auction, every Wednefday, and Saturday Mornings at 11 o'clock, on the North Side of Vine Street between Sixth and Seventh Streets, ~~in the Northern Liberties~~, where they will be thankful for the favors of their ~~former~~ friends ~~and cuftomers, pledging themfelves~~ to ufe every exertion in their power for the Intereft of their employers, the practice and experience which they have had for thefe feveral years paft in conducting the fales at the Horfe Market, induces them to believe that they can ferve their friends with the fame ufual attention and punctuality which they have heretofore done.— They return their hearty and fincere thanks for the repeated favors which have been conferred upon them and refpectfully folicit a continuance of the fame.

THOSE who have Horfes, Carriages, &c. for public fale, will pleafe to enter them at the Auction Room, No. 34, Dock-Street, any day in the week or at the above place of Sale, after 9 o'clock on Wednefday, and Saturday Mornings.

☞ All Horfes fold will be paid for unlefs they are warranted, after 4 o'clock on the fame afternoon, and if warranted after 9 o'clock, in the Morning on the fucceeding Market day.

EDWARD POLE, & Co. *Auctioneers.*

APRIL 24, 1799.

Philadelphia: Printed by R. Aitken, No. 22, Market-Street.

A broadside dated 1799 promoting the business of Edward Pole & Co., an auctioneer of horses and carriages in the city of Philadelphia.

early as 1729, the Council commented on "the general complaint of the irregular methods of selling merchandise by public vendue" and acted to quiet the city's merchants who – while both buying and selling through the vendue masters – found the knockdown prices that Father Abraham and Poor Richard observed to be injurious to their businesses.

The order came in September 1730 "that the Vendue Master for the time being not to sell goods at Vendue under the value of fifty shillings in one lot, except for wearing apparel or second-hand goods". This represented a concession to the city shopkeepers who wished to see auctioneers sell only in bulk. It was among the first in a long series of regulatory measures that were subtly designed to maximize taxation revenues while appeasing the vocal retail community.

In theory, at least, heavy penalties were incurred by unlicensed persons attempting to sell by auction. In the case of livestock for example – for which an auctioneer was specifically appointed to sell on Wednesdays and Saturdays in the southeast part of Centre Square – an additional charge could be levied on each horse or head of cattle sold outside these prescribed limits. Those who were caught by the justice of the peace conducting a black-market auction were liable for a stiff fine.

Among the earliest surviving Philadelphia auction catalogues, A Catalogue of Books, to be sold, by public auction, at the City Vendue-Store, in Front-Street printed by William and Thomas Bradford, 1769.

THE HISTORICAL SOCIETY OF PENNSYLVANIA

But just how successfully these elementary rules were enforced is subject to debate. Shopkeepers of the city frequently complained of violations, particularly among the boat builders, lumber yards, and warehouses of the Northern Liberties and Southwark where "every man set up for himself whenever he pleased" to conduct a sale without paying their dues to the government.

*   *   *

Mordecai recalled several vendue stores in the Liberties, all on Second Street above Vine. "They were wooden buildings, seldom open but on vendue days. The Vendue Masters were Footman and Jeyes, William Sitgreaves, and some others not remembered."

These out-of-town duty-dodgers – according to J.F. Watson, the first was Jonas Phillips who held his sales in a large brick house on the rising ground over the Middle Ferry of the Schuylkill River – were certainly a resourceful bunch. It was not unusual, for example, for unlicensed auctioneers in the Northern Liberties to lure potential bidders to sales across the Schuylkill at the Upper Ferry or across the Delaware at Cooper's Ferry with a free carriage ride from the city center. After the conclusion of the afternoon sales, the goods were packed in trunks and cases and brought to the city

limits. From there they would be delivered to purchasers the next morning.

It was in this environment, and following the repeal of the Townshend Acts that effectively cut all duties on imports into the colonies except for tea, that the city's retailers petitioned to exercise a partial boycott of the vendues in 1770. "We, the shopkeepers of Philadelphia, and places adjacent ... labouring under many and great difficulties ... have found it necessary and expedient to come into an agreement not to purchase any goods so exposed to publick sale, but under the following regulations." Pledging to buy only in quantity and to shun those auctioneers they considered guilty of malpractice was an early grassroots attempt to regulate the auction business before its legislation would become ever more tangled.

This was not the only broadside discussing the merits, or otherwise, of the auction system that circulated through the streets of Philadelphia in the days prior to the Revolution.

As early as 1770 upping the duties imposed on goods sold at auction was being solicited as perhaps a more effective way to lessen the impact of the secondary economy in the nation's biggest city. Others, fearful that a heavy auction tax would see imports migrate to neighboring ports as they had when taxes were raised in New York, favored regulation and not taxation.

The broadside *A Few Reasons in Favor of Vendues* – an anonymous document, likely printed by John Dunlap in 1772 – argues the case for free trade. It opens thus: "It has always been considered a general rule, that trade will regulate itself; and that this being granted, vendues or auctions will be found rather advantageous than destructive." The regular vendues in Philadelphia were, said the author, simply a reflection of the large surplus of goods imported into the city. Their success had encouraged increasing numbers of merchants from Britain and Ireland to engage in transatlantic commerce while low prices brought as many benefits as they might hardship. Suppression of this trade would endanger Philadelphia's position as America's commercial powerhouse and encourage pawnbroking, an "evil [that] must be confessed to be much greater than the most extravagant description given of vendues".

Regulation and not taxation was largely what the city's auction business got shortly after Independence. Wartime laws were designed to hit the duty-dodger hard. In 1779, *An Act for the effectual suppression of public auctions and vendues* ... set the fine for unlicensed auctioneering at an astronomical $20,000. To crack

down on horse stealing, "so frequent in this and neighbouring states, as to render every precaution and remedy necessary and proper," the city's legitimate auctioneers were asked to keep a detailed register of all livestock sold.

Adding to the red tape was *An Act Laying Duties on Property sold at Auction* enacted by the Third Congress in 1794 in the hope of replicating the regulatory systems employed in the great trading cities of Europe.

Fines for unregulated sales were set at a more modest $400 for each transgression but Congress required a minimum bond of $1,500 from each auctioneer, detailed accounts and a quarterly pound of flesh on the first day of January, April, July and October.

And yet there were considerable perks to be had as a member of Philadelphia's exclusive club of governor-appointed auctioneers.

As merchandise arrived at the docks in increasing tonnage and as the city expanded at rapid pace, there was a steady supply of goods for sale on commission. If all was in order the auctioneers themselves were entitled to a one percent share of the total auction duties given to the taxman and, when selling dry and household goods, were permitted further concessions.

Monopoly, taxation, legislation, division. This was the world T.B. Freeman entered in November 1805 when he became an auctioneer.

A TYRANNICAL EMBARGO

Among the loudest voices that have come down to us from the final quarter of the 18th century is that of Robert Bell. Self proclaimed as a "born and bred book auctioneer", Bell came to Philadelphia from Great Britain in 1767 and operated a publishing business and the city's first circulating library from High (Market) Street. His shop could be found "at the sign of the sugar loaf" between King (Water) Street and the Delaware River. He would eventually gain the reputation of being the most progressive publisher in the colonies but he was also among the first men to conduct regular book auctions in North America, shipping material from Philadelphia to neighboring states. Boston, where legislation would allow him to conduct sales by public outcry, was a regular destination for his merchandise.

Prohibited by the laws from holding sales in Pennsylvania, he got wind in 1783 that an application had been made to appoint a book auctioneer to the city and petitioned the General Assembly for a piece of the action. However, his apparently successful application for a specialist license to sell literary property from the "upper vendue house on Second Street, near Vine" (one of the regular city auction marts in the Northern Liberties) met tremendous opposition from the Philadelphia's vocal and powerful publishing lobby. An embargo was imposed and Bell was found guilty in the courts of conducting a sale by public outcry without a license. Such "an invidious indictment against the propagation of literature" prompted Bell to publish a series of tracts petitioning anyone who would listen on the rights and wrongs of the auction process and a "tyrannical embargo now laid upon the free sale of books by auction." This from a four-penny pamphlet dated 1784: Pray stop, Master Bell, with your selling of books, Your smart witting sayings, and cunning arch looks, By auction I Mean 'tis a shocking offence, To sell wit, or humour, or e'en common sense, Unsanctioned by law on any pretence: Read the Act of Assembly, by Mood, and by Tense, There's none can vend Knowledge without a lie–cense.

But for all his crusading words on liberty, monopoly and free trade, in a city where printers and engravers were only second in numbers to sailors and merchants, Bell would lose the battle. He changed tack and again began shipping books out of Pennsylvania to sell at vendues in states with more favorable legislation, but died soon afterwards in Richmond, Virginia.

The business end of Philadelphia, circa 1800. A hand colored engraving titled *Arch Street Ferry* from William Russell Birch's *Views of Philadelphia*.

T.B. Freeman Years

CHAPTER THREE

"Sales of Dry Goods on Tuesday afternoon at 2 o'clock, at T.B. Freeman's auction store, No. 177 Market-street"

POULSON'S AMERICAN DAILY ADVERTISER, NOVEMBER 23, 1805

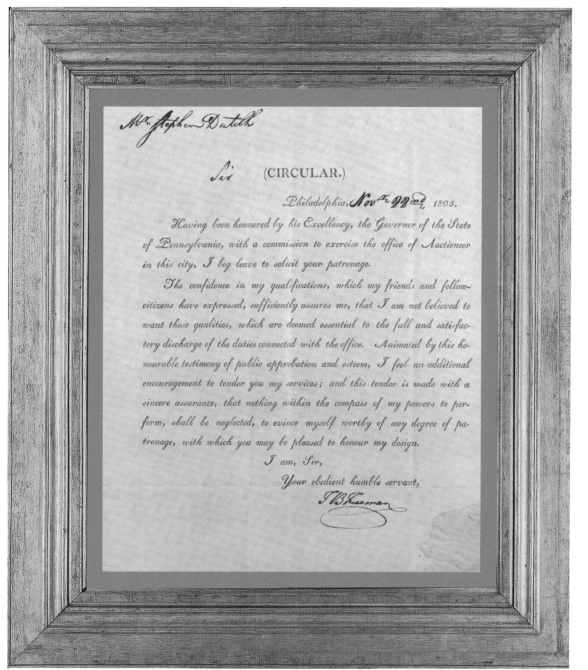

Mr. Stephen Dutilh

Sir   (CIRCULAR.)

Philadelphia, Nov. 22nd, 1805.

Having been honoured by his Excellency, the Governor of the State of Pennsylvania, with a commission to exercise the office of Auctioneer in this city, I beg leave to solicit your patronage.

The confidence in my qualifications, which my friends and fellow-citizens have expressed, sufficiently assures me, that I am not believed to want those qualities, which are deemed essential to the full and satisfactory discharge of the duties connected with the office. Animated by this honourable testimony of public approbation and esteem, I feel an additional encouragement to tender you my services; and this tender is made with a sincere assurance, that nothing within the compass of my powers to perform, shall be neglected, to evince myself worthy of any degree of patronage, with which you may be pleased to honour my design.

I am, Sir,

Your obedient humble servant,

T.B.Freeman

"The confidence in my qualifications, which my friends and fellow citizens have expressed, sufficiently assures me, that I am not believed to want those qualities, which are deemed essential to the full and satisfactory discharge of the duties connected with the office." A solicitation letter dated November 22, 1805 addressed to the merchant Stephen Dutilh and signed by T.B. Freeman.

Similar circulars were issued by other Philadelphian auctioneers. An almost identical document was printed for a newly-appointed auctioneer Peter Kuhn in 1809 in which he announces his recent move into the "auction stores lately occupied by Mr T.B. Freeman…"

A signer of the Declaration of Independence, Revolutionary War colonel and member of the Continental Congress, Thomas McLean (1734-1817), a fiery radical turned old-school Democrat instrumental in Jefferson's electoral victory on an anti-Federalist ticket in 1800, was beginning his third term as governor of Philadelphia in 1805.

"Sales of Dry Goods On Tuesday afternoon at 2 o'clock." T.B. Freeman's first advertisement as an auctioneer as it appeared in Poulson's *American Daily Advertiser*, November 23, 1805.

In early November the good news had arrived from the governor's office. Zachariah Poulson's *American Daily Advertiser* reported on November 13, 1805, that Tristram Bampfylde Freeman, had, by order of Thomas McLean, governor of the State of Pennsylvania, been appointed to the office of auctioneer for the city of Philadelphia and Districts. He had set up business at 177 Market Street. According to the executive minutes taken the previous day, McLean – a tall, choleric and volatile Scots-Irishman whose third term in office was notable for a campaign to remove political opponents from state-appointed positions – had recently accepted the resignation of the auctioneer Edward Pole. He had commissioned as his replacement a man who, not seven years before, had tasted destitution.

A bond for the not inconsiderable sum of $5,333 and 33 cents had been in place two days later, with two Philadelphia merchants, Edward Shoemaker and William Page, acting as sureties. Lewis and Clark had reached the Pacific Ocean on the same day.

*   *   *

"Two bales of fine and common cloth, three dozen striped blankets, one dozen bales of worsted hosiery, four trunks of chintz-printed cotton, three bales of India muslins and a box of Irish linens ..." It was with these goods imported from the textile mills of Great Britain that T.B. Freeman would commence his trade as an auctioneer in Franklin's town.

Early 19th century Philadelphia, an urban but pre-industrial settlement numbering perhaps 60,000 people, was a city that looked out to sea. In 1805, when Philadelphia's maritime trade was near its peak, 547 ships and 1,169 coasters from overseas sailed up the Delaware River. In total 3,564 vessels had dropped anchor to unload finished goods and reload with agricultural produce and raw materials.

Of these cargos – American imports had surged to a lofty $138.5 million by 1807 – some immediately found their way to the city shopkeepers. Some would be peddled in the taverns, while others would appear in small ads in the press. The option was there to employ the local knowledge of a commission merchant, but if no immediate customer could be found, the quickest place to turn assets into cash was the auction room. In the busier trading months, with six men permitted to sell by public outcry in the city, there would be more than one sale on most days of the week. T.B. Freeman took the auctioneer's stand every Friday morning and Tuesday afternoon in "the warm season." The winter months, when the port was prone to freezing and transatlantic

trade limited, prompted auctioneers to look closer to home and develop the relationships that make the auctioneer as important to the local community as the preacher and the doctor. Sales of local real estate, minor libraries and estate goods provided the vendue master with a sense of place. They would be supplemented by the unsold stock of the city shopkeepers who, campaigning against the vendues during the day, might under the cover of darkness, consign goods by night.

Freeman's inaugural sale would be followed in December with opportunities to purchase the fast-sailing schooner *Betsy*, "a recently-received cargo of white and brown sugar from Havanna [sic]", cases of English woolen hats and seven pipes of Spanish brandy. January 9, 1806, brought four lots of woodland from the estate of James Logan sold "at Samuel Deal's tavern, on the township Line Road" on the instructions of James Vaux of number 72, North Third Street.

Account books and correspondence have not survived, but circumstantial evidence suggests Freeman's enterprise enjoyed a prosperous beginning.

In 1808 the Freemans adopted Isabella Hodgkiss, the eight-year-old daughter of the late Michael Hodgkiss and Sarah Dewees of Frederick, Maryland. She was given a private baptism into the Freeman family at Christ

Church on September 9. Isabella – she was the same age and name of a daughter the Freemans had lost to the fever three years prior – would marry John Norwell, editor of *The Franklin Gazette*, in 1822.

As business allowed, T.B. Freeman had also become more and more involved in life beyond the shop door. He joined a number of the city's émigré societies, devoted time to the Masonic duties he took so seriously and directed a few dollars into the path of the city's poor with whom he could empathize closely. Early biographers unsure of their subject's nationality can only have been perplexed by his membership in the Society of Sons of St George (1799), the St Andrew's Society (1804), the Hibernian Society (1808); and the Friendly Sons of St. Patrick (1808). Remembered by his obituary writers as a kind and generous man, T.B. Freeman also had exceptional talents as a networker.

In December 1808, he had snared a substantial consignment of the type Philadelphia auctioneers welcomed in the winter months. Better still, it was an estate associated with the patriarch of a celebrated military family.

The sale of his father's effects is not among the best-chronicled moments in the remarkable life of Barbary Wars hero Commodore Stephen Decatur.

Philadelphia Gazette, December 15, 1808

"For Sale At Publick Vendue On Monday the 19th inst. At 10 o'clock A.M. at the late dwelling house of Capt. Stephen Decatur, near Frankford".

A silver bookplate depicting the Decatur family engraved by Henry Dawkins circa 1783. This oval plate, engraved to the obverse with the arms of the Decatur family, depicts the sitters Captain Stephen Decatur (1752-1808), his wife, the former Ann Pine; and their three children, the future naval hero Stephen (1779-1820), Ann Pine (1776-1819) and the baby James Bruce (1782-1804). According to family tradition this bookplate passed from Stephen Decatur Snr. to his son, Commodore Stephen Decatur, who died without issue. It was sold by Christie's New York on January 20-21, 2005 for $32,000.

© CHRISTIE'S IMAGES LIMITED 2005

A portrait of Stephen Decatur engraved by A.B. Durand after T. Sully.

Stephen Decatur Sr., the son of a French lieutenant who came to Newport, Rhode Island, about 1750 and Philadelphia soon afterwards; had died November 11, 1808, at the age of 57. He had lived long enough to know of his son's dashing leadership and feats of derring-do at Tripolian Harbor in 1804 but not his heroics in the War of 1812. Decatur Jr. and Francis Gurney (1738-1815), a Philadelphia merchant who served as a captain in the militia, were named executors of the will, with the entire estate to be sold at auction to benefit Decatur Sr.'s widow, Ann (neé Pine). She would die four years later, to be buried alongside other family members in St. Peter's churchyard.

Like his better-known son, Decatur Sr. had also had been a naval officer of some note. During the Revolution he was engaged in privateering, commanding a succession of Pennsylvania vessels. In partnership with the Philadelphia merchants Gurney & Smith, Decatur later became part-owner, and commander, of the ships *Pennsylvania* and *Ariel*. At the age of eight, Decatur Jr. accompanied his father to Bordeaux, an exposure to life at sea that would lay the groundwork for his future career.

At the outbreak of hostilities with the French, the elder Decatur had been commissioned as a captain in the U.S. Navy, May 11, 1798, and again saw action off northern Cuba. He had captured five prizes in the new frigate *Philadelphia*.

However, unlike his son who would die in 1820 from a wound incurred on the dueling ground in Bladensburg, Maryland, his life after honorable discharge from the military was spent in relative peace on the Millsdale estate, near Frankford, Pennsylvania. There, he established a gunpowder works – a clue to some of the more atypical estate goods sold by T.B. Freeman on Monday December 19, 1808.

But when three years later, James Mease, a chronicler of local current affairs, recorded the six auctioneers "appointed by the governor for the sale of goods of all kinds and household furniture in the city of Philadelphia," his list did not include T.B. Freeman.

Freeman had lost or relinquished his auctioneer's license in the spring of 1809.

It is possible, given the political impulses associated with the office of auctioneer, that the new governor failed to look kindly upon an application for a periodic license renewal. Simon Snyder, a New School Jeffersonian Democrat, was a staunch opponent of Thomas McLean. However, there may be no need to look for conspiracy theories. The demise of a fledgling firm is equally in tune with the economic realities of the second decade of the 19th century.

The year 1807 had signaled the start of a tumultuous ten years for the city's merchants and shopkeepers. Jefferson's Embargo Act, intended to damage the British in the midst of a war against France, had been a disaster for Philadelphia's maritime economy. The only beneficiaries would be the profiteers and the first American manufacturers. As hungry sailors marched on City Hall in 1808, Mayor Robert Wharton wrote to his brother: "Our city as to traffic is almost a desert, wharves crowded with empty vessels, the noise and buzz of commerce not heard, whilst hundreds of labourers are ranging the streets without employ or the means of getting bread for their distressed families."

During the dry port of 1809, the total state yield from legitimate vendues would plummet to $33,635.22 from something closer to $45,000 in previous years.

Perhaps Freeman was simply unable to supply the necessary security when his license came up for renewal.

Tristram would be succeeded to the position of auctioneer by the business of Peter Kuhn & Son. Kuhn let it be known by a circular dated April 24, 1809 that his company had "taken over the auction stores lately

The Ruinous Tendency of Auctioneering and the Necessity of Restraining it for the Benefit of Trade demonstrated in a letter to the Right Hon. Lord Bathurst, President of the Board of Trade in England, 1813. First published in London this pamphlet was reprinted in New York in 1813 and again in 1828. The author dictates that the retailer should be protected from cut-price auction goods "inasmuch as the shop keeper has as great a right to have the profits of his business secured to him, as the public officer has to have his salary, the clergyman his tythes, the lawyer his fees or the landlord his rent."

occupied by Mr. T.B. Freeman" and was "now prepared to execute the duties of auctioneers and commission merchants." His name appeared in Mease's list of the city's six licensed auctioneers alongside John Dorsey, Frederick Montmollin, Thomas Passmore, John Humes and Silas E. Weir.

Without a license to wield the gavel – a hiatus in his life that would last a turbulent ten years – T.B. Freeman nevertheless endeavored to stay close to the auction business. Passmore and then Kuhn would become business associates.

For the next decade he again operated as a commission merchant but this time chose to source dry goods, foodstuffs, liquor and books for regular sales "at the new city auction store" hiring a licensed auctioneer to conduct proceedings. This was blurring the traditional boundaries that existed between auctioneer, consignor and buyer and a loophole that would be closed in the legislative purge of the 1820s. Such, however, were the necessities during a mercantile crisis.

As war was declared against Philadelphia's greatest trading partner over the issue of impressment in 1812, a British blockading squadron cruising off the capes of the Delaware ensured barren times for a local economy. Again, the ordinary mode of bargain and sale was found

THE
RUINOUS TENDENCY
OF
AUCTIONEERING,
AND THE
NECESSITY OF RESTRAINING IT
FOR
THE BENEFIT OF TRADE,
DEMONSTRATED IN A LETTER
TO
THE RIGHT HON. LORD BATHURST,
PRESIDENT OF THE BOARD OF TRADE.

—A-going ! a-going !! a-going !!!

NEW-YORK:
PUBLISHED BY EASTBURN, KIRK, & CO.
NO. 86, BROADWAY.

1813.

A portrait of Tristram William Lockyer Freeman (1792-1846) in militia uniform.

PRIVATE TRISTRAM WILLIAM LOCKYER

On March 20, 1813, as alarming news of the presence of the British fleet off the coast of the Delaware Bay and River reached Philadelphia, the young men of the defenseless city met at Stratton's Tavern. Around 70 men – many of them members of the Young Men's Democratic Society of Philadelphia – immediately formed a volunteer company for artillery service to re-enforce the 11 recruits manning the garrison at Fort Mifflin. The Junior Artillerists were shortly joined by three volunteer detachments under the command of Colonel Lewis Rush: the Philadelphia Blues; the Independent Volunteers and a newly organized company under "America's first economist", Captain Condy Raguet, called the Washington Guards. Each consisted of 100 privates, 15 officers and two musicians. Among the Guards was Private Tristram William Lockyer Freeman, age 22. At the time, the second son of T.B. Freeman and the future head of the family business was operating a "fancy warehouse" at 51 Chestnut Street and had revived the family printing business with "a picturesque Printing Office & A Manufactory for Carving and Gilding". Wearing a cockade in his hat, a blue coat trimmed with gold braid epaulettes and buff pants, he left the city for the state of Delaware on the afternoon of May 12.

They made camp, first at Staunton on the Baltimore road, from May 16 to June 2; and then near Hamilton's Landing at Shellpot Hill, three miles north of Wilmington, after hearing rumors that the enemy intended to destroy the duPont powder mills on the Brandywine River. Around July 12, they took up a new station at Oak Hill, near Stille's Run, but as the British descended onto the Chesapeake Bay, the Philadelphia troops returned home on July 28. T.W.L. Freeman would, nevertheless, remain a militiaman, reveling in the pomp and ceremony and the occasional skirmish with the unruly mob.

THE *Taking of* MAJOR ANDRE.
By the Incorruptible PAULDING, WILLIAMS *and* VANVERT.

"That the Auction System is a monopoly, cannot be denied; that it is calculated to aggrandise a few at the expense of many; that it is ruinous to regular trade; that it is detrimental to the morals of the community, and calculated to impoverish the country, can, and I think will be, satisfactorily shewn."

The pamphlet *An Exposition of some of the evils arising from the Auction System* published in 1821, is representative of a deluge of literature on the subject of auction practice, and the secondary economy in general, circulating in the port cities of early 19th century America. The writer, identified only as "A New York Merchant," depicts the auction system as inherently unfair,

occasionally corrupt and – as a service to the English importer who "occupies for a season a seat at the table of a boarding house who bears none of the burdens and performs none of the duties of the citizen" – detrimental to the American economy.

Conscious of the dumping tactics of British industry, the publisher Mathew Carey was among those who advocated tariff protection for the products of American industry.

THE LIBRARY COMPANY OF PHILADELPHIA

wanting. Again, it did little for the popularity of auctioneers and commission merchants.

Believe the pamphlets that anyone with an opinion and some spare cash could publish and auctioneers were prone to fraud, deception and greed, anathema to the spirit of honest trade and traitors to Quaker ideals of good merchandise at fair prices. It was an issue on the other side of the Atlantic too. *The Ruinous Tendency of Auctioneering ...*, a popular auction-bashing pamphlet circulated freely in 1813, was authored not in New York, Boston or Philadelphia but in London. Its sentiments were, nevertheless, familiar. The auctioneer's stand, the author suggests, was "a machine contrived to diminish the number of hands employed in trade." He continues: "it will be the force of law alone that can effectively check this evil and if that power be not very quickly exerted we shall very soon find that the auction mart is an infinitely worse enemy to us ... than the armies of Bonaparte." These lively words were reprinted in New York twice, in 1813 and again in 1828.

The relationship between America's auctioneers and her merchants – rival channels through which foreign goods might reach the consumer – would deteriorate yet further with the peace treaty of 1815. As British merchants and manufacturers flooded the ports of

Philadelphia, New York, Baltimore and Alexandria with cheap, surplus goods, the auction stores were filled to brimming. The honest American shopkeeper was again at the mercy of the deceitful English importer and his stooge the auctioneer.

"It was soon discovered," wrote the New Yorker who authored *An Exposition of some of the evils arising from the Auction System,* "that half a dozen privileged persons in our principal cities had monopolised that trade, which once gave a livelihood to hundreds."

When, during a severe postwar depression, T.B. Freeman successfully reapplied for his auction license (probably in 1819), great profits were made hammering down the deluge of imported merchandise sold on foreign account. Philadelphia, however, would be spared the worst by the passage of importer-friendly auction legislation effected in New York in 1817. It was there, helped by a more accessible and ice-free harbor, where tons of excess cottons and wools would be offloaded at advantageous tariffs to buyers from all over the country. After the War of 1812, Philadelphia never regained its position as the trading capital of America.

But it was politics, not economics, that led to wholesale reform of Philadelphia's auction system in April 1822. Sixteen months previously, with impeachment

AN

EXPOSITION

OF SOME OF THE EVILS ARISING FROM THE

AUCTION SYSTEM.

———

The mode of offering and disposing of Goods at a public meeting, collected together by previous advertisement, had its origin in the best motives, and was the dictate of sound policy. It was devised as the most effectual means of preventing fraudulent collusion in assignees, executors, agents and other persons, holding property in trust, to be realized for the benefit of the parties interested; who in the ordinary course of things are often minors, unskilful in business, or resident at a distance, or in various

One of a group of three surviving invoices issued to the merchant William Cramond for services rendered by the commission merchant T.B. Freeman in 1816. Cramond, the owner of Sedgely Park estate on the grounds that now form the northern part of Fairmount Park, was charged a five per cent commission and advertising costs for the sale of five dozen silk hats sold at $3 apiece for a total of $180 in April. A similar consignment of hats was charged at two and a half per cent in May and when Cramond asked T.B Freeman to negotiate the sale of 192 English hats on June 5 he was charged only one per cent of the realized price.

THE HISTORICAL SOCIETY OF PENNSYLVANIA

proceedings hanging over the incumbent William Findlay, the Revolutionary War veteran Joseph Hiester had been voted into the governor's new Harrisburg residence on an anticorruption ticket. The system of appointing auctioneers – if not a source of actual corruption then certainly the source of much suspicion – would be among the casualties of Hiester's new broom.

An Act Relating to Auctions and Auctioneers became law on June 1, 1822. Wiping away the old appointment system, permission was granted to "make sale by auction of all and every kind of merchandise, estate and property" to any who had the wherewithal to stump up a license fee of $2,000 and "give proper security of $6,000." For half of these fees ($1,000 to the treasury and a bond of $3,000), a license would be granted to conduct sales of either "household and kitchen furniture, at the dwelling of the house thereof, of ships or vessels, and of real estate" or "of hardware, books, stationery, paintings, prints, watches, jewelry and furniture." Closing the legal loophole that had allowed T.B. Freeman to operate as an auctioneer in all but name from 1809-1819, a clause made it unlawful for "any auctioneer to associate with a commission merchant who shall derive profit or advantage from any sales by auction".

The oldest Freeman's catalogue extant, dated November 9, 1827, is a *Catalogue of Books ... suitable to the antiquarian and scholar* sold by Freeman, Son and Potter. The addition "Potter" to the company name appears to have been short-lived, and is first recorded in this publication. By 1829 the name had reverted to T.B. Freeman & Son.

CATALOGUE

OF A

PRIVATE LIBRARY,
(Edwd. Penington's)
COMPRISING MORE THAN

6000 VOLUMES OF BOOKS

In the different departments of

LITERATURE AND THE SCIENCES;

MANY OF WHICH ARE

EUROPEAN EDITIONS

WITH FINE ENGRAVINGS,

EXTREMELY RARE AND VALUABLE.

THE SALE

WILL TAKE PLACE AT THE LONG ROOMS

OF

FREEMAN, SON & POTTER,

NO. 8, SOUTH THIRD STREET,

ON TUESDAY EVENING, NOVEMBER 7, AT SIX O'CLOCK.

PHILADELPHIA:

PRINTED BY WM. STAVELY, 70, SOUTH THIRD STREET.

1826.

CATALOGUE

OF

LATIN, GREEK, HEBREW, FRENCH, GERMAN, AND ITALIAN

BOOKS, *12*

JUST RECEIVED ON CONSIGNMENT FROM EUROPE,

COMPRISING

SCARCE, RARE, AND VALUABLE WORKS

OF MANY OF THE ANCIENT WRITERS;

BEING A

Curious and Extensive Collection,

SUITABLE TO THE

ANTIQUARIAN AND SCHOLAR.

TO BE SOLD

ON THURSDAY MORNING, SEPT. 10, 1829, AT NINE O'CLOCK, BY

T. B. FREEMAN & SON, Auctioneers,

No. 8, SOUTH THIRD STREET,

PHILADELPHIA.

J. CLARKE, PRINTER, NO. 7, FRANKLIN PLACE.

1829.

At a time when the average weekly wage of a Philadelphia weaver was a mere $5, the reality was that license fees at these prices did not occasion a flood of would-be auctioneers – but that would arrive in 1826 when fees were scrapped in favor of an increase in the duties of goods sold at auction.

✶   ✶   ✶

With the legislative flurry of the 1820s, new avenues of specialization appeared.

Anxious to display the style and knowledge befitting a true gentleman, Americans had been buying new and antiquarian books since the very earliest days of the colonies. Tradition has it that Benjamin Franklin purchased books from Samuel Baker and John Sotheby who, like fellow Londoners Thomas Dodd and Walter Bonham, began life as book auctioneers. However, in the face of Philadelphia's muscular publishing lobby that objected vehemently to the idea of a book auctioneer for the city in the 18th century, it was not unusual for major American antiquarian libraries to be shipped back to London for resale. It was not until the decades after the Civil War that the movement of literary property from old world to new would become a tidal wave, as the great libraries of America were assembled.

Among those to purchase a $1,000 license to conduct auctions devoted to new and antiquarian books was Moses Thomas, the publisher of the *Analectic Magazine*, whose earliest auction catalog extant dates from 1823. Freeman's, who sporadically in its early history had sold new and used books imported from Europe, would begin to conduct weekly sales the following year.

On August 10, 1824, as the city readied itself for the arrival of the old warhorse Marquis de Lafayette, the *National Gazette* carried a notice from T.B. Freeman and Son (the company name had changed the previous year when Tristram William Lockyer joined the family firm) wishing to "respectfully acquaint the city and country dealers, that they intend regularly to hold public sales of Books, during the warm season, only on Saturday evenings. The rudimentary book catalogues produced by Freeman's for this period when the company was based on South Third Street are the earliest to have survived.

✶   ✶   ✶

With more auctioneers selling more merchandise, the meetings against auction sales did not dissipate during the doldrums of the 1820s. And, as Philadelphia's foreign commerce declined to a poor third or fourth place among the nation's trading capitals, some members of the retail community were arriving at the conclusion that

state auction legislation did not work. Increase local auction taxes and the market simply moved along the coastline to find more advantageous tariffs in the faster-growing cities of Baltimore, Boston and New York.

On June 27, 1828, a large meeting of merchants was held at the Clements Hotel to appoint a committee under the belief "that the system of sales by auction is a great and increasing evil, and highly injurious to the interests of every class." A memo was prepared for Congress objecting to "foreign speculators … incessant fluctuations in prices injurious to commerce … fraudulent debtors, thieves, heedless and guilty clerks, smugglers and others." It was signed by "several merchants of great respectability and intelligence, delegates from New York, Philadelphia, Baltimore and Alexandria."

It did not lead to the blanket rise in taxation on the sale of goods by auction that the merchants had hoped. However, given their primary interest to preserve the revenue laws from violation, in January 1829 the Committee of Ways and Means of Congress provided to tighten up on import duty dodging. "In all sales by auction of foreign goods, the invoice shall be produced, and a schedule of the goods, with all the marks and particulars or importation, shall be published."

CATALOGUE OF
THE GENUINE ELEGANT
Household Furniture,
French China, English Cut-glass, Piano Forte, Paintings, &c.

The Property of a Gentleman going to Europe.

To be sold on Thursday morning, April 10, 1828, at ten o'clock, at No. 251 Arch street, by

T. B. FREEMAN & SON.

FRONT PARLOUR

No.
1. fine toned Piano Forte, with additional keys, by Clementi of London
2. music stool
3. very superior mahogany Sideboard, with elegant knife cases
4. do do do card tables, harp pattern
5. two scarlet table cloths
6. fire screens, superior brass shifting mountings, inlaid
7. ten mahogany chairs, first quality, expressly made to order
8. breakfast table, claw feet, strong supporters
9. noble pier glass, 1st qual. French plate
10. mantel do do do
11. alabaster clock (10 day) mounted with the figure of truth
12. one pair bronze mantel lamps
13. one pair French china double gilt vases
14. amber lamps for sideboard or table
15. Brussels carpet, first quality, medallion centre
16. one pair foot stools
17. andirons, shovel, tongs and fender, with two slabs
18. thermometer, by Pool & Sons, London
19. sett of waiters, seven pieces
20. sett damask silk curtains with cornishes, the silk of the first quality
21. one pair venetian blinds
22. painting of Jesus brought before Pilate, fine picture
23. do representing a storm & wreck of a vessel
24. do landscapes, morning & evening
25. two col'd prints, mail coaches
26. 1 sett of French breakfast china, flowered and gold
27. 1 sett do do do white and gold
28. 1 rich harlequin sett, ornamented with different patterns
29. 18 claret glasses
30. 27 wine do
31. 13 tumblers
32. 2 finger glasses
33. 2 decanters

BACK PARLOUR

34. sett of yellow damask silk curtains and cornishes
35. noble French plate mantel glass
36. splendid pair mantel lamps, bronze and glass drops
37. do lustres, 1st qual. cut glass
38. one pair vases
39. small urn
40. one pair rich gilt brackets
41. sofa, 1st qual. materials, made to order
42. 10 chairs, mahogany, do do
43. Brussels carpet, first quality
44. pair foot stools
45. a double dinner sett of French white and gold china
46. dessert sett, with flowers
47. 2 pair quart and pint decanters, strawberry cut, 1st qual. English glass
48. pair rich cut pint decanters, do
49. 3 decanters do
50. 24 rich cut tumblers do
51. 23 do wines do do
52. 24 do jelly glasses do
53. 22 do ice cream do do
54. 16 champeigne do do

55. 3 pair salt cellars do
56. large cut glass dish, same pattern do
57. cellary do do do
58. 4 pair do dishes do
59. 4 fruit china baskets
60. 3 do do
61. bowl and pitcher
62. 2 superior cut glass pitchers
63. 1 do do pint pitcher
64. sett of rich cut glass castors, with silver mounting
65. do liquor stand, silver mounting
66. plated cake basket, silver mounting
67. do bread do do rim
68. 2 pair plated candlesticks, do
69. 1 do snuffers and tray, do
70. china butter boat and stand
71. andirons, shovel, tongs, fender and slabs
72. pair plated nut crackers
73. 2 venetian blinds

ENTRY

74. range of dining tables, made to stand upright, claw feet, made to order
75. entry carpet
76. hat stand
77. entry lamp
78. stair carpet, first and second story

BREAKFAST ROOM

79. pier glass
80. dinner sett of heavy stone Canton china
81. cups and saucers do do
82. 2 window curtains
83. 2 venetian blinds
84. very fine large mahogany book-case and secretary
85. 6 chairs
86. carpet and rug
87. 2 arm chairs with cushions
88. Spanish chair
89. pair vases
90. do jars
91. do plated candlesticks
92. do do snuffers
93. 2 glass shades, one broke
94. 4 paintings, Dutch views
95. 1 do landscape
96. 1 do philosopher
97. mahogany breakfast table, green cover
98. 2 maps
99. mahogany stand, claw feet

Front Bed Room Chamber—2nd floor.

100. 2 very superior pier glasses
101. 1 large do wardrobe
102. 2 ornamental pier tables
103. wash stand, bowl and pitcher
104. small tables
105. wash stand, marble slab, bowl & pitcher
106. 2 small towel stands
107. 9 chairs
108. neat mahogany bureau
109. dressing glass
110. large easy chair, chintz covers, extra cover, dimity
111. small stove and chair
112. andirons, shovel and tongs
113. pair plated chamber candlesticks
114. mahogany bedstead
115. chintz curtain, with silk fringe, for do and three window curtains to match
116. very first quality feather bed, bolster and pillows
117. do do large hair mattrass

118. 2 pair blankets, large size, No. 4 & 5, 12 quarters
119. carpet, fine print Magdalen
    1 painted chamber pan

Back Bed Chamber—2nd floor.

120. mahogany bedstead
121. fine feather bed, bolster and pillows
122. do large hair mattrass
123. 2 pair large blankets, Nos. 1 & 6—10 and 11 quarters
124. 2 pair do on bureau, Nos. 2 and 3—10 quarters
125. dimity curtains for bedstead and two windows
126. 2 superior bureaus
127. large mahogany wash stand
128. pier glass
129. chairs, gilt
130. carpet
131. 2 basins and pitchers—chambers, &c.
132. book shelves
133. fancy pier table
134. andirons, shovel, tongs and fender, with hearth brush
    1 painted chamber pan

ENTRY—2nd FLOOR

135. entry Venetian carpet
136. fancy sofa and 2 arm chairs with cushions to match

ENTRY—3rd FLOOR

137. Venetian carpet

Back Chamber—3rd story

138. Brussels carpet
139. field bedstead
140. chintz curtains for do and two windows
141. low bedstead
142. bed, bolster and pillows, on the field bedstead
143. hair mattrass, do
144. single bed and bolster
145. do hair mattrass
146. 1 painted chamber pan
147. 4 pair blankets, Nos. 8 9 10 & 11
148. brass stair rods

Front Chamber—3rd story

149. small bureau
150. low post bedstead, bolsters and pillows. No. 1—bed for do
151. low double post bedstead, No. 2—bed, bolster and pillow for do
152. lots of carpet—6 chairs
153. 2 window curtains
154. table and glass
    1 painted chamber pan

ENTRY—3rd STORY

155. carpet

GARRET

156. bedstead, bed & bedding, table, 2 chairs and small glass
157. a general assortment of kitchen furniture

CLARET WINES

5 boxes of one doz. best quality Latour
12 or 13 doz. St. Julien

first rate close Carriage
first rate gig, nearly new, made by Weaver, with harness and trunks
2 gentlemens' saddles and bridles
1 lady's do with stable furniture, &c

T.B. Freeman's Real Estate Register is one of several surviving broadsides providing details of the latest properties for sale at auction or by private treaty. This one, dated February 23, 1833, announces the forthcoming sale at the Merchant's Coffee House of the 109-acre Hugg's Meadow Farm, 'situate [sic] at the mouth of Timber Creek, one mile below Gloucester ferry, and four miles from Philadelphia."

Interpreting the revenue figures, one might conclude this had a substantial impact upon the trade in Philadelphia as it began a painful transition from mercantile seaport to manufacturing center. Duties on goods sold at auction in the city, valued at $124,937.31 in 1830 and $139,361.22 in 1831, fell into sharp decline after the severe winter of 1831-32, generating only $93,552.40 by 1832 and a mere $78,063.60 in 1833. Of the 45 auctioneers J.F. Watson lists as operating in Philadelphia between 1828 and 1850, he observes most were in business for just one or two years.

As foreign commerce declined, other auction businesses came and went. But Freeman's survived.

Just as a seaport found it could excel in heavy industry, technology and transport, so, too, an auctioneer of more than 20 years' experience found profits in more inward-looking ventures as the second generation approached. As the city's population grew by 50 percent with each successive decade, T.B. Freeman would sell the real estate of "the Athens of America" and conduct low key estate sales with a frequency that reflected the average life expectancy of the day. Most citizens lived only to see their early forties.

By 1836, as he assumed the position of Right Worshipful Grand Master at his lodge, T.B. Freeman chose to relinquish his auctioneer's license yet again. But this time it would be to hand over the reins to his son.

An announcement appeared in the debut issue of Philadelphia's first penny paper, *The Public Ledger*, dated March 25, 1836. It read:

"T.B. Freeman respectfully informs the gentlemen of the Bar and others that he has made such arrangements in his present business as will enable him personally to devote the whole of his time to sales by order of the courts of law and the appraising of all descriptions of personal property which might be required by order of executors, administrators etc. The experience of 30 years practice which he has had in the sales of real estate and personal property, he flatters himself, will enable him to give personal satisfaction."

He was 59 years old.

No. 1836 T. B. Freeman's Real Estate Register.

HUGG'S
MEADOW FARM.

Will be sold on Wednesday evening, the 20th of March, 1833, at seven o'clock, at the Merchants' Coffee House, in the city of Philadelphia, the following described Real Estate:—

The valuable Farm, long known as "Hugg's Meadow Farm," situate at the mouth of **Timber Creek**, one mile below **Gloucester** ferry, and four miles from **Philadelphia**, containing **109** acres more or less, about 66 of which are first rate bank Meadow, and the remainder upland of good quality.

The facility of water carriage afforded by the situation of this place, being at the junction of **Timber Creek** with the river **Delaware**, and its proximity to the city, contribute to render it very desirable and profitable for the production of hay or the grazing of cattle, and for the raising of vegetables, or "truck" for the Philadelphia market.

The buildings consist of a comfortable two story **Frame Dwelling**, spacious **Frame Barn** and large **Hay House, Corn Crib**, stone **Spring House** over an excellent and never failing **Spring**, stone **Smoke House**, &c. &c.

If agreeable to the purchaser, $2500 may remain secured on the premises in the usual way.

Terms made known at the time of sale, by

T. B. FREEMAN,
Auctioneer, No. 8 South Third St.

February 23, 1833.

Printed by J. Richards, No. 13 Church Alley, Philadelphia.

Freeman's portrait as Right Worshipful Grand Master hangs above the sweeping staircase of Philadelphia's magnificent Masonic Temple. Freeman (top center) hangs to the right of George Mifflin Dallas, mayor of Philadelphia in 1828, vice president under James K. Polk and the man who gave the city of Dallas, Texas, its name.

RIGHT WORSHIPFUL GRAND MASTER
T.B. FREEMAN

Tristram B. Freeman, who likely became a Mason while living in London, would assume a prominent role within Lodge No. 51 in Philadelphia. He was admitted to "the 51" (instituted in January 1792) as a Master Mason in 1805, on the day of Jefferson's second inauguration. At the time Robert Polk (circa 1771-1836), an auctioneer known to every grocer in the city was also a member. By 1836, Freeman had risen to the position of Right Worshipful Grand Master. A noted speaker on Masonry, his most important address titled *Principles of Masonry* was delivered on June 22, 1821, at the English Presbyterian Church in Germantown, and was published nine years later by the Philadelphia printer Robert Desilver. His tenure oversaw a turbulent period in the history of the Pennsylvanian Masonry. It included the Panics of 1837 and 1842, that necessitated the temporary sale of Freemason's Hall on Chestnut Street, and the defense of the fraternity at a time when anti-Masonic feeling was at its height. When, in 1835, the House of Representatives appointed a committee to investigate "the evils of Freemasonry," Brother Freeman was among those called upon to vigorously rebuff its detractors' charges.

A chapter of the Royal Arch Masons – the Tristram B. Freeman Royal Arch Chapter No. 243 of Philadelphia – was also named after him, although it now has been disbanded. Tristram's first son, Henry Gibbard Freeman (1789-1875), who chose law over the family business, was also a member of Lodge 51.

"We perceive by an advertisement in our paper this morning, that Mr. Ohl, the administrator upon the estate of the late Mr. Maelzel, will, on the 1st day of September next, cause to be sold at public auction, the whole of the curious automata and machinery which constituted Mr. Maelzel's exhibition, the principal one of which is DeKempelen's celebrated chess player."

UNITED STATES GAZETTE, AUGUST 10, 1838

"An old and highly respected citizen of Philadelphia…" The death of
T.B. Freeman as it was recorded on the front page of the
Philadelphia *Inquirer* dated March 29, 1842

☞ In the obituary column this morning, will be found a notice of the death of T. B. Freeman, Esq. an old and highly respected citizen of Philadelphia— one whose generosity has been conspicuous, and whose liberality and charity has made for him a fame that wealth could never purchase. He has, in a good old age, sunk away into rest, and after an active and useful life. he met death with an humble cheerfulness, relying on other merits than his own for that happiness towards which he looked

Mr. Freeman has left no enemy, we believe; and many who knew the kindness of his heart, will lament that they shall no longer enjoy his intercourse. But they will find a consolation in the reflection, that whither he has gone, pain and anguish, such as have wasted him away, cannot come.

Brief obituaries of the man the *Philadelphia Inquirer* called "an old and respectable inhabitant of this city" were carried by most of the major newspapers. Slowly relinquishing the auction business to his son in the 1830s, T.B. Freeman had continued to trade as a merchant into his 76th year but, diagnosed with cancer, was confined to his house during the final three months of his life. He died on March 28, 1842, the date of his 44th wedding anniversary. Freeman's male friends and family members, his Masonic brethren and the members of the St. George and other societies to which he belonged were invited to attend his funeral on March 30. He apparently left no will, and no valuation of his estate is known to exist. However, he had lived long enough to see his son sell one of the best-known and most remarkable objects of the age.

✶   ✶   ✶

Of all the exotic characters to pass through the royal courts of Europe during the late 18th century, none were more enigmatic than left-handed, hookah-smoking chess player called "the Turk." Outfitted in lavish robes and seated at a maple cabinet, the Turk spent 65 years traveling the Continent, stunning Europe's crowned heads and literati with his uncanny prowess at the game of kings. His record of chess victories included matches against Frederick the Great, Napoleon Bonaparte and Benjamin Franklin. What made this player so special? He was a machine.

The chess-playing Turk, the product of six months' labor for its inventor, the Hungarian nobleman and scientist Baron Wolfgang von Kempelen (1734-1804), made his debut at the royal court of Austria's Empress Maria Theresa in 1770. The cabinet's doors were ceremoniously opened and the drawers pulled out to reveal for the audience an elaborate clockwork mechanism. The hookah was removed, a lighted candelabrum placed atop the cabinet, while the gears were wound slowly and deliberately to heighten the sense of anticipation. Members of the court were then invited to challenge the mechanical marvel. Most would lose.

At critical points in the game, the Turk would issue physical challenges to his opponent. Each time the automaton prepared to make a move, the mechanism could be heard whirring inside. The Turk would turn its head as though perusing the board, then raise its hand, select a chess piece and consummate the move by setting it down on the chosen square. To indicate "check" to its adversary, the Turk would shake its head three times and declare, in French, "échec!"

If checking the queen, it remained silent, but would shake its head twice. It also seemed to know if its opponent had made an unacceptable move, as it would shake its head negatively, lift the piece from the incorrect square and return it to the square previously occupied.

There was widespread conjecture over a machine with apparent human intelligence. In 1789, a German, Joseph Friedrich, set about designing a replica Turk before authoring an exposé on how the chess player might function with a concealed human collaborator. Others saw strange magnetic phenomenon or even evidence of a Faustian pact.

When von Kempelen died in 1804, the famed automaton was sold to a Viennese musical engineer and personal friend of Ludwig van Beethoven, Johann Maelzel. The pair travelled to the new Napoleonic courts of Germany where it was seen by Prince Eugène de Beauharnais. The stepson of Napoleon Bonaparte became besotted with the mechanical amusement and in 1811 reportedly paid Maelzel 30,000 francs to purchase the automaton and learn its secrets. Six years later, Maelzel repurchased the Turk, agreeing to pay the prince from profits earned by the attraction's future appearances.

By 1818, Maelzel and his machine were enjoying London's fashionable Belgravia quarter. In a small candlelit salon, the Turk was displayed together with other prized attractions including a mechanical trumpeter and a spectacular moving diorama called The Conflagration of Moscow. The show was the talk of the town, and ran twice daily through the summer of 1820. Newspaper ads invited any opponents to try their hand against the Turk, offering a first-move advantage.

But it was at the end of this two-year exhibition that the mystique began to unravel and the Turk was soon to begin its path to Freeman's. A brilliant young London mathematician named Robert Willis had devised a theory about the automaton after studying all published accounts of games it had played and won. He attended one of the London performances at Spring Gardens to get a close-up look. Standing before the Turk and using an umbrella as a makeshift measuring stick, Willis confirmed his suspicions and went on to publish his thoughts in *An Attempt to Analyse the Automaton Chess Player of Mr. von Kempelen*.

In this pamphlet, Willis suggested that, based on his estimate taken with the his umbrella, the Turk's cabinet could sufficiently accommodate an adult player – no doubt a talented one. The gears and interior mechanism

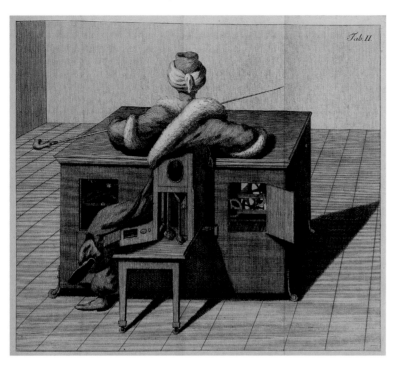

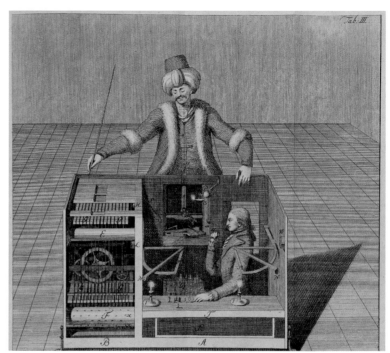

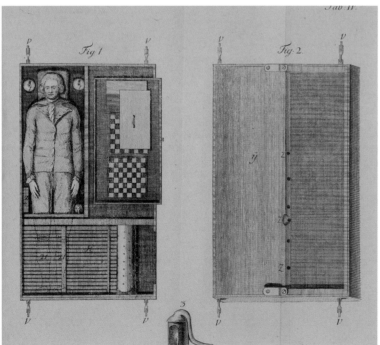

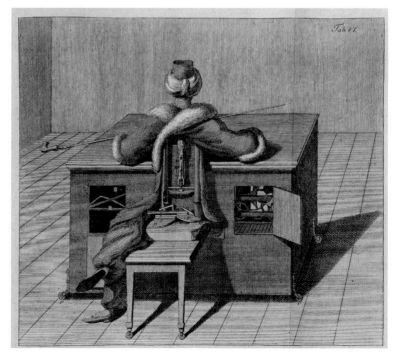

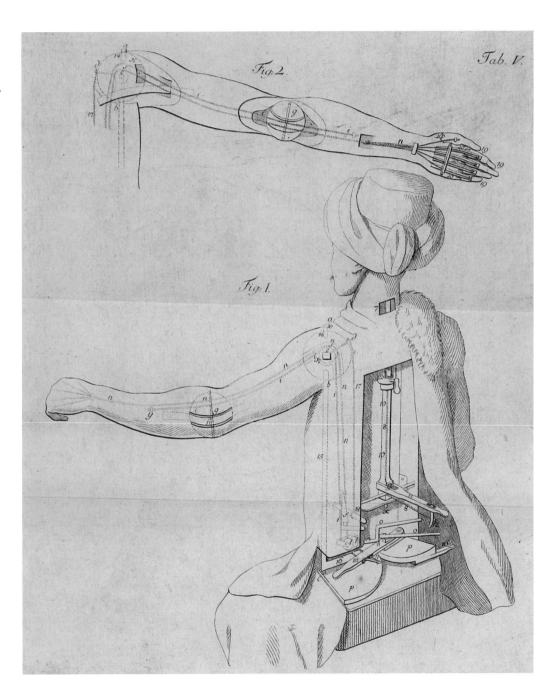

SALE OF FURNITURE,

At No. 292 Market street, between Eighth and Ninth.
On Wednesday morning,

At 10 o'clock, will be sold, at 292 Market street, the furniture of a lady relinquishing housekeeping, consisting of ingrain carpets, venitian blinds, mahogany tables, looking glasses, chairs, stair and domestic carpets, and-irons, shovel and tongs, Liverpool and glassware, a number of excellent feather beds and good bedding, single and double bedsteads, washstands and bureaus, with many other articles of furniture; also, several stoves with an assortment of kitchen furniture.

Public Sale of the Valuable Exhibition of the late Mr Maelzel.

By order of the Administrator.
On Saturday morning,

Sept. 1, at 10 o'clock, will be sold, at the store No. 229 south Front street, the effects of the late Mr. Maelzell, all of which are carefully packed up in their respective cases and boxes, and properly assorted, containing

The Automaton Chess Player,
Do   Trumpeter,
Do   Rope Dancers and Speaking Figures,
Six or 7 Automaton Figures for the small theatre,
The Whist Player,
The grand Panorama of Moscow,
The Carousal or Tournament,
The Pyric Fire,
A Piano,

All these objects being of such a peculiar nature, the Administrator has no more knowledge of them than the purchaser, and will therefore sell them as they are, without guarantee as to their perfectness, good order, or numbers. Terms made known at the sale.

JOHN F. OHL, Adm'r.

Public Sale of Machinery for Cleaning Flaxseed.

On Saturday morning,

1st Sept. will be sold at the store adjoining 229 south Front street, and immediately after the sale of the effects of the late Mr Maelzel a set of machinery used for cleaning flaxseed, consisting of 4 wire screens, 10 and 12 feet long and 30 and 32 inches in diameter; a large fan, with other fixtures; also, sundry iron frames and doors for ovens and furnaces.

N.B.—The above articles may be seen any time previous to the sale.

Engravings by Carl Gottlieb von Windisch from his 1783 pamphlet *Lettres sur le jouer d'echecs de M. de Kempelen* showing how the masterful automaton concealed its human secret. Windisch's findings following a series of correspondence with his associate De Kempelen were published in France but reprinted and translated into English in 1819 as the Turk moved first to London and then to Philadelphia.

were nothing more than a smokescreen to cover up sounds of the concealed player.

Some were not entirely convinced by Willis's argument. A human arm reaching up through the cabinet couldn't possibly fit into the Turk's arm. But with the publication of Willis's paper and other exposés, Maelzel sensed his good thing soon could be coming to an end.

Fearing the inevitable, and still in debt to the heirs of now-deceased Prince Eugène de Beauharnais to the tune of 30,000 francs, Maelzel fled the Continent in 1825. He would cultivate the fresh fields of America.

The Turk, with the hidden assistance of a young Frenchwoman, made its American debut in 1826 in New York. The Big Apple was followed by appearances in Boston, Philadelphia, Washington, Pittsburgh, Richmond, Virginia, and Baltimore. In Philadelphia its presence had inspired the formation of America's first organized group devoted to the game of chess, the Franklin Chess Club. Its performance in Baltimore, in 1836, had been witnessed by Edgar Allan Poe.

In 1838, at the height of its popularity in North America, the Turk's career came to an abrupt halt. Maelzel and the Turk's final operator, French chess master William Schlumberger, were in Havana when Schlumberger suddenly fell ill with yellow fever. He declined rapidly

and died before the two men could arrange passage back to the United States. Without his human chess player, a disheartened Maelzel crated his automata and, on July 14, boarded a ship bound for Philadelphia. But like Schlumberger, Maelzel would never make it back. A week into the voyage, as the ship approached the South Carolina coastline, Maelzel was found dead in his cabin. He was buried at sea, a four-pound shot attached to his feet. His worldly effects arrived in Charleston without him – his dismantled and crated automata, 12 gold doubloons, some personal papers, a gold medal given to him by the King of Prussia, and his chessboard.

All of the goods ended up in the custody of Maelzel's friend, John F. Ohl, one of several Philadelphia merchants involved in the Latin-American shipping trade. He had owned the vessel on which the showman had died.

The United States Gazette carried Maelzel's obituary while Ohl arranged for the shipping crates containing his possessions to be delivered to the premises of T.W.L. Freeman at 8 South Third Street for a sale on September 14.

Brief details of the auction appeared the next day in *Poulson's American Daily Advertiser*. "Mr. Freeman sold yesterday morning the valuable 'exhibition' of the late Mr. Maelzel, at the following prices: Chess Player $400,

Carousal [sic] $200, Fire Works $250, Whist Player $40, Trumpeter $675, Rope Dancers $225, Organ $35, Piano Forte $55, Seven small Figures for Theatre $160, and Panorama of Moscow $900. Total $2,940."

It emerged that Ohl, himself, had purchased the Turk at Freeman's sale, hoping to resell it for a profit above his $400. To his disappointment, a buyer did not materialize until the following spring, when it caught the eye of local physician Dr. John Kearsley Mitchell. He later sold shares to 75 curiosity-seekers who together reassembled the Turk to learn its mechanical secrets.

In 1840, Mitchell briefly reprised the automaton's career, but its public performances – minus the benefit of Maelzel's personality and showmanship – failed to strike a chord with spectators. The number of paid admissions dwindled in a matter of weeks, prompting shareholders to donate the Turk to the local Chinese Museum, where it spent its final days in a seldom-visited corner of the building. On July 5, 1854 the Turk perished when a fast-moving fire spread from the nearby National Theater and consumed the museum's contents.

Fortunately for future students of illusion, the Turk's secret did not die with it. In 1857, Mitchell's son, Silas Weir Mitchell, published a series of articles that came very close to detailing how the Turk operated. He confirmed that the cabinet was capable of housing an average-size adult – albeit uncomfortably. The player could be hidden from the public during the ceremonious opening of doors and drawers by executing a skillfully choreographed sequence of movements on a sliding seat. The elaborate mechanism was merely a decoy activated to mask sounds while the candelabrum beside the board was helpful in masking the smell of the candle providing visibility to the operator. In his final playing position, leaning forward with knees up and breathing through small air holes drilled into the cabinet, the operator faced a chessboard that replicated the one placed before the Turk. By means of an ingenious, articulated metal rod that ran vertically upward into the Turk's torso then down its left arm, the operator was able to orchestrate the chess moves, opening and closing the Turk's hand to pick up and relocate chess pieces. A voicebox, when activated, emitted the warning "échec!"

Keeping track of the game's progress required intense concentration on the part of the operator. The only way he or she could follow the opponent's moves was by watching for the movement of magnets suspended on wires overhead. On their own chessboard, operators conducted a mirror image of the game as it took place

overhead, and would execute the Turk's moves by means of the metal rod.

A letter written by the Turk's last operator at the Chinese Museum, a young Philadelphia man named Lloyd Smith, is held in the archives of the Library Company of Philadelphia. It is the only known first-hand account from any of the Turk's operators explaining how the automaton worked.

Conducting business against the backdrop of ugly racial violence and the second severe economic depression of the century, T.W.L. Freeman would also be fortunate to find himself at the center of the forgotten mulberry tree craze that swept the East Coast states during the 1830s.

With Europe's upper classes clamoring for silk finery, arborists from Long Island to Virginia had been quick to seize on the idea of promoting a new home industry. Cultivation of mulberry trees – whose leaves are the preferred food of silkworms everywhere – would provide work for new settlers, silk fibers for the new mills of New England and riches for the adventurous farmer.

Silkworm cultivation had occupied colonial Virginians before tobacco became the state crop, and had been endorsed by Franklin as a method of subsistence

suitable for the Commonwealth of Pennsylvania. The burgeoning industry had been given a kick-start by a state society, a deluge of literature tailored to the would-be cottage cocoonist and the enterprising American Silk Agency on Bank Street, Philadelphia, who touted silkworm breeding as a "profitable branch of NATIONAL INDUSTRY" – with the patriotic emphasis as shown.

Buoyed by overstated newspaper accounts of the fortunes to be made from silkworms and their ease of cultivation in the Mid-Atlantic climate, the farms of new and old Pennsylvanians changed from breadbaskets and orchards to mulberry plantations. In 1830, the frenzy reached a new plateau as the first shipment of genuine Chinese mulberry trees (the *morus multicaulis*) arrived on American soil from the Orient. Speculators attempted to corner the market for this superior species, buying the seedlings as they arrived at the docks from China and reselling them at auction as they approached maturity.

Farmers and speculators would travel to the Philadelphia area to bid on young trees as they stood in the ground. Some bought for cultivation; others only had an eye towards reselling them for profit at a later date. At one recorded auction of the period, 260,000 trees were sold at prices varying from 17 to 37 cents per tree, with the entire gross coming in at $81,218.75.

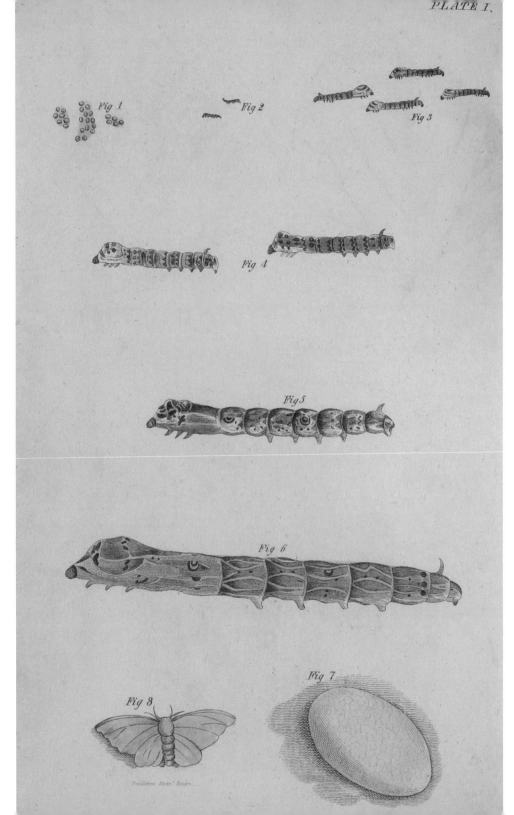

Hand-colored engravings from Jonathan Holmes Cobb's *Manual containing information respecting the growth of the mulberry tree with suitable directions for the culture of silk,* a 68 page booklet printed in Boston in 1831.

The leaves of the *morus multicaulis* as depicted in an *Essay on the cultivation of mulberry trees, and the culture of silk taken from the Transactions of the Essex Agricultural Society*, Massachusetts, 1832.

Despite a landscape now inundated with mulberry trees, auction prices for *multicaulis* rose steadily into the late 1830s as cocoonists, undeterred by the economic panic of 1837, continued to buy trees from wholesalers and patiently tended their silkworms in hopes of future reward. Dramatic price rises occurred toward the end of 1838 when a bill to promote the culture of silk was passed by both houses of the legislature, offering every silk farmer a premium of 20 cents per pound of cocoons raised in the state of Pennsylvania.

T.W.L. Freeman's, with its reputation already well established as a commodities clearing house, found itself at the center of the mulberry tree boom, conducting countless on-site sales and sometimes holding multiple tree auctions on a given day. On September 18, 1839, for example, Freeman's auctioned 20,000 *morus multicaulis* "in a very thriving condition and large growth … in quality equal to any in the market" at Hamilton Village, the settlement laid out in the western part of the city in the earlier years of the century. Immediately afterward, the company auctioned a further 16,257 of the same species "about 100 miles west of the Permanent Bridge" on Market Street, describing the trees as "admired by all who had an opportunity of seeing them."

As the bubble reached its greatest circumference in 1839, one report of the day stated Chinese mulberry trees were commanding as much as $100 apiece. It was certainly more than the silk produced from the worm progeny of such a tree could ever hope to recoup in one investor's lifetime. And this at a time when thousands of unskilled Philadelphians toiled at the hand looms for 60 cents a day or in the match factories for $2.50 a week.

Inevitably, this latter-day version of the 17th century tulip mania ended with a catastrophic market crash at the close of the decade. As investments imploded, many farmers dug up or axed their mulberry trees in disgust and returned to more traditional crops that now would have to be started from seed. Others stubbornly soldiered on, only to fall victim to competition from China. Ultimately a blight wiped out mulberry orchards all up and down the East Coast. Freeman's however, would find other goods to sell.

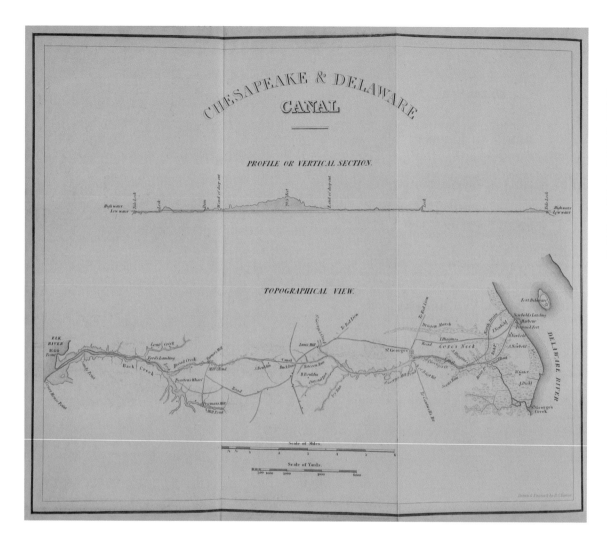

CHESAPEAKE & DELAWARE CANAL

PROFILE OR VERTICAL SECTION.

TOPOGRAPHICAL VIEW.

In 1802 the Chesapeake & Delaware Canal Company formed with the idea of connecting the Chesapeake Bay with the Delaware River. When work on the 14-mile waterway was finally completed in 1829 at a cost of $2.5 million, the sea route between Baltimore and Philadelphia was 300 miles shorter. As detailed in *The 16th General Report of the Chesapeake & Delaware Canal Company* dated June 1, 1835 the company was experiencing great financial difficulties in its early years, a possible reason why on April 28, 1835 T.W.L. Freeman was offering for sale "the Elegant canal boat Pennsylvania formerly belonging to the line between this city and Baltimore...20 feet long, 19 feet beam."

Purchased by the US Government in 1919, the Chesapeake & Delaware Canal is the only canal from the heyday of American canal building that remains in constant use today.

HORSES, COWS, HOGS AND HAY ...

Changing legislation allowed for the rise of specialist auctioneers in real estate, books or livestock in Philadelphia, but the firm of T.W.L. Freeman would remain very much a jobbing concern. Second-hand furniture and local real estate would provide the bread-and-butter existence in the difficult years as Philadelphia came to terms with the Industrial Revolution. However, this list of some of the more unusual items that went under the gavel is more revealing:

Elegant canal boat Pennsylvania formerly belonging to the line between this city and Baltimore, and the Chesapeake and Delaware Canal 20 feet long, 19 feet beam, April 28, 1835

Perpetual Motion ... the machinery of the late James L. Vauclain ... together with a regular journal of his proceedings and calculations thereon ... being the product of 23 years labor, March 1, 1839

The fine Philadelphia-built brig Ann Eliza ... now lying at Lombard Street wharf, 110 tons, April 30, 1839

70,000 burnt and 37,000 raw bricks with a large quantity of dry clay, September 21, 1839

Horses, cows, hogs and hay, March 6, 1843

At private sale, Pew No. 40 in the Fourth Presbyterian Church in the corner of Fourth and Pine Streets, which will be sold low, March 6, 1843

Two first-rate locomotives with engines, April 19, 1843

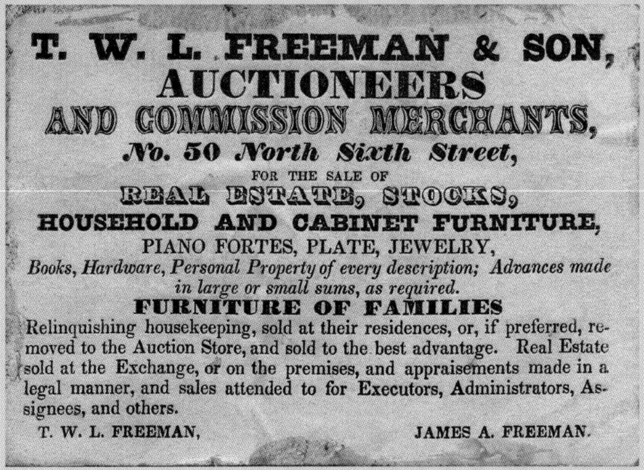

T. W. L. FREEMAN & SON,
AUCTIONEERS
AND COMMISSION MERCHANTS,
No. 50 North Sixth Street,
FOR THE SALE OF
REAL ESTATE, STOCKS,
HOUSEHOLD AND CABINET FURNITURE,
PIANO FORTES, PLATE, JEWELRY,
Books, Hardware, Personal Property of every description; *Advances made in large or small sums, as required.*
FURNITURE OF FAMILIES
Relinquishing housekeeping, sold at their residences, or, if preferred, removed to the Auction Store, and sold to the best advantage. Real Estate sold at the Exchange, or on the premises, and appraisements made in a legal manner, and sales attended to for Executors, Administrators, Assignees, and others.
T. W. L. FREEMAN,   JAMES A. FREEMAN.

The Merchants' Exchange designed by William Strickland as depicted in William Russell Birch's *Views of Philadelphia*. Built in 1832, on the north side of Walnut between Third and Dock streets, the white marble building is now part of Independence National Historical Park.

1850-1900

CHAPTER FIVE

"*The present auction system – be it right or wrong – sees the auction stores strewed thick as the autumnal leaves with multitudinous bales of English merchandise.*"

ANNALS OF PHILADELPHIA AND PENNSYLVANIA IN THE OLDEN TIME,

JOHN FANNING WATSON AND WILLIS P. HAZARD, 1877

James A. Freeman (1820-1896). Born in Chester County but moving to the city early in his life, James Freeman was the figurehead of the family business for 40 years. In his prime he was acknowledged as a great auctioneer whose wit and versatility could hold an audience and bridge a potentially awkward silence. The *Public Ledger* reported his technique at the Philadelphia Exchange in 1890: "Come, what do you bid." There was no response. "Why do you hesitate, stocks have gone up again." Still no bid. "The Panic's over, you know". Bidding resumed.

A local councillor, prison inspector and appointed President of the Board of Charities and Correction in 1892, James A. Freeman would also generate column inches by the manner of his death on April 8, 1896. According to the front page of the *Public Ledger* of the following day: "He left his office, 422 Walnut Street at 12:30, presumably to go to his home, 1713 Vine Street. He boarded a Fifth Street car and was carried to the depot in Frankford when the conductor discovered that his aged passenger was in a comatose state and unable to speak. An ambulance was summoned and Mr. Freeman was conveyed to the Episcopal Hospital where he was diagnosed with Bright's disease of the kidneys, put in a hot bath and subjected to other treatments but without success."

By the third quarter of the 19th century, there were close to 30 auctioneers operating in Philadelphia. A dozen of those companies could be found within a 10-block stretch of Chestnut Street. Almost as many populated Market Street, while two firms occupied forgotten icons of colonial Philadelphia.

It had been the source of discomfort for the city's antiquarians that the City Tavern, dining room of the First Continental Congress, had been reduced to little more than a storeroom for the auction firm Thomas Birch & Son before its demolition in 1852. One can only imagine the scene described by historian and preservationist Benson J. Lossing after laying eyes on Carpenters' Company Hall in 1848.

There in the hall "consecrated by the holiest associations which cluster around the birthplace of our republic" he encountered the auction business of C.J. Wolbert & Co., and something akin to the moneychangers in the temple. "What a desecration! Covering the façade of the very Temple of Freedom with placards of grovelling mammon! If sensibility is shocked with this outward pollution, it is overwhelmed with indignant shame on entering the hall where ... the godfathers of our republic convened ... to find it filled with every species of merchandise." In 1856, the Carpenters' Company took

heed and decided to evict its tenants and make repairs and restorations.

Legislation was at the root of the mushrooming number of Philadelphia auctioneers. A six-tier licensing system was introduced to the city's auction laws in 1859 – the cost of the license depending upon the annual value of the merchandise the auctioneer was expecting to sell. For as little as $100 any citizen of the United States could trade as an auctioneer in the Commonwealth of Philadelphia providing the annual value of the goods sold did not exceed $50,000. The price rose incrementally up to a ceiling of $2000 to be paid by those who anticipated sales of more than $750,000. And by 1900 Freeman's would hold a first category license.

Directories mention no fewer than 12 different locations for Freeman's in its first 50 years, but moving with the westward flow of the city, the company would spend the second half of the century on Walnut Street. From 1846 it would operate from number 106 and then at number 422 from 1858.

In 1853 *A New and Complete Gazetteer of the United States* had called Walnut the "ton" street of Philadelphia's most fashionable quarter. The throughfare "thronged with spacious and elegant residences ... giving

The emergence of photography by the 1840s took the gloss off many of Philadelphia's buildings, previously depicted free from the grime of industrialization in paintings and lithographs. Freeman's home from 1858 to 1898 was 422 Walnut Street. Before becoming an auction house, the building was "an elegant boarding house for gentlemen," owned by a Mrs. Crim, whose guests included the infirm Chief Justice Marshall, who died there on July 6 1835. It was at Marshall's funeral that the Liberty Bell would be tolled for the last time.

United States Gazette, February 25, 1846
"T.W.L. Freeman: The Subscriber, having relinquished the General Auction Business in favor of his son and late partner, JAMES A. FREEMAN, proposes giving his attention to the sales of real estate made under the order of the Orphans' Court, or by Executors, Trustees, or Assignees. He will also attend to the sales of Personal Effects of persons deceased ..."

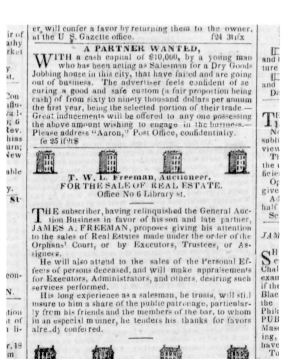

abundant evidence of affluence, taste and luxurious ease, and comfort," but behind the tree-shaded sidewalks were small-scale manufacturers and the early suggestions of a downtown shopping district. Number 422 – it was one of thousands of addresses in the city that had just changed in the newly consolidated city – had been "an elegant boarding house for gentleman" and the guesthouse where Chief Justice Marshall had spent his final days in 1835. Its fine classical facade and walls of pressed-brick would serve as Freeman's base until 1898.

∗   ∗   ∗

It was the English author Anthony Hope who, in his novel *A Servant of the Public*, said: "Three generations it takes to make a great concern." Tristram William Lockyer Freeman had five sons, but it was his eldest, James A. Freeman, and his youngest, Samuel T. Freeman, who would carry on the family business into the 20th century.

The company had moved into its third generation early in 1846. T.W.L. Freeman had taken a small notice in the *United States Gazette* to announce his decision to spend what would be the final year of his life brokering property sales in and around the city, and relinquish the General Auction Business to his eldest son. Samuel T.

Freeman, plus James' two sons, Erasmus and Harold A. Freeman, would soon join the company.

Like the man himself, who juggled the family business alongside public service duties as a councillor and prison inspector, James A. Freeman's General Auction Business remained a multifarious operation. At the center of the operation there were still the "multitudinous bales of English merchandise" to which Willis P. Hazard referred. But this period would see the emergence of the wholesale dealer with storage warehouses on the banks of the Delaware that would usher in a pattern of commerce more like that of today.

James A. Freeman was as likely to be conducting regular sales of real estate, office and household furniture, minor libraries and the occasional casualty of industrial progress. More unusual, but certainly revealing, were the burial plots at the Odd Fellows Cemetery, 20 cases of Dom Perignon champagne, 50 shares in the Steubenville and Indiana Railroad, and a "Newfoundland dog ... 14 months old sold for want of room". Surely, however, the company motto – *Omnia praeter amicos vendimus* (We sell everything but our friends) – was never more relevant than in February 21, 1866, when James A. Freeman brought down the gavel on 500 tons of "manure and composts of meats, bones etc. of great

Catalogue
of
Peale's Gallery of American Portraits

8

MODE OF SELLING.

N. B.—To afford an opportunity to preserve this valuable collection entire, the choice will be sold with the privilege,—i. e., the choice of any Painting of the entire collection will be sold to the highest bidder, allowing him the privilege of taking one or any number he may wish. After he shall have made his selection, the choice of the remainder will again be put up, and so continue until the whole collection is sold.

CATALOGUE.

NO.

1. Columbus.

2. Americus Vespucius.

3. Magellan.

4. Hernando Cortes.

5. General Washington, painted in 1783.

6. General Henry Knox, of the Army of the Revolution, and Secretary of War in 1789.

7. General Nathaniel Greene, Commander-in-Chief of the Southern Department in the Revolution.

8. General Henry Knox.

9. General Daniel Morgan, of the Army of the Revolution.

10. General Arthur St. Clair, of the Army of the Revolution, Commander-in-Chief of the North Western Army, and Governor of the North Western Territory.

11. General Anthony Wayne, of the Army of the Revolution, and Commander-in-Chief of the North Western Army.

12. General Benjamin Lincoln, of the Army of the Revolution.

13. General Horatio Gates, the Hero of Saratoga.

14. General Richard Montgomery, of the Revolution.

15. Christ Healing the Sick, an Original Picture, by REMBRANDT PEALE.

16. General Sumpter, of the Army of the Revolution.

17. The Marquis De Lafayette.

18. General Lacklan Macintosh, of the Revolution; a Member of Congress from Georgia, in 1784.

1

"One of the most attractive sales of paintings ever made in the United States ..." The rudimentary catalogue published by Moses Thomas for the sale of 269 portraits by Charles Willson Peale from the Philadelphia Museum on October 9, 1854.

Combining natural history with Charles Willson Peale's personal choice of candidates for the national pantheon of heroes, the Philadelphia Museum, more familiarly known as Peale's Museum, had been making Americans feel special for more than half a century. Portraits of Revolutionary War generals, products of the great men of science, a menagerie of stuffed animals and birds, and a mastodon skeleton unearthed in Ulster County, New York in 1801 were some of its featured displays. For the admission price of 25 cents, Philadelphians could gaze upon one man's vision of "a world in miniature ... little inferior to the imperial Museums of Europe".

Charles Willson Peale, *George Washington at Princeton*, oil, 1779. This iconic image of the pater patriae, was among the works sold by the descendents of the artist at the Peale auction conducted by Moses Thomas in 1854. Purchased as the "first choice" it sold at $360. The heirs of the buyer presented it to the Pennsylvania Academy of Fine Arts in 1943.

strength." It could, said a notice in the *Public Ledger*, "be examined at any time."

Freeman's would occasionally handle a more rarefied consignment. In 1854, the company would clear the warehouse of Ignatius Lutz, one of many French-trained cabinetmakers in American cities at that time, who had come to Philadelphia in 1844. His shop employed 30 craftsmen who worked mainly without power machinery to produce laminated, bent and carved rosewood and walnut parlor furniture in the rococo style. On October 12, 1854, "as Mr Lutz [was] about rearranging his business," James A. Freeman offered what he called "the most elegant stock of furniture ever sold in Philadelphia."

No sale records survive, but the Lutz enterprise did continue into the next decade. In *Philadelphia and its Manufactures of 1859*, Edwin T. Freedley wrote of the lamination process: "In Mr. Lutz's establishment in Eleventh Street, my attention was attracted to an ingenious method adopted by him to prevent the liability of carved mahogany to break. In carved chair work, for instance, he divided the mahogany into several lateral parts, and joins them by glue in such a manner that the grain of the wood runs in different directions. The strength of the wood is, by this method, increased in proportion to the number of times it is divided ...

Mr. Lutz has supplied furniture to some of the finest mansions in this city."

Nevertheless, in art historical terms, the memorable sale of the antebellum was not the unsold stock of Philadelphia's answer to Joseph Meeks or John H. Belter, but rather a series of dispersals associated with the demise of the best-known museum of the early republic. These sales would be conducted by M. Thomas & Son, a rival auction business but one that, in time, would become part of the Freeman's empire.

The closure of Charles Willson's Peale's Philadelphia Museum – a magnificent monument to science, patriotism and curiosity – had its roots in its relocation upon the founder's death. Secured by a $200,000 loan from the troubled Bank of the United States that exaggerated receipts and valued its portraits at a colossal $150,000, the Philadelphia Museum had moved in 1827 from its second-floor rooms in the State House to more expensive premises across the street. The ambitious move had not paid off, and the institution's financial crisis only worsened during the Panic that ensued when the bank finally closed its doors in February 1841.

As the city plunged into depression, sheriff's sales of natural history specimens from the museum had

provided showman P.T. Barnum with some of his prized exhibits at knock-down prices. A famous mastodon skeleton unearthed in Ulster County, New York in 1801 had been among them .

As the collection ebbed away the rechartered United States Bank made efforts to minimize its losses. The portrait collection was seized, a sale to the Smithsonian was attempted and then – having rejected an offer of $6,000 for the collection from a group of city worthies – the 269 paintings were consigned for sale on October 9, 1854.

Sharing the bill with "Polley's Patent Globular Elastic Adjustable and Expanding Bucket examined and approved by the most scientific men of Philadelphia," was, said auctioneer Moses Thomas, "one of the most attractive sales of paintings ever made in the United States." The sale venue was the smart second floor gallery of Thomas' recently opened brownstone store on South Fourth Street.

Rejecting the best offer for the entire gallery (again $6,000, tendered this time by the City Council), the pictures were instead sold painting by painting by "choice." This time-honored method of sale is still practiced today in many small American auction houses. Bidding is opened on the understanding that the

purchaser of the 'first choice' will have the privilege of taking any number of items he or she wishes at the bid price. When the pick has been made, the bidding restarts to determine the "second choice" winner, and so on.

First choice on October 9, 1854 was, said the *City Bulletin*, "knocked off to Mr. Edward Ingersoll for $360." At this price he took both Peale's portrait of Benjamin Franklin and a full-length painting of George Washington executed shortly after the Battle of Trenton. The second choice was secured at $175 by Mr. Lewis H. Newbold. He took Martha Washington, Peale's famous full-length self-portrait, *The Artist in His Museum,* and a dozen others. Heroic images of Revolutionary War generals Lafayette and Wayne were sold at $165 each.

Carrying away a great number of pictures at lower price levels, and contributing $5,113 to the overall total of $11,672.06, was one Mr. P.C. Erben of New York. That in 1845 Philadelphia had 10 personal fortunes of $1 million or more (25 by 1857) supports the belief of a local antiquarian in attendence at the sale, John McAllister, who opined: "The paintings generally did not bring exorbitant prices."

The *North American* was certainly not satisfied. "It is with a feeling of deep regret that we record this dispersion of

"Harness, saddles, musical instruments, fixed ammunition..."
James A. Freeman advertises his second sale of military surplus at
the City Arsenal in the wake of the Civil War.

JAS. A. FREEMAN, AUCTIONEER,
No. 423 WALNUT Street.

Second Sale at the City Arsenal, Race street, below
Broad.
HARNESS, SADDLES MUSICAL INSTRUMENTS
FIXED AMMUNITION, &c.
ON TUESDAY MORNING, Jan. 30,
At the City Arsenal, Race street, below Broad,
will be sold a large quantity of fixed ammunition,
harness, saddles, drums, fifes, bugles, cushions,
boxes, tarpaulins, condemned muskets and rifles,
stoves, iron, &c., &c.

a collection of paintings that had been so long among us that we had begun to consider them as our property." The reporter continued: "We do not think the limit of the sum to be offered by the committee on City Property was a wise one under the circumstances. There might have been a slight stretch to suit this occasion and there would have been no grumbling among our citizens."

In fact, it emerged later that Mr. "Erben" – a pseudonym and a play on the word "urban" – had been the city's silent buyer. The 87 portraits he secured, most of them of signers of the Declaration of Independence and the Constitution, were purchased for the gallery of Independence Hall, and would be augmented by subsequent acts of benevolence by members of the community. But some important works were lost. Nobody seemed to want a tarnished figure such as Thomas Paine, whose portrait (its whereabouts now unknown) sold for a mere $6.50.

＊   ＊   ＊

War arrived in Philadelphia in 1861 but, as a business that serviced the consequences of dying, the city's auctioneers hardly had to worry about the long-term impact of the first total conflict upon their turnover. On any given week in the Civil War years, James A. Freeman might offer more than 50 properties or lots of land "new and finished with every improvement and to be sold on easy terms."

During the invasion crisis of 1863, as black soldiers took up arms and 2,000 men were found to dig entrenchments around the city, more than 20 auctioneers were enjoying Philadelphia's position as a center for northern mobilization. As supplies backed up in storage warehouses, this number grew although occasionally it would be left to the soldiers to conduct less official auction sales among themselves. The title "colonel" is still occasionally used today to denote the status of an auctioneer – a reference to the days of the war when men of that rank were responsible for auctioning government surplus and livestock.

If auctioneers were among those like the shipbuilder William Cramp or the Baldwin & Company Locomotive Works for whom war was no financial tragedy then the immediate aftermath would also be a boon. The ink of Appomattox was barely dry before auctioneers along the East Coast were clamoring to conduct the government sales of mules, harnesses, medical supplies, ocean and river craft, gallons of whiskey and other condemned ordnance that was now surplus to requirements. Once again historical events helped determine the nature of the merchandise under the auctioneer's gavel.

On a local level, James A. Freeman had a piece of the action, occasionally advertising sales of horse tack, tools, drums, fifes, bugles, condemned muskets, rifles and ammunition at the City Arsenal. No surprise that as the red, white and blue victory ribbons on Chestnut Street turned black to mark Lincoln's assassination, the auctioneers were among those at whom charges of profiteering were lodged.

But while enjoying the cold prosperity that war stimulated in Philadelphia, the city's auctioneers had also participated in the great fundraising venture of the period.

During the first of the many fairs conducted by the redoubtable women of the U.S. Sanitary Commission – that held in Chicago for two weeks in the fall of 1863 – the largest single contribution to the cause of Union soldier relief had been made at an auction.

In 1863, at the request of commission leader Mary Livermore and founding Chicago Historical Society member Isaac N. Arnold, Abraham Lincoln had agreed to donate the original draft of the Emancipation Proclamation to the Northwestern Sanitary Fair. The document was sold on the understanding that the buyer would then donate it to the Chicago Historical Society. It

had been purchased for $3,000 – although history remembers the CHS building would be destroyed by fire, the Proclamation with it, on October 9, 1871.

Such a feat could not, of course, be repeated for the Philadelphia effort held at Logan Square from June 7-29, 1864, but keen not to be outdone were two Princeton-educated Philadelphia Unionists: the journalist Charles Godfrey Leland and George Henry Boker, the scion of a local banking family. It was Leland, who in his role as the editor of Boston's *Continental Monthly*, claimed to have coined the term "emancipation" as a substitute for "abolition."

Passionate "emancipationists" with an eye for a collectible, the two men commissioned 48 special printed copies of the Proclamation that the President, his secretary of state, William H. Seward, and his private secretary, John G. Nicolay, all agreed to sign. Helped by the presence at the fair on June 16 of Lincoln himself, the Leland-Boker editions, as they are now known, were sold to the highest bidder – as just occasionally they are today. Freeman's sold one as part of a sale marking the nation's bicentenary in November 1976, for $22,500.

Despite its conservative voice on the Negro question and the solicitude often expressed for the constitutional rights of the neighboring South, the spirit of Philadelphia

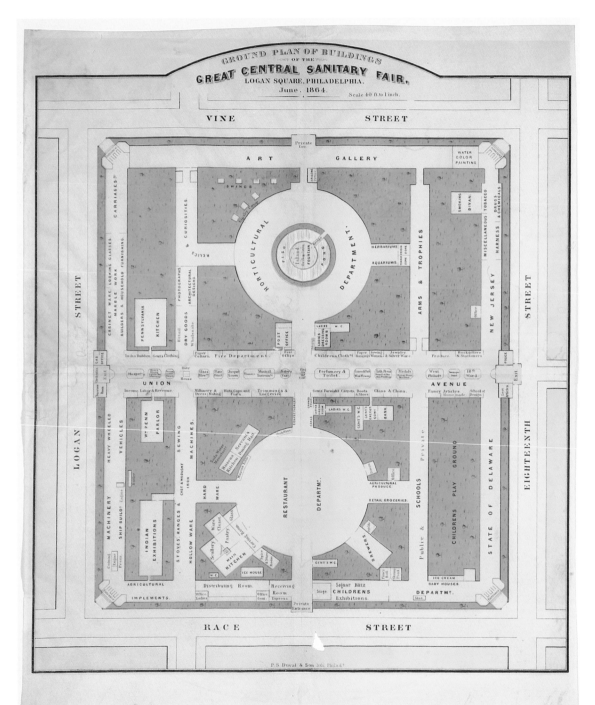

What the *Daily Fare* called "the noblest and greatest work of human benevolence the world has ever seen," the Great Central Fair would realize over $1 million for the Sanitary Commission, supplying relief to wounded Union soldiers.

benevolence peaked in 1864 with the Great Central Fair. Spurred on by the $100,000 raised in Chicago and proud in the knowledge that hometown hero General George G. Meade had out-generalled Robert E. Lee at Gettysburg, the fair ran for three weeks. Close to 5,000 people a day passed through the turnstiles. Most were there to get a meal in a restaurant in which well-to-do women of the city played hostess, or to attend the formal performances that persuaded visitors to return night after night. Others went to marvel at captured Confederate battle relics, the Great Belt of Wampum or a recreated Germanic homestead carrying the banner *Grant's Up to Schnitz*. But many items were also for sale. Local merchants contributed from their stock, wealthy members of the community brought from their homes a valuable stick of furniture, a treasured brooch or a letter from an old Philadelphian; while others would demonstrate their needlework skills fashioning a lock of Lincoln's hair into a heart or the tunic of a dead Rebel general into a pincushion.

In a popular section carefully designed to connect Philadelphians with their past titled Relics, Curiosities, and Autographs, William Vaux had purchased an 18th century curly maple dressing table that carried a label reading: *The table on which Franklin and Washington*

This 'Franklin' Queen Anne curly maple dressing table that had been sold at the Sanitary Fair to a member of the Vaux family was hammered down for $386,000 at Freeman's in 1999.

Long after the tented buildings had been taken down, Philadelphia's auctioneers were adding to the $1 million that three weeks in June had raised for the Union's wounded. Six months after the close of the Great Central Fair, Philadelphia auctioneers Thomas Birch & Son offered this array of unsold exhibits, including 24 letters signed by General Lafayette, manuscripts by Harriet Beecher Stowe and "a piece of the shirt bosom of the Rebel General Barksdale who was killed at Gettysburg".

Thomas Birch Jr., who operated from the City Tavern before moving on its demolition to 1110 Chestnut Street in 1852, was among the Philadelphia auctioneers to take advantage of the legislation of the 1820s. In September 1845, he conducted a sale of "valuable paintings & statuary, the Collection of the late Joseph Bonaparte, Count de Survilliers at the mansion at Bordentown, New Jersey."

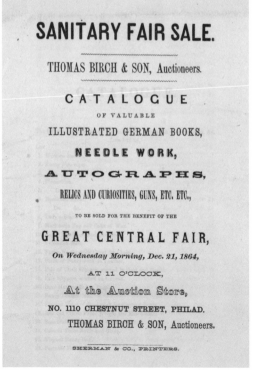

SANITARY FAIR SALE.

THOMAS BIRCH & SON, Auctioneers.

CATALOGUE

OF VALUABLE

ILLUSTRATED GERMAN BOOKS,

NEEDLE WORK,

AUTOGRAPHS,

RELICS AND CURIOSITIES, GUNS, ETC. ETC.,

TO BE SOLD FOR THE BENEFIT OF THE

GREAT CENTRAL FAIR,

On Wednesday Morning, Dec. 21, 1864,

AT 11 O'CLOCK,

At the Auction Store,

NO. 1110 CHESTNUT STREET, PHILAD.

THOMAS BIRCH & SON, Auctioneers.

SHERMAN & CO., PRINTERS.

The massive organ built by Hilborne E. Roosevelt of New York
for the Music Pavilion of the Main Exhibition Hall at a cost of
$22,000 was sold by M. Thomas & Son on behalf of the
Fairmount Park International Exhibition Company in the fall of
1881 for $5,000.

THE LIBRARY COMPANY OF PHILADELPHIA

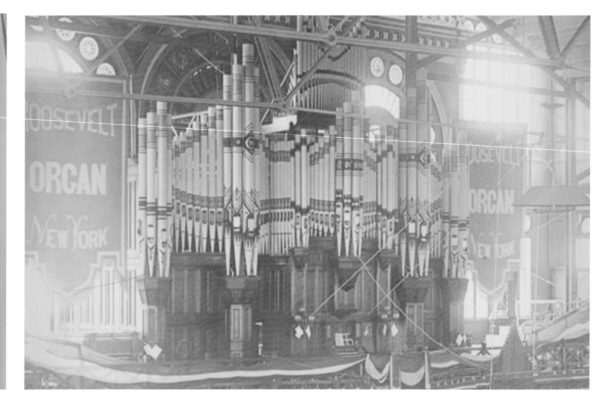

"The Workshop of the World" - stereoscopic images from the
Centennial celebrations.

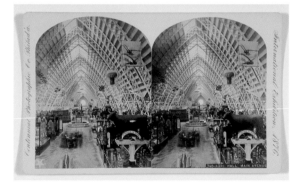

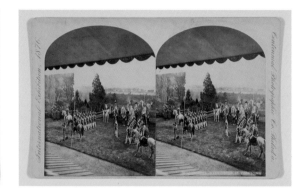
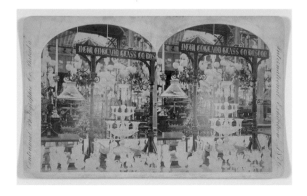

Frank Leslie's *Historical Register of the United States Exposition*, 1876, Frank Leslie's Publishing House, NY, 1877

"Our illustration presents a scene which was quite common in New York and Philadelphia after the close of the Centennial, when all sorts of Centennial articles – particularly ceramics and bric-a-brac generally – were offered at public auction, and eagerly purchased by the public, whose taste for this class of ware had been developed by means of the Centennial itself. Within a few years auction sales of this class of wares have become very frequent, and quite a mania for collection has begun to grow among our cultivated people."

played chess. It had possibly been donated by a member of the Bache family (through which some of Franklin's furniture descended) given that Alexander Dalls Bache was vice president of the Sanitary Commission and his brother, R. Mead Bache, was on the editorial committee of the house newspaper *The Daily Fare*. It would remain in the Vaux family until 1999, whereupon this important example of colonial cabinetmaking would be sold at Freeman\Fine Arts for $386,000.

Exhibits that had not been snapped up in June found their way into a series of onsite auctions held after the closing day of the fair. Offering their services gratis, the city auctioneers drew large crowds until midnight on July 6, when the final lot, an oil painting of the fair itself, was sold.

Much more has been written about the Centennial as a defining event for American decorative arts – a first taste of Japanese arts and crafts, a shot in the arm for the colonial revival style and a key moment in popular collecting. In engravings, advertisements and popular commentaries, tantalizing scraps of evidence also survive to suggest the celebration of Franklin's Town, the city they called "The Workshop of the World," provided

Samuel T. Freeman (1839-1913).

Between Samuel T. Freeman and his older brother James was a span of 19 years. and it would not be until around 1870 that the man who gave his name to the company in its second century would be taken into the partnership. It would adopt the name Samuel T. Freeman & Co. in 1898, two years after James A. Freeman's death.

an opportune moment for Philadelphia's auctioneers to showcase their trade on the international stage.

Sales of the unsold pottery, porcelain, metalwares, furniture and industrial innovations that Europe's exhibitors chose to leave behind were "quite common in New York and Philadelphia after the close of the Centennial," according to Frank Leslie's *Historical Register of the United States Exposition, 1876.* "All sorts of articles – particularly ceramics and bric-a-brac generally – were offered at public auction, and eagerly purchased by the public, whose taste for this class of ware had been developed by means of the Centennial itself."

Perhaps the last and the largest of these Centennial breakdown sales was conducted by M. Thomas & Son on behalf of the Fairmount Park International Exhibition Company in the fall of 1881. The main attraction of this three-day dispersal "including flags, chandeliers, lanterns, remaining exhibits, etc." had been a massive organ built by Hilborne E. Roosevelt of New York for the Music Pavilion of the cavernous Main Exhibition Hall.

An opening bid of $2,500 had been tendered before competition narrowed down to the Rev. Mr. Mutchmore of the Alexander Presbyterian Church, who bid $4,950, and a Mr. Bradley representing the Massachusetts Mechanics' Charitable Institution of Boston, who offered

$5,000. It was then that the organ, which had cost Centennial organizers $22,000, came into his possession.

★   ★   ★

It was not for the first time in the century that members of the Freeman family would have cast jealous glances across town in the direction of 139 and 141 South Fourth Street, where the business of M. Thomas & Son was conducted. However it was not through fine art that the lion's share of Philadelphia's auction duties of $130,000 per annum were exacted. The big money was in real estate.

It was the outward march of the city, viewed against the backdrop of remarkable population growth from 409,000 bodies by 1850 to 1.3 million by 1900, that would ensure Freeman's rise, by 1900, to pre-eminence among Philadelphia's auctioneers.

As the last vestiges of Penn's Greene Country Towne died among the smog of heavy industry, property values were soaring across the city. Between 1850 and 1900 real estate on Market, Walnut, Broad and Chestnut increased as much as ten-fold as the neighborhood completed its the transition from fashionable residential sector to thriving business arena. Steep price rises in the newer residential districts of Germantown, Port

Established Nov. 12th, 1805.

FREEMAN & CO.

AUCTIONEERS,

STORE: 422 WALNUT ST.

Sale, Nov. 27th, 1889.

Real Estate

STOCKS, &c.,

TO BE SOLD AT PUBLIC SALE ON

Wednesday

November 27, 1889, Commencing at 12 o'clock, noon, precisely,

AT THE PUBLIC SALES-ROOM

IN THE

PHILADELPHIA EXCHANGE,

N. E. cor. Third & Walnut Streets.

NO POSTPONEMENT ON ACCOUNT OF WEATHER.

SPECIAL ATTENTION GIVEN TO

Furniture Sales: For Executors, Administrators and others, who are settling estates, closing business, or relinquishing housekeeping, held at the Auction Store, or at any other location, as desired, and so carefully conducted as to secure the fullest returns to our Employers.

Machinery Sales: For Assignees, Receivers, Masters and others, acting under direction or by authority of the Courts, advertised, arranged, catalogued and sold so as to afford perfect security to the accountants.

Miscellaneous Sales: Every form of personal property; useful or ornamental; disposed of at Public Sale to the best possible advantage.

PLEASE PRESERVE THIS CATALOGUE FOR USE AT SALE.

TELEPHONE No. 1154

A Freeman & Co. real estate catalogue for a sale conducted at the Public Sales-Room of the Philadelphia Exchange the late 1880s.

Richmond and Frankford dictated that, alongside mercantile pursuits and intermarriage, real estate speculation predominated as the way to wealth.

The money was not just in the castles being built close to the neo-gothic stations of the Main Line or in collecting rental income from the immigrant populations who inhabited the decaying precincts of Southwark and Moyamensing. In between the extremes of rich and poor were the 4,500 owner-occupied, one-family dwellings that were being added to the city every year by the 1870s. It was this remarkable period of homebuilding in a landscape that allowed Philadelphians to build out rather than up, that, by the late 19th century, had earned 129 square miles of urban sprawl the sobriquet City of Homes.

On the instructions of the venerable Orphans' Court, with its wide-ranging jurisdiction in matters relating to personal and property rights, inheritance and estate tax, the sale of row houses was a constant source of business for 422 Walnut Street. Equally lucrative would be the large tracts of mineral or timber-rich lands in upstate Pennsylvania, sold to speculators in the era of Reconstruction.

More spectacular were the plots of downtown real estate that filtered onto the market during an

In the early 1880s, the old United States Post Office and
Courthouse building at 426-428 Chestnut was sold by James
A. Freeman & Co. for $425,000, a record for a single building
sold at public auction. The building was demolished to make
way for the Drexel Building built by 1885 to operate as the city
stock exchange. It too was demolished in 1955.

THE LIBRARY COMPANY OF PHILADELPHIA

unprecedented period of civic and commercial
building.

As Philadelphia lost and acquired some of its most
recognizable landmarks, the handsome white marble
auction mart, the Merchants' Exchange, provided the
venue for many of the largest property transactions of
the final quarter of the century. As it passed its three-
quarter-century, Freeman's began to make its first
newspaper headlines.

Sometime in the early 1880s, Samuel T. Freeman, now a
partner in the firm and fast becoming an acknowledged
expert on the city's real estate market, had got his hands
on the magnificent but obsolete United States Post
Office and Courthouse building that had stood for a
generation at 426-428 Chestnut. Scheduled for
demolition the old Post Office plot would be gaveled
down for $425,000 to make way for the Drexel Building
built by 1885 to operate as the city stock exchange. At
the time it was a record for a single building sold at
public auction.

Calvin Coolidge was in the White House. Income was on the rise. New consumer goods were pouring into the marketplace, and Americans had discovered credit. But important anniversaries were not forgotten, and many Philadelphians hoped for a party with deeper significance at the Sesquicentennial International Exhibition of 1926.

The event, while beleaguered by rain throughout, had its high spots – 120,757 spectators had gathered, on September 23, to see Gene Tunney defeat Jack Dempsey in a heavyweight title bout (it rained then too). But in retrospect, the Sesquicentennial is remembered for its poor attendance and financial overambition.

War and Industry
CHAPTER SIX

"There is no picture of community life more attractive than when sons take up the work to which the father has devoted a life of honorable effort and carry it on with undiminished ability and reputation."

PUBLIC LEDGER, DECEMBER 31, 1907

Addison B. Freeman (1885-1962) ranks among the most remarkable of all members of the dynasty. Freeman's current chairman, Beau Freeman, recalls his uncle Addison as a formidable "Victorian" gentleman – tall, slender, straight-talking and very proper. But he also remembers a thinker who would furnish his employees with insightful judgements on issues as diverse as Cold War politics and closed-circuit television, a writer with a pleasing turn of phrase and a businessman with the gift of prescience.

In 1913, the year Samuel T. Freeman died, age 74, at his home in Germantown, the company that would continue henceforth to carry his name handled more than 85 percent of all the bankruptcy sales in Philadelphia. Of all auction sales of real estate in and about the city of Philadelphia that same year, 88 percent of them were conducted by Samuel T. Freeman & Co.

The company considered itself unique in the country as an auction house with specialist departments in real estate, stocks and bonds (introduced in 1911), furniture, machinery, merchandise, bankruptcy, antiques and fine art. Freeman's had become part of the fabric of the community. And yet – save the occasional foray into the Mid-Atlantic states – Samuel T. Freeman & Co., essentially remained a concern whose sphere of influence was eastern Pennsylvania. For further growth, the company needed a catalyst. And, when Woodrow Wilson's neutrality policy gave way in 1917, that catalyst was The Great War.

Samuel T. Freeman and his wife, Sarah H. Clendenin (they may have also been first cousins), had five sons. All, with the exception of Paul Freeman (1884-1959), who chose the law profession over auctioneering, found work in the growing family business. Albert L. Freeman (1893-1941) worked in the gallery. Eldest son George C.

Freeman (1875-1955) oversaw small industrial sales in the Philadelphia area, while the forte of Samuel M. Freeman (1879-1958) was real estate. But it was Addison B. Freeman (1885-1962) who became the dominant personality of the fourth generation.

It was through a war buddy that Addison secured Freeman's its first contracts outside the Mid-Atlantic states. Called to the trenches with his brother Samuel for what would prove to be the last days of the 1914-1918 war against Germany, Addison B. Freeman had there befriended H. Gates Lloyd, a prominent Philadelphia businessman and secretary of the Navy. Addison, a great champion of the auction method – "its fairness, its efficiency, its expedition and, above all, its glass bowl qualifications" – had been remembered by Lloyd upon his return home when Armistice presented to him a problem that, in scale, was entirely new.

Beguiled by the belief that the first global conflict would be the last, the government instigated a rapid and extensive disposal of war surplus that dwarfed those conducted in the wake of the Civil War. This first involved the entire domestic wool clip of 1917 and 1918. Millions of tons of wool had been commandeered by the Army and the Navy during mobilization (primarily for the creation of cellulose used in the gunpowder process)

but would shortly to be dumped back onto the market. Upon consultation with the nation's largest wool brokers, auction was the procedure recommended, and Freeman's was chosen to conduct the sales between December 1918 and the end of 1919. They were held not just in the Bellevue in Philadelphia but also in the Copley Plaza in Boston. In one sale, Samuel T. Freeman & Co. – regrettably working for a fee rather than a percentage – knocked down $17 million worth of the commodity in a matter of two hours. The total amount of wool sold on behalf of the government approximated $350 million. And that was back in the days when a $5 bill could still be exchanged for a gold coin.

The money was good, but politics dictated that it would not last. Congress decided auction sales of war surplus should be conducted by local auctioneers. Faced with the end of a New England venture, but reluctant to remove his foot from this lucrative door, Addison B. Freeman seized upon the opportunity to purchase the name and goodwill of J. E. Conant Co., an auctioneer in the cotton town of Lowell, Massachusetts. It would prove a prescient decision – not least because it would place Freeman's in the heart of a declining textile industry where bankruptcy sales would be plentiful. More immediately it prolonged the good working

STEEL –
ARMOR PLATE

NON FERROUS METALS

To be Removed from
U.S.S. MICHIGAN
U.S.S. KANSAS
U.S.S. MINNESOTA
At Public Auction

NAVY YARD
League Island
PHILADELPHIA

on Wednesday January 23, 1924
10 A.M.
Eastern Standard Time

Central Sales Office
Navy Yard
Washington, D.C.

Samuel T. Freeman Co.
Auctioneers
Philadelphia, Pa.

Catalogue Nº
542 A

Three of the World War I battleships sold for scrap by Samuel T. Freeman & Co. in the wake of The Treaty on the Limitations of Armaments.

U.S.S. Kansas, a 16,000-ton *Connecticut*-class battleship built at Camden, New Jersey in 1907 had been used in training and escort roles. She was dismantled at Philadelphia Navy Yard.

U.S.S. Minnesota, a 16,000-ton *Connecticut*-class battleship built at Newport News, Virginia in 1907 was part of the Great White Fleet and later a gunnery and engineering training ship in WWI, during which she was damaged by a German mine.

Laid down by New York Shipbuilding Co., Camden, New Jersey, the 16,000-ton battleship *U.S.S. Michigan* was assigned to the Atlantic Fleet in 1908. After putting to sea to protect American interests in Mexico and Cuba, she engaged in fleet maneuvers and battle practice during and after the war.

relationship with the armed forces. And Addison was now thinking big.

According to the terms of The Treaty on the Limitations of Armaments signed by the United States, Great Britain, France, Italy and Japan on February 6, 1922 and effective from August 17, 1923, the U.S. Government proposed to dispose of a number of battleships. Slated for the scrap heap were the two ageing *Connecticut* class battleships *U.S.S. Minnesota* and *U.S.S. Kansas*, troop carriers *U.S.S. South Carolina*, *U.S.S. Michigan* and the British-built servant of both the 3rd and 4th battle squadron, the *H.M.S. Dreadnought*. There was also the small matter of 2,500,000 pounds of ferrous metals intended for the construction of the *U.S.S. Saratoga* and the *U.S.S. Washington* in Camden, New Jersey, that now had become surplus to the military's requirements.

Of course the easiest way to comply by the treaty was to tow the vessels out in mid-ocean and scuttle them. Certain naval officers recommended this route as the proper resting place for old men-of-war. But such romantic notions found no favor with the authorities for whom several thousand tons of ferrous metal represented a clear revenue stream and a potential source of employment opportunities during a postwar recession. A break-up program and the jobs it might

create for local communities appeared a far more attractive social as well as financial alternative.

When offered for sale by sealed bids, the break-up values had been depressingly low and were rejected out of hand. Addison B. Freeman undertook to offer the ships, rendered unfit for war purpose, at auction as parcels of scrap iron to be cut up at the Naval yards where they resided. Selling ships from Philadelphia's docks had, after all, been part of the family business for more than a century.

Dates were set for sales at the destroyer and submarine base, Squantum, near Boston; the U.S. Navy Coaling Station, East Lamoine, Maine; and the Navy Yard, League Island. Their net result was – crowed the Postmaster General's report of the following year – triple what had been achieved under sealed-bid conditions.

★   ★   ★

This new national perspective and the decision to position Freeman's as industrial clearance specialists for the big occasion gained its greatest momentum in 1922 in a West Virginia town called Nitro.

The name is a clue to its explosive beginning. At the turn of the 20th century this lumber camp located on a bend in the Kanawha River numbered 24 houses, two

churches, a school, a company store and a post office. And it might have remained that way had not this spot 14 miles west of Charleston in the heart of the bituminous and natural gas fields been chosen as the location to redress the critical gunpowder shortage that quickly became apparent as the doughboys prepared to journey to the trenches in France.

The proposed name Redwop (powder spelled backwards) was shelved for its possible ethnic misinterpretation. Instead the Ordnance Department chose a name that referred to its primary product, the chemical compound nitro-cellulose. In America, where so many cities share the same name, state to state, it became the first and only place to be dubbed Nitro.

Ground was broken on December 23, 1917. Overnight, a project was masterminded and trainloads of workers and materials began pouring into a muddy pasture on the banks of the Kanawha River. With wages close to $120 a month, more than 100,000 were on the payroll during the 11 months of building time. The Powder City Boys, as they were known, came from Boston, Baltimore, Chicago, Denver, New York, Omaha, St. Louis and Los Angeles. A young 17-year old called Clark Gable was among them, hired in as a laborer to push wheelbarrows and dig ditches.

"13,594 wooden nose plugs, 25,183 metal transit plugs, 10,580 tops and bottoms for bouchon and grenade boxes ..." The catalogue for the Nitro, West Virginia, sale of May 22-May 26, 1922, includes this fold-out panoramic view of the city.

NiTRO
W.VA.

As a plant capable of producing 700,000 pounds of gunpowder per day emerged on the river bank, so did 1,500 homogenous brown-stained houses built in rows. They were numbered 1 to 57 and designated an area letter from A to ZZ according to the nationality and color of their occupants.

On May 7, 1918, a record 60 of these ready-built housing units were erected in a single day, furnished identically with iron beds, wicker furniture and grass rugs, and occupied almost as soon as they were completed.

James J. Gotch was a plant worker who arrived in Nitro from Sioux City, Iowa, in the summer of 1918. He and his family lived in Area A.

"We were employed by the Hercules Powder Company, and we wore large badges with our pictures on them. I was employed on one of the many tall 'press' buildings in the plant. This appeared like a coal tipple, with the huge brass press on the top floor. A cake of raw powder, the size of a 50lb piece of cheese, was placed into the press and the steam power turned on, and small strings of powder like spaghetti appeared on the next floor below. This was led to wooden pails and then fed into slicing machines which cut it into lengths of about one-half inch, after which it was placed in warming ovens and dried. Later it was weighed and placed into silk bags for use in the field."

By November 1918, Explosive Plant C was 90 percent complete and housing 24,000 people. But then came Armistice Day. Two weeks later, row after row of houses had fallen empty as families packed up and returned home. The plant was mothballed and the entire reservation declared "surplus".

What to do with Nitro was a question first answered by The Charleston Industrial Corporation (CIC) that, backed by six West Virginia businessman and five investors from New York, successfully bid $8,551,000 for the city's entire industrial and residential facilities. They had experienced some success selling American industry relocation packages "in the finest manufacturing locality the country has to offer," enticing workers with cheap housing.

However, enormous quantities of machinery, equipment and stock, and some 400 buildings and bungalows still remained when Samuel T. Freeman & Co. was invited by the United States Army Ordnance Salvage Board and the CIC to clear the decks without limit or reserve in spring 1922.

To date, it is the largest sale the company has ever conducted. Addison B. Freeman and his road crew – the "outside division" as they were known in Philly – began at 10 a.m. sharp on Monday, May 22, 1922, with material located in building 1246. Lot number one, 644 lbs of aluminium and cast-iron welding rods. Lot number two, 190 lbs of wrought-iron asbestos gaskets (assorted). Lot number three, 42 sets of metallic bored packing (assorted sizes). And so it went on for five days. One hundred lots an hour. Seven hours a day,

By the end of 1922, the CIC had managed to pay the government more than half of the purchase price, and five years after the war, Nitro was on the way to becoming a permanent community. Remodeling and paintwork ensured that few of its makeshift structures would survive as historical testaments, but in 1982 a Congressional Resolution recognized a landmark in U.S. engineering when it established Nitro as a Living Monument to World War I.

"Quiet, please, ladies and gentleman. My name is George C. Freeman, and I would like to welcome you today to Philadelphia's Exposition Grounds for this the fifth in a series of six sales conducted to benefit the creditors of the Sesquicentennial Exhibition Association. And we can begin with lot number one, an 80ft replica of the Liberty Bell. Included in the lot are 26,000 15-

WAR & INDUSTRY

The group of 22 buildings from the Franklin Book Shop to the Declaration House that together reconstructed Philadelphia High Street at the time of the American Revolution.

THE LIBRARY COMPANY OF PHILADELPHIA

watt light bulbs and 30,000 feet of wire. There you are. You've all seen it working. Ladies and gentleman, what am I bid for this lot?"

The Sesquicentennial International Exhibition of 1926 had not been a great success. The big idea was to create an international gathering 150 years after the signing of the Declaration of Independence, where once again Americans would converge upon the birthplace of the nation to celebrate its struggle and its achievements.

A 450-acre plot at League Island near the U.S. Navy Yard in South Philadelphia was selected as the meeting place and a committee was formed. Numerous voluntary boards staffed by pillars of the community were asked to plan appropriate events and activities in such fields as athletics, business and industry, fine arts, medicine, music, transportation, and black history. And the centerpiece of it all was an elaborate gateway built at the entrance of the exposition – a gigantic steel replica of the Liberty Bell designed by engineers of the Westinghouse Electric and Manufacturing Company. Together its 26,000 bulbs would light those prophetic words from Leviticus 25:10 across the night sky: *Proclaim Liberty throughout all the Land unto all the inhabitants thereof.*

The centerpiece of the Sesquicentennial Exhibition was this elaborate gateway – an 80ft replica of the Liberty Bell incorporating 26,000 light bulbs.

THE LIBRARY COMPANY OF PHILADELPHIA

This was the vision. The reality was overambition, miserable weather, a palpable lack of excitement, and logistical and financial problems that dogged the project from beginning to end. Even the Liberty Bell entrance gate, chosen to feature on the cover of the official guide, was still not ready by opening day. and the industrial parade of 1,000 bands and 135 floats quickly passed by its scaffold on June 4.

By November 30, as perfunctory ceremonies formally closed the rain-sodden exposition and representatives of 30 nations packed up and returned home, financial disaster loomed.

Against a backdrop of bank failures, financial scandals, postwar unemployment and corruption, paying visitors during the 159 open days had numbered just eight of the expected 50 million. Little in the way of rescue dollars and cents had been forthcoming from the federal government. The Sesquicentennial Exhibition Association, established more than a decade earlier, passed into receivership in 1927.

It would be several years before the claims of the organization's many creditors were resolved in the U.S. District Court and the 40 cubic feet of paper records from this forgettable episode could be laid to rest in the Philadelphia City Archives. However, the immediate

action of the receivers was to call in a company who in the previous decade had proved itself adept at crisis management on a big scale.

The dispersal of the relics of 1926 represented the sort of logistical challenge at which Freeman's industrial clearance division now excelled.

Four sales were conducted "in situ" on the expo grounds from July to August. On July 18, police, restaurant and theatrical equipment was sold, including the hundreds of costumes worn by actors recreating moments from the Battle of Gettysburg and characters from Philadelphia's High Street at the time of the Revolution. The electrical equipment sold on July 28 included the Electrical Fountain, which was lit by 24 light clusters in the basin and 85 single bulbs in the tower, and capable of pumping more than 2,000 gallons of water per minute. The uncompleted Tower of Light, upon which $290,000 was lavished before the city concluded it was too expensive to finish, brought $1,000.

Oak and mahogany office furniture followed on August 2, as did a Graham 20-passenger bus, while August 8-9 saw the sale of the cavernous steel-framed exhibition buildings that had been erected at a cost of more than $3 million. The auctioneer began with the 110,000 square feet steel-framed auditorium, the Palace of

Education, which had cost $1 million but brought only $10,750 at auction.

The circular World Acquaintance Cafeteria, The India Building, better known as the Taj Mahal, and buildings for Liberal Arts and Manufacturers, Fine Arts, Agriculture and Foodstuffs all followed. Most of them were simply sold as scrap to a wrecking company from Cleveland, Ohio. And the Liberty Bell? It brought just $60.

The roots of American industry and the roots of American working people can be found in the suburban Boston mill town of Lowell, Massachusetts, where Freeman's cut its first New England foothold in 1920. A century before, a Scottish visitor had marveled at the massive brick-built mills lining a mile of the Merrimack River and its adjoining village where workers lived, schooled and churched. "Niagara and Lowell," he said, "are the two objects I will longest remember in my American journey, one the glory of American scenery, the other of American industry."

It was in buildings like these, turning raw cotton into one million yards of cotton cloth per week, where America had evolved from a rural society ruled by the changing seasons and the rising and setting sun to another where

Views of the Hog Island Shipyard during its heyday in 1918: a bird's-eye view of the barracks for 30,000 men; the launching of *Quistconck*, the first of 328 standard-design merchant ships built at the Hog Island before closure in 1921; learning to countersink rivet holes at the Hog Island training school; night illumination of the shipways.

HAMMER THE RIVETS HOME!

Stick to the job, boys. Hammer the rivets home! Think of every one as a blow to the Kaiser.

America needed warships and the Virginia Shipbuilding Corporation shipyard at Jones Point, Alexandria, was there to provide them. This 430-something acre plot was one of 111 yards constructed in suitable American coastal towns between 1917 and 1918. Extending a shipbuilding tradition that dated back to the 1750s, the new yard possessed all the necessities to build, launch and repair a dozen 9,400-ton steel cargo ships: a fabrication shop, a blacksmith shop, a boiler shop, two craneways, four massive concrete shipways and rail links. The site was constructed in a mere 85 days. President Woodrow Wilson drove the first rivet into the keel of the merchant ship *Gunston Hall* on May 30, 1918, and she was launched from the yard on February 27, 1919. A decade later, in 1928, with all outstanding contracts cancelled, the corporation was bankrupt, its plant sold at auction on July 24-25.

During this period, Samuel T. Freeman & Co. would sell the machinery and equipment of 15 shipbuilding yards from the Detroit Shipbuilding Co., in the north, to the New Orleans-based Jahncke Dry Dock Co. However, the largest and closest to home was the sale

announced in the fall of 1922 following the closure of the Hog Island Shipyard in 1921. Ship construction in Philadelphia, on the decline before the war, had rapidly escalated to meet the needs of the Atlantic supply line. Organized as the Delaware River District under the Emergency Fleet Corporation, the Philadelphia area built a total of 328 standard-design merchant ships or 20 percent of the total tonnage constructed in the United States for the war effort.

Philly's great achievement of the mobilization program was the new yard at Hog Island. It rose out of 947 acres of swampland (now occupied by Philadelphia International Airport) in a matter of months at the end of 1917. When finished, its 50 shipways, employing 30,000 workers and using fabricated parts, would launch a new cargo and transport vessel every four working days. Hog Island also gave its name to an Italian luncheon sandwich preferred by the South Philly workforce, known then and forever more as the "hoagie."

Freeman's conducted the sale from November 1-3, beginning at 10:30 each day, to disperse 400 searchlights, boilers, tanks, anchors, traveling cranes, 80-ton ice machines, pipe fittings, pumps and engines, machine tools and ship equipment.

work was the same all year round, where the machines continued to grind after nightfall and where the beginning and end of the day were determined by the sound of the factory bell.

The cotton goods industry in the North had been instrumental in America's rapid rise to industrial pre-eminence by 1900 but would suffer steady decline into the 20th century in the face of low prices resulting from overproduction, labor unrest and competition from new factories closer to the cotton fields of the South. Sales at auction would provide a footnote to this particular moment in history.

Textile mills from Maine to Pennsylvania were struggling to stay afloat as Samuel T. Freeman & Co., first moved to Lowell. Those mills were going under as the company became one of the first tenants in Boston's new Chamber of Commerce building. An auction schedule surviving from the years 1926-32 indicates remarkable levels of business for the "outside division" during the Depression years. A total of 35 dyeing and finishing works, hosiery manufacturers, knit goods manufacturers, silk manufacturers, woolen and worsted manufacturers were liquidated – each sale no doubt the final chapter in a tale of upheaval and hardship.

THE PROBLEM OF THE MILL VILLAGE

"If you have money to invest; if you want to buy attractive real estate that can be quickly sold at a profit; or if you're looking for a home that will reduce your present cost of living ... here is your chance of a lifetime." Freeman's liquidates the mill village of Cheney Brothers in 1937.

AT PUBLIC AUCTION

BY ORDER OF CHENEY BROTHERS, Owners ... IN SEPERATE PARCELS for HIGHEST BIDDERS

245 DWELLING PROPERTIES of CHENEY BROTHERS

144 COTTAGES · 20 THREE AND
79 DOUBLE DWELLINGS · FOUR FAMILY DWELLINGS
COMMERCIAL PROPERTIES · GARAGES

ALL SALES ON THE PREMISES

THURSDAY·FRIDAY·SATURDAY SEPT. 23, 24, 25, 1937.

STARTING AT 10 A.M. 75% CAN REMAIN ON MORTGAGE 75% A Complete Descriptive
D.S.T. EACH DAY Catalogue Is Mailing For You

Samuel T. Freeman & Co. Auctioneers Established
80 FEDERAL ST. BOSTON, MASS. NOV. 12, 1805.

LOCAL OFFICE OF THE AUCTIONEERS

Parcel No. 34
Sold at Auction on the Premises
Thursday, Sept. 23, 1937 at 10.00 A.M.
SAMUEL T. FREEMAN & CO.

COMMISSION PRÉPARATOIRE

POUR

L'ORGANISATION INTERNATIONALE POUR LES RÉFUGIÉS

GENÈVE. SWITZERLAND · PALAIS DES NATIONS

OFFICE OF THE EXECUTIVE SECRETARY
BUREAU DU SECRÉTAIRE EXÉCUTIF

August 1, 1948.

Samuel T. Freeman & Co.
1808-10 Chestnut Street
Philadelphia, Pa.

Dear Sirs:

The Preparatory Commission for the International
Refugee Organization, acting through its Merchandising
Advisory Committee, has decided to give you the management of
an initial sale in Philadelphia of rugs, silver and other
objects of value now in its possession.

As you have been informed, the entire net proceeds realized from these sales will be used to rehabilitate
and resettle eligible non-repatriable victims who suffered
heavily at the hands of the Nazis. The background of this
humanitarian undertaking will be of interest to you.

In Germany and Austria the Allied Armies recovered a vast quantity of miscellaneous personal property
which had been confiscated by the Nazis from their victims.
The disposition of that portion of the property which could
not be identified either as to individual ownership or national origin was provided for under Article 8 of Part I of the
Final Act of the Paris Conference on Reparation, and the Five
Power Agreement of June 14, 1946. These International
Agreements directed the transfer of the unidentifiable looted
property to an appropriate international refugee organization,
to be liquidated and the proceeds used for the rehabilitation
and resettlement of non-repatriable victims of German action
--- persons who suffered heavily at the hands of the Nazis
but who were unable to claim the assistance of any Government
receiving reparation from Germany.

The property which you have undertaken to sell
is a substantial part of the unidentifiable looted property,
and is officially designated in the above mentioned Treaties
as "non-monetary gold."

COMMISSION PRÉPARATOIRE

POUR

L'ORGANISATION INTERNATIONALE POUR LES RÉFUGIÉS

GENÈVE. SWITZERLAND · PALAIS DES NATIONS

OFFICE OF THE EXECUTIVE SECRETARY
BUREAU DU SECRÉTAIRE EXÉCUTIF

2.

Samuel T. Freeman & Co.

The Government of the United States played a
leading role in securing allocation of "non-monetary gold",
as reparations, for the assistance of non-repatriable victims;
and it acted most promptly in implementing this provision of
the Reparation Agreements. Some time ago it directed that,
upon determination of unidentifiability, the looted property
in the US Zones of Germany and Austria be transferred by the
Occupying Authorities to the appropriate international
refugee organization, formerly the Intergovernmental Committee
on Refugees and subsequently the Preparatory Commission for
the International Refugee Organization. In accordance with
the Treaty obligations, the property must be liquidated by
PCIRO and the proceeds used for the rehabilitation and resettlement of eligible non-repatriable victims.

Upon completion of the transfer of the property
in the US Zones of Germany and Austria, it was shipped by the
Preparatory Commission to the United States for liquidation.
To assist PCIRO in disposing of the property, the Merchandising
Advisory Committee, a voluntary board, was established to effect
the liquidation.

Our aim is to receive the highest possible proceeds from the sales, so that the maximum assistance may be
extended to the greatest number of victims.

Successful sale of this property will contribute
materially to mitigate the suffering of innocent men, women
and children -- victims of the Hitler holocaust, and offer
them hope for a happier future.

We are confident that the public will support
us in this humanitarian undertaking.

Yours very truly,

W. HALLAM TUCK
Executive Secretary

THE AUCTIONEERS' NATIONAL ADVISORY COMMITTEE, 1946

"Probably every auctioneer of competency and possibly some incompetents have solicited employment by the Government for the sale of Government surplus. Generally speaking, little has come of it, and [this] meeting in New York was born out of that discouragement."

Frustrated by the reluctance of the U.S. Government to use the auction process in the sale of domestic war assets after victory in the Second World War, the Auctioneers' National Advisory Committee met in New York on April 1 and May 20, 1946, with the goal of lobbying the War Assets Administration for more business. Chaired by Addison B. Freeman – who had recently opened a short-lived office in the Big Apple at 27 William Street – the coittee would produce a document titled *On the Use of Auctions for the Sale of Government Surplus* to promote the auctioneers as creators of the best immediate market. And its sound bite? "Auction – there is no better, no fairer, no more American way of sale."

Success was met on a limited scale. This would not be the great free-for-all of the late teens and the early twenties, but in August 1948, Samuel T. Freeman & Co. would receive a letter from the Preparatory Commission of the International Refugee

Organization, granting them management of a substantial portion of the Nazi war loot in its possession. "In Germany and Austria the Allied Armies recovered a vast quantity of miscellaneous personal property which had been confiscated by the Nazis from their victims," wrote Mr. W. Hallam Tuck, the executive secretary of the commission. "The disposition of that portion of the property which could not be identified either as to individual ownership or national origin was provided under Article 8 or Part 1 of the Final Act of the Paris Conference on Reparation, and the Five Power Agreements of June 14, 1946 … As you have been informed, the entire net proceeds realized from these sales will be used to rehabilitate and resettle eligible non-repatriate victims who suffered heavily at the hands of the Nazis. Successful sale of this property will contribute materially to mitigate the suffering of innocent men, women and children – victims of the Hitler holocaust, and offer them hope for a happier future."

The sale of approximately 1,500 pieces of Continental silver, 87 Oriental rugs and hundreds of pieces of gold and gemstone jewelry was conducted over four days from September 27 to October 1, 1948.

CONTINENTAL SILVER
JEWELRY AND ORIENTAL RUGS

To be sold for the
Resettlement and Rehabilitation
of Victims of Nazi Action
PREPARATORY COMMISSION
INTERNATIONAL REFUGEE
ORGANIZATION
OF THE UNITED NATIONS

☆ ☆ ☆

Public Auction Sale

September 27th, 28th, 29th, 30th and
October 1st at 2 P. M. each day

At the Art Galleries of

SAMUEL T. FREEMAN & CO.
Established November 12, 1805

AUCTIONEERS

1808-10 Chestnut Street   -::-   Philadelphia, Pa.

1948

Addison B. Freeman Jr. (1920-1960) smiles for the camera in 1955 after signing a $1 million check following Freeman's record-breaking industrial clearance sale conducted on behalf of Lockwood Dutchess Inc. of Waterville, Maine.

The passing of a plant that had been part of the life of the city for more than half a century would not be marked without a display of sentiment. Dozens of old employees, their ages accelerated by years of service in the mill, were present to see it sold by "the big firm from Philadelphia." Some jobless, they manifested a keen interest in the identity of the bidders, harboring the possibility that the auctioneer's gavel might just fall to some entrepreneurial spirit that could mean a livelihood for themselves and their families. Rumors would be rife regarding representatives from this company or executives from that company who had been spotted in town.

On occasion, among the audience of scrap dealers and those looking for parts and machinery at a bargain-basement price, a new owner would be found for the mill that might promise a stay of execution. During the 1920s and '30s the ordeal would become commonplace for the many mill workers who frequently moved, either from one mill village to another or between the farm and mill village. Load the furniture and other personal belongings onto a flatbed truck during daylight hours, then drive through the night to a new destination while the children slept.

It was, however, not always necessary for the mill to close. Of the many addresses that Addison B. Freeman gave to the financial and legal institutions that might send business his way, all helped cultivate the impression that the industrial auction was a science and something best left to the experts. There was pride in a mailing list accumulated from U.S. and Canadian telephone books that boasted approximately 1 million names and addresses in 150 different classifications, and in experience that, by the 1930s, would include sales conducted in more than half of the states in the Union and in two Canadian provinces. Using this early database, a Freeman specialty was the mill tenement property sale.

Pioneered by Samuel Slater in the Blackstone Valley and perfected in Lowell, the planned industrial village had been emulated by mill owners from Maine to Louisiana. It was in these company villages that workers could rent a good house with electricity and indoor plumbing for as little as $4 a month, have credit at the company store, attend church and school, play ball or go bowling. It was also an opportunity for the 'benevolent' white-collar mill owner to control almost every aspect of the blue-collar existence and squeeze 100 percent efficiency from his workforce.

At the beginning of the 20th century, the village remained a necessary adjunct to a mill, but that would change with the automobile and hard-surfaced roads, which made it practicable for "operatives" to travel up to 20 miles to and from their place of work. The mill owners began to look at the villages as stagnant assets that were expensive to maintain. Handled properly, the sale of the tenement properties back to the workers could secure the loyalty of mill operatives, instill the pride of individual ownership in the workforce and release funds at a time when working capital was short.

Among the many companies who took up the offer from Samuel T. Freeman & Co. to liquidate inactive capital was Cheney Brothers of South Manchester, Connecticut, the largest manufacturer of silk in the United States. The first American company to master the intricate art of silk weaving – but bankrupted by investments in Chinese mulberry trees – the Cheney fortune was rebuilt in the 1840s around the invention of a spinning machine that had the ability to double, twist and wind raw silk. Over the course of 50 years, a model manufacturing community was built on Cheney family farmland.

By 1920, the company employed 4,000 operatives, but it would be hit hard by both the invention of rayon, a cheaper and more consistent man-made fiber, and the Great Depression.

The announcement went out over the radio in the weeks preceding the sale in 1937: "If you have money to invest; if you want to buy attractive real estate that can be quickly sold at a profit; or if you're looking for a home that will reduce your present cost of living ... here is your chance of a lifetime."

In the context of the time, the Cheney buildings were of unusually high quality, rendered in a variety of turn-of-the-century architectural styles, from simple vernacular cottages to houses in the Craftsman and Eclectic idioms. The sale, the first of its type in Connecticut said the local papers, involved the dispersal of the entire compound of 245 residential parcels with a total of 747 dwelling units inhabited by more than 40 different ethnic groups. The Boston team (Addison B. Freeman, Colonel William "Billy" Hoey, Jim Moran and Mike Shaughnessy) set up an office on site for several weeks. Mortgage financing of up to 75 percent of the purchase price was assured to every buyer (more than was typical at these sales), with 10 per cent of the price due on the day of purchase. The Federal Housing Administration also encouraged locals to explore financing possibilities with the slogan: "With a small down payment your rent money will buy a home."

From September 23-25, a crowd followed Freeman's staff from parcel to parcel as each of the dwellings was sold for a grand total of $831,215. More than 200 individuals were added to the list of the town's property owners over those two days, while the $800,000 availed by the Cheney Brothers after fees, represented close to 80 percent of the company's debt. The Cheney Brothers Mill Village is now listed on the National Register of Historic Places.

At the time, this sale – one with the happy coincidence of pleasing consignor, buyers and the people of the city – ranked as the highest-grossing New England real estate auction on record. It would be matched by the highest-grossing New England industrial machinery sale in 1955.

The last of the great mill sales in the North was conducted by Freeman's for Lockwood Dutchess Inc. of Waterville, Maine. The textile conglomerate with interests across several states had auctioned all buildings and land not directly connected with the Waterville plant in the 1930s, but was rapidly downsizing its industrial real estate in the 1950s after a brief war bounce. Addison B. Freeman Jr., who had joined the Boston crew alongside his father in 1946, would sign a $1 million check to Lockwood Dutchess on September 21, 1955, after completing a two-day sale of

In the 1920s as automobiles were beginning to change the appearance of Philadelphia's streets – most notably the addition of the Delaware River (Benjamin Franklin) Bridge – Samuel T. Freeman & Co. was selling those companies that didn't quite make it. Between 1924 and 1928, the auction house's industrial division traveled to conduct liquidation sales at more than 20 defunct automobile plants. In geographic reach they spanned the Luxor Cab Manufacturing Corporation and the Harley Co. (a division of the Indian Motorcycle Co.) in Massachusetts to the Rutenber Motor Company and the Apperson Automobile Co. (the birthplace of the pneumatic tyre) in Indiana. Closer to home were the Fox Motor Car Company, Ace Motor Corporation and the Commercial Truck Company of Philadelphia, the Stanley Steam Vehicle Corporation of America of Allentown, the Rowe Motor Manufacturing Company of Lancaster and the Owen Magnetic Motor Car Company of Wilkes-Barre.

How the *Philadelphia Inquirer* reported the news of the Boston Harbor Air Crash on October 4, 1960.

machinery that totaled $1,200,550.30. Shortly after, his father announced his intention to retire and Addison B. Jr. (he was affectionately known simply as "B") took the company into its fifth generation as a proprietorship. It was a time when Freeman's seemed to have it all.

No one could have foreseen what lay ahead. October 4, 1960 had been another day at the office. Attending a liquidation sale in Methuen, Massachusetts, the new proprietor had raced down to Boston Logan Airport to catch the Eastern Airlines Electra flight to Philadelphia. He had made it just in time.

As the plane became airborne, a flock of starlings crossed its path and the birds were ingested by all four of the craft's turbine-propeller engines. The plane crashed into Boston Harbor, killing 62 of the 72 people on board.

Back in Philadelphia was Samuel M. "Beau" Freeman II, the son of Samuel T. Freeman II who had joined the family firm in 1958. He was awaiting the return of his cousin. After two years of working in the gallery (he had taken his first full mezzanine sale on September 22, 1959), he wanted to know his career prospects and was plucking up the courage to confront him on the matter.

"Did you see the news?" his mother asked. "I think B was on that plane." It was the end of an era.

The Philadelphia Inquirer

PUBLIC LEDGER

An Independent Newspaper for All the People

FINAL
CITY EDITION

THE WEATHER
U. S. Weather Bureau Forecast
Philadelphia and vicinity:
Mostly sunny Wednesday and
Thursday. High both days near
70. Variable winds 5 to 10 miles
an hour.
COMPLETE WEATHER DATA
ON PAGE 16

August Circulation: Daily, 619,414; Sunday, 1,001,937   132d Year   WEDNESDAY MORNING, OCTOBER 5, 1960   WFIL 560 KC • WFIL-TV 6   FIVE CENTS

60 Killed as Phila.-Bound Airliner Crashes Into Harbor at Boston

Dr. Ralph W. Sockman, principal speaker at the United Fund drive opening dinner at the Bellevue-Stratford, lights the torch held by Sally Stevenson, student nurse at Pennsylvania Hospital. R. Stewart Rauch, Jr., chairman of the drive, is an interested spectator.

United Fund Drive

Gloom Fills Airport Here As Kin Wait

News Brings Relief To One Family, But Grief to Others.

By SAMUEL ETTINGER

Philadelphia International Airport's terminal building, normally ablaze with life, was a gloomy shell Tuesday night.

Relatives of eight persons who were aboard the Eastern Air Lines Electra that crashed in Boston Harbor huddled in the terminal's "VIP Lounge" waiting for news.

For the family of Sidney W. Popkin, of 113 Pond st., Bristol, there was joy. He survived. For the seven other families there was only heartbreak.

38 DUE TO DISEMBARK

The plane, bound from Boston to Atlanta, Ga., was due at Philadelphia International Airport at 6:49 P. M. Thirty-eight passengers were scheduled to disembark here, 30 of them from the Philadelphia area.

Relatives arriving to meet passengers were told at the

Firemen and volunteers search through the tail section of an Eastern Air Lines turbo-prop Electra that crashed in shallows of Boston Harbor just after taking off from Boston's Logan International Airport.

Spring Summit Slated by Nikita

Broken Bodies, Wreckage Floated In With the Tide

11 Survive As Electra Falls Apart

30 From Here, U. S. Top Secret Papers Missing

BOSTON, Oct. 4 (AP).—A 60-ton airplane suspended Tuesday night an Eastern Air Lines Lockheed Electra, the airliner of 11 of the victims crashed on take-off into Boston Harbor.

An eye-witness said the Philadelphia-bound plane appeared to explode as it hit the water and split in two.

"Trustees' sale in bankruptcy…" Samuel T. Freeman & Co.,
announces the wartime sale on the premises of the buildings,
library, furniture and machinery of the *Evening Public Ledger*
newspaper on September 15-17, 1942.

READ ALL ABOUT IT

Alongside a host of specialist periodicals, Philadelphians
had five major newspapers from which to choose at the
beginning of the 1930s: the morning and evening issues
of the *Public Ledger*, the *Inquirer*; the *Evening Bulletin*
and the *Record*. But with advertising dollars in short
supply, Depression economics affected the newspapers as
much as the news they printed.

The *Inquirer* would survive a scandal that saw its owner,
Moses Annenberg, spend three years in prison and pay
$10 million for tax evasion; but David Stern's *Record,* a
partisan Democratic daily, folded during bitter strike
action in 1946.

The *Public Ledger*, a pioneer of investigative news
reporting when it first launched, and for close to a
century the voice of Philadelphian Republicanism,
disappeared from the newsstands during the Second
World War. Samuel T. Freeman & Co. was a regular
advertiser in its pages – T.B. Freeman had chosen the first
issue of Philadelphia's first penny paper dated March 25,
1836, to give notice of his intention to devote his time to
sales by order of the courts of law and was given the task
of liquidating the plant and machinery of the *Evening
Ledger* in September 1942.

Fine Art

The third floor gallery at 1808 Chestnut Street as it appeared shortly after opening in the 1920s. The Ionic columns and hanging lanterns remain *in situ* today.

"During the past ten years we have been developing an antique department which has a reputation among buyers of which we are most jealous. No piece is sold as an antique unless our expert is confident of its authenticity and his knowledge and honesty are recognised by all our customers. In this department we can offer our clients probably the finest rooms in their own property of any auctioneer in America. We have spent a large sum in re-decorating the Gallery. The color scheme of green and white with indirect lighting for the room and special reflectors for illuminating the side walls enables us to display fine furniture, bric-a-brac and paintings to the best possible advantage."

EDMUND B. BRICKLEY, 1914

In a patriarchal company – one where the eldest son is groomed to inherit – losing the leader is acutely felt. Difficult challenges and difficult decisions lay ahead.

Addison B. Freeman Jr. had left no obvious heir to succeed him, and by default, it was his mother, Mary Freeman, who inherited the proprietorship. It was the only moment in the company's history that a woman would hold title, and the first time that the succession would not move from father to son. After a frustrating hiatus of several months – one that prompted the Freeman family to end its long-standing relationship with the Provident National Bank – a deal was struck in September 1961 that saw three new names on the headed notepaper. They were: John M. Freeman, only son of George C. Freeman; the young Beau Freeman; and a retired railroad executive related to the Freemans by marriage, Lester C. Boslar.

It was, however, too late to save the Boston office, where the loss of a figurehead and his little black book of lawyers, bankers and industrialists was most acutely felt. With the high-profile Nitro and Lowell sales now mere memories, Freeman's presence in Massachusetts faded into history. In a brief note to staff in 1961, Addison B. Freeman, a broken man following the death of his son and heir, announced the closure of the Boston office after 40 years of operation.

In Philadelphia, Freeman's business was also in flux. The flood of industrial and real estate sales of the first quarter of the century, which had leveled to a steady stream in the second quarter, had become no more than a trickle. Industrial sales numbered fewer than half a dozen a year by the mid 1960s; likewise, competition and economic change saw fewer and fewer urban properties sold from the rostrum.

Hence, by the outset of the 1970s, Freeman's, the company that once prided itself on its diverse activities in the auction business, was almost exclusively operating in the field of estate sales, fine art and antiques.

Freeman's serious interest in the fine art trade began not in the postwar era but in February 1903 with the arrival of Edmund B. Brickley, a young retail specialist from John Wanamaker's. Brickley was given charge of Gallery sales, the name that survived at Freeman's until the 21st century to denote auctions of selected merchandise from the field of art and antiques.

From his time with Philadelphia's top department store, Brickley had a natural affinity for the fine art business.

The craft of fine art auctioneering did not reach too far back in American history but he grasped immediately that this was about class. Not about social class (although it certainly helped in a town like Philadelphia, where the "old" families still counted), but about style, veneer, polish and a sense of theater. To Freeman's, he brought window displays, vases of fresh flowers, subtle lighting and carefully chosen color schemes suitable for showing paintings and fine furniture to their best advantage. It was not quite New York, where leading auctioneers had recently began conducting the formal black-tie evening sale, but in the green-and-white painted walls of 1519-21 Chestnut Street, Philadelphia's leading real estate and industrial clearance business could now pass muster with ladies who lunch. He could boast of "probably the finest rooms in their own property of any auctioneer in America."

Samuel T. Freeman & Co. had made its move from a building at 12th and Walnut to Chestnut Street in 1908 with the break-up of rival auctioneers M. Thomas & Sons. Number 1519 – three blocks east of the building that would become most identified with the Freeman's brand – brought the company close to one of the best shopping districts of the city and back to the street where the first members of the dynasty had worked as

printers a century earlier. A porter had got it in the neck when the boss's desk smashed as it tumbled from a cart during the move, but little will have dampened Samuel T.'s spirits. The acquisition of the premises of M. Thomas & Sons represented much more than a real estate transaction.

Moses Thomas (1776-1865) had been a contemporary of Tristram Bampfylde Freeman, and like that other "old and respectable inhabitant of the city," he was both a member of Lodge 51 and an influential figure in the history of American printing. Born of "poor honest parents of old English extraction," he had started work at the Bradford & Inskeep bookstore, opening his own retail store on Chestnut at around 25 years of age. In between brief militia service (the 4th C. Frankford Volunteer Artillerists) and membership of two local fire companies (the Resolution Hose Co. and the Neptune Hose Co.) he negotiated to buy the *Analectic Magazine*. Under the editorship of his friend Washington Irving and with the contributions of other members of the so-called Knickerbocker School, the *Analectic* would take on new life. It was in Thomas's magazine that Americans encountered the early efforts of the aspiring young naturalist Alexander Wilson and, two decades before Currier & Ives, would see the first American lithograph.

Jno. A. McAllister

FINE ARTS.

M. THOMAS & SON,

WILL SELL BY AUCTION,

At their Auction Rooms, No. 105½ Chesnut Street—Up Stairs,

THE

ELEGANT PAINTINGS,

DRAWINGS, ETCHINGS AND ENGRAVINGS,

Lately in the Rembrandt Exhibition *at its close.*

The sale will take place without any reserve, whatever, excepting the protection to be offered to the two Rembrandts, and will commence precisely at 11 o'clock, on Wednesday Morning, May the 2nd, and will continue until the 38 lots of Paintings are sold. The same evening, exactly at 7 o'clock, the sale of the Prints, Drawings, Etchings and Engravings will commence, and be continued that and the ensuing evening, until the whole are sold.

Catalogues, price 12½ cents, to be had at the Auction Rooms. His catalogue money will be allowed to every purchaser.

☞ OBSERVATIONS *respectfully addressed to the Public by the Proprietor of this Collection.*

The change of climate having, unexpectedly, called forth the incipient infirmities incidental to the Proprietor's very advanced age, (now entered on his seventy-ninth year) and aggravated some chronic ailments, to which he is subject, his illness at length reached an *extremity* which deranges his plan of an extended pictorial tour in the UNITED STATES, and disables him from all further active professional exertions, although it has pleased God to leave him in possession of an unimpaired mind. After his having been so long a sufferer, struggling between life and death, unable even to return the attentions of courtesy and kindness, for which he is a grateful debtor, the entire prostration of his bodily strength and the weight of years, have warned him "TO SET HIS HOUSE IN ORDER," and close all professional concerns, *without the loss of an hour.* In this solemn emergency, he has been necessitated to hazard this auction, *as a winding up of all.—* Whether this movement be considered an act of wisdom or of folly of provident speculation, or of unworthy panic under an imaginary alarm of immediate or speedy mortality, all surmises must end as they have so far ended, in one palpable conclusion, that the risks o

However, to the next generation of Philadelphians, the company of M. Thomas & Son was auctioneer first and publisher second. It was, like most other auction houses in the city, a jobbing firm – no estate too big or too small – but Moses and his brother and partner Samuel (both literary types according to the Masonic biographers) had been among the first to take advantage of the emancipation of the book trade in the early 1820s.

From as early as 1823, they handled the antiquarian libraries of learned Philadelphia including, in 1844, that of lawyer, American Philosophical Society president and Historical Society of Pennsylvania founder member Peter S. Du Ponceau. Thomas also cut a profitable niche as proprietor of Philadelphia's annual Book Trade Sales – an idea first mooted by that great Irish immigrant publisher Mathew Cary and successfully resurrected by his eldest son Henry. Thomas ran the book auctions as weeklong, trade-only affairs from his store at 105 Chestnut Street, clearing sometimes half a million dollars worth of new and used books to American retailers. Famously good refreshments kept his customers in the building and spending money until close to midnight.

Books evolved into real estate. M. Thomas & Son had taken a tidy 1 percent commission when in 1875 upon instructions of Congress the defunct Navy Yard sold to a representative of the mighty Pennsylvania Railroad Company for $1 million. Books had also evolved into fine art – a major sale of Old Master paintings in 1838, the sale of the Peale Museum in 1854 and the estate of artist Rembrandt Peale in 1862. As Freeman's occupied itself with the lucrative but less-than-glamorous world of bankrupt stock, industrial clearance and urban decay, it was often M. Thomas & Sons to which the city lawyers turned when the ace cards were being dealt.

Catastrophe had struck on the evening of July 1, 1882 when Thomas's brownstone store on South Fourth Street was gutted by fire, incurring an estimated loss of $20,000. It was a bitter irony for a company whose founder had devoted so much energy in his youth to putting out the city's frequent fires. But to its credit, M. Thomas & Sons re-established itself in new premises at 1519-21 Chestnut Street. In 1908, the business's family lineage ended with Freeman's acquisition of this slice of Philadelphia's fine art heritage.

Two key hands were not absorbed into the new operation. Samuel S. Ellis (auctioneer) and Harry Bare (manager) would set up shop on the second floor of a building on the southeast corner of 15th and Chestnut. Their business, the Philadelphia Art Galleries, would continue to advertise under the name M. Thomas &

The first appearance in Philadelphia of 'the Swedish nightingale'
Jenny Lind on October 17, 1850 had provided Moses Thomas with
his oddest, but perhaps most famous, moment in auctioneering.
Orchestrated by the showman Phineas Taylor Barnum, all previous
musical spectacles in the city were outshone by the tour of the
European chanteuse, the tickets to her opening performance at the
Chestnut Theatre sold at auction to the highest bidder. The highest
bidder of the first ticket was the well-known city daguerreotypist
Marcus Aurelius Root. He was even better known around town
when the newspapers advertised his ability to pay $625 for a single
seat.

Sons but with the caveat "late of" before the company
logo.

Freeman's found instead the expertise and experience to
handle the illustrious collections of Philadelphia's new
and old money in another former Thomas employee.
Stanislaus Vincent Henkels was that rare combination
the fine art trade occasionally breeds – the merchant-
academic.

"Stan" V. Henkels had joined M. Thomas & Son in his
teens, working his way up through the ranks before
running a rare book emporium and auction business
from the 1890s. He was a recognized expert in
American autographs and American portraiture, and
scarcely a Washington signature or book of Audubon
plates passed through Philadelphia without the approval
of his sharp eye. If that were not enough, Henkels also
had an extraordinary gift for persuading monied
collectors to buy from him and cash-strapped families to
sell through him.

Thomas Birch & Sons, another of the city's major late
19th century auctioneers, had been willing to oblige
Henkels' need for suitable premises to showcase the
remarkable things he selected for auction. Working in
tandem in the early 1890s, Henkels and Birch & Sons

A letter written by Nathan Hale to Miss Betsy Christophers of New London, Connecticut while a captain in a Revolutionary Army unit stationed at Camp Winter Hill. Dated October 19, 1775, the two-page letter was written less than a year before the Martyr Spy would be executed in New York. At Freeman's sale of the Valuable Collection of Autographs gathered by the late John Mills Hale Esq. of Philipsburg, Center County, Pennsylvania, it sold on February 14-15, 1913, for $1500.

conducted remarkable sales. They sold a group of documents, memorabilia and relics from the rump of the Washington family estate in 1890-'91 and the James Madison correspondence (some 2,900 documents) from the estate of James C. McGuire the following year. The collection of books from the library of George Washington collected by John R. Baker Sr. of Philadelphia (1891); the Lincoln Memorial Collection (1894) and the first of eight sales to disperse the Franklin collection of Governor Samuel W. Pennypacker (1905) have all become part of the Stan Henkels legend. In between, he found the time to edit the five volumes of *The Bibliographer's Manual of American History* (published in 1907) and to become embroiled in an unsuccessful attempt to save a valuable William Penn document, the Charter of Liberties, for the citizens of Pennsylvania.

But, with Freeman's move in 1908, Henkels' allegiance shifted to the new residents of 1519-21 Chestnut Street.

That, in April 1909, Samuel T. Freeman found itself in the happy position of disposing the important collection of engraved portraits of Washington and Franklin assembled by Henry Whelen Jr. suggests that Henkels' impact was almost immediate. Whelen, a retired naval officer and head of the banking house of Townsend Whelen & Co., was among those who had gazed upon

the relics and images of the "father of our country" at Fairmont Park in 1876, and had chosen to become part of the mythmaking. His pioneering collection of Washington engravings was second only to that of his father-in-law, the retired conveyancer turned arts author and historian William Spohn Baker. Baker's assemblage of Washingtoniana – comprised of 1,092 engraved portraits that formed the basis of his book *Engraved Portraits of Washington* (1880), plus 1146 coins, medal and tokens – had been gratefully received by the Historical Society in 1898.

First in the minds of collectors at the Whelen Jr. sale was a mezzotint of General Washington engraved by V. Green after a bust-length portrait by John Trumbull. It sold at $370, followed by a Green/Trumbull full-length at $310 and a mezzotint done by P. Dawe from a three-quarter-length portrait by Wright of Philadelphia of the general in uniform ($260.)

Basking in the glow of a sale whose novelty and subject matter had received widespread press coverage, Henkels followed up in February 1913 with the autographs gathered by his long-standing client and friend, the late John Mills Hale Esq. of Philipsburg, Center County, Pennsylvania. A collector for close to half a century who had sought out the letters of luminaries from all walks of

life, Hale had already willed a complete set of autographs by the signers of the Declaration of Independence to the University of Pennsylvania, but his archive was so vast as to be barely diminished.

"Letter of Hale sells for $1500" was the headline in the *Inquirer*, which provided day to day coverage of the event. The Hale to which the newspaper referred was the Martyr Spy, whose two-page note had been written to Miss Betsy Christophers of New London, Connecticut while a captain in a Revolutionary Army stationed at Camp Winter Hill on October 19, 1775. Less than a year later he would be executed for espionage in New York.

Sold at $900 the following day was a Lincoln campaign letter written from Springfield, Illinois, on April 14, 1860 to Connecticut journalist James F. Babcock, then editor of the *New Haven Palladium*. Lincoln gave the names of politicians from Illinois, Ohio and Iowa he believed were sympathetic to his nomination for the presidency. Purchased for $650 was an undated but fully signed letter from Martha Washington discussing the delivery of supplies, including 37 pounds of butter and a cask of apples. "Mr Wa'n would have sent them but he had no barrel that [they] could be put in," she explained.

It was not just the caliber of merchandise that was changing at Freeman's. Under Henkels' supervision,

Camp Winter Hill Octo: 19th 1775

Dear Betsey,

I hope you will excuse my Freedom in writing to you, as I cannot have the pleasure of seeing & conversing with you. What is now a letter would be a visit were I in New London, but this being out of my power suffer me to make up the defect in the best manner I can. I write not to give you any news, or any pleasure in reading (though I would heartily do it if in my power) but from the desire I have of conversing with you in some form or other.

I once wanted to come here to see something extraordinary, my curiosity is satisfied. I have now no more desire for seeing things here, than for seeing what is in New-London, no, nor half so much neither. Not that I am discontented — so far from it, that in the present situation of things I would not accept a furlough were it offered me. I would only observe, that we often flatter ourselves with great happiness could we see such & such things; but when we actually come to the sight of them, our solid satisfaction is really no more than when we only had them in expectation.

All the news I have, I wrote to John Hallam, if it be worth your hearing he will be able to tell you when he delivers this — It will therefore not worth while for me to repeat.

I am a little at a loss how you carry on at New-London. Jared Stam I hear is gone. The number of Gentlemen is now so few, that I fear how you will go through the winter, but I hope for the best.

I remain with esteem,

Yr. Sincere Friend
& Hble Set.
N. Hale

Arthur J. Sussel was a Polish immigrant who arrived in Philadelphia shortly after the turn of the 20th century, at age 15. While working as a hat-check boy at Kugler's Restaurant on Chestnut Street, Sussel, around 17 when this picture was taken, became acquainted with Samuel T. Freeman. His conversations with Mr. Freeman, and his subsequent visits to the nearby auction house, inspired Sussel to enter the antiques trade. He would go on to become the city's premier antiquarian, selling to blueblooded familes and movie stars alike from his shop on Pine Street.

ARTHUR J. SUSSEL (1889-1958)

By virtue of its longevity, Freeman's has provided a constant point of reference for the dealing profession. In some ways it could be said that Philadelphia's antiques trade was a sibling that grew up alongside America's oldest auction house. Certainly it was the bustling, charged atmosphere at Freeman's that inspired the dean of Philadelphia's antiquarians, Arthur J. Sussel (1889-1958), to take the plunge into antique dealing.

In his unpublished autobiography, whose typescript is now part of the Joseph Downs Collections of Manuscripts and Printed Ephemera at Winterthur, the Polish émigré wrote of the awakening he experienced during the first decade of the 20th century when observing and then partaking in the flurry of activity at Freeman's gallery.

"It all started many years ago," Sussel wrote in his 1945 memoirs, "when I worked at Kugler's [Restaurant on Chestnut Street]. An old gentleman, Samuel T. Freeman, auctioneer, used to come in with his three sons every day, for luncheon." Sussel, who had bypassed secondary education and found work as a hat-check boy, recalled how the elder Freeman – "perhaps to atone for the smallness of [his] tips" –

would tell him about the auction house, suggesting he pay a visit sometime and "buy some bargains."

His curiosity piqued, Sussel walked the short city block to Freeman's one afternoon when he had some free time, and was mesmerized by what he saw. "It was all new and strange to me," he wrote, "but somewhat devilish and witty, too. I just walked about – studied things…the people, the noise of the auctioneers, the handlers. And there sure were bargains in those days."

A year after his introduction to the auction world at Freeman's, Sussel became acquainted with an antique dealer and furniture maker on Pine Street whose daughter he was courting. It would convince him of the correctness of his career direction, and in 1913 he would open the first of several shops he would own over the next 45 years.

In the words of Sussel's daughter-in-law, Sonnie Sussel: "He sold to many of the society people of Philadelphia – the Drexels, the Biddles and Dr. Albert Barnes (founder of The Barnes Foundation), who would come in with Violette (de Mazia, vice president of The Barnes Foundation). He also sold to a lot of movie stars, including Katharine Hepburn and Claude

Rains, some of whom would come in from New York or wherever to his shop. They loved him. He knew how to talk to them from his experience as a hat-check boy. In later years, when he became ill, they were very attentive and showered him with flowers and gifts."

Attending auctions was integral to her father-in-law's existence. The family joke was that he had not been born at a hospital at all; his parents had bought him at an auction. Sonnie Sussel relates the event that ignited Arthur Sussel's interest in buying at auctions for resale. "I think he might have been at a Freeman's auction and scratched his nose or something, and in so doing bought a set of cups and saucers. On the way out of the gallery, a dealer came up to him and said, 'Would you like to sell them?' He immediately saw that he could make a profit that way." Sussel would go on to become an expert buyer and an habitué of Freeman's sales, usually bidding with a wink or the subtle lifting of an eyebrow.

previously rudimentary catalogues acquired a more scholarly edge and – with the introduction of the occasional image – a sophistication. If he said a picture was by Benjamin West, then it would be accepted as such. If he opined a painting was "circle of" Benjamin West, then there was the likelihood that the work was of the period of the artist and closely related to his style, but not from his brush. A work from the "studio of" was possibly executed under the supervision of the artist but not wholly by his hand, while the caveat "school of" indicated a work in the style of the artist but probably of a later period. These are accepted cataloguing terms in the modern auction world, but at a time when the norm was to present the object with a description corresponding to the most optimistic expectations of the owner, they were unusually precise. Specialization in niche categories of the fine art business – one of the central tenets of the rebirth of the Freeman's enterprise in the late 1990s – first arrived at Freeman's with Henkels in 1908.

With Brickley providing the style and Henkels the substance, Freeman's sold its most valuable work of art to date in 1919. There had never been a tradition of selling museum-quality works at public auction – that was typically left to the discretion of the private dealer –

but Gilbert Stuart's small full-length portrait of George Washington was the second major Stuart portrait to be sold in Philadelphia in that decade. The splinter of the M. Thomas & Son operation, trading as Philadelphia Art Galleries, had sold a major Stuart half-length portrait of Washington just six years previously as part of the final dispersal of the collection of the industrialist and art collector Joseph Harrison Jr. Named after its first owner, the Philadelphia merchant John Vaughan, Stuart's first portrait of the first President from life had been acquired by Harrison around 1851, passing to his widow Sarah Poulter Harrison before it was sold by on March 12, 1912. It would enter the Andrew W. Mellon Educational and Charitable Trust in 1936, and the National Gallery of Art, Washington D.C. in 1942.

The portrait that crossed Freeman's path in 1919 was a small version of the so-called Lansdowne type. Its exemplar was painted in 1796 at the behest of wealthy Philadelphia merchant William Bingham and his wife, Anne, as a gift for William Petty, the First Marquis of Lansdowne. Courtesy of a $20 million gift to the Smithsonian in 2001, it still resides in the National Portrait Gallery.

Reproduced time and again on creamware, silk handkerchiefs and whisky bottles, in the Lansdowne

portrait, Washington stands before us with his right hand extended palm-upward and his left hand holding the hilt of a sword. He wears a black frock coat fitting for a leader of a new republic. An oval medallion on the back of a gilt armchair is draped with the laurels of victory, the rainbow emerging from stormy clouds suggests hope, while a stack of books are carefully chosen to underline Washington's military and civilian leadership.

The previous owners of this artist's copy were two Philadelphia notables. A handwritten note to the back detailed the first owner of this small full-length portrait as Henry Kuhl, one of the founders of the Pennsylvania Academy of Fine Arts. His daughter, Margaret John Kelly had sold it in 1857 to Thomas Skelton Harrison, the grandson of the chemist John Harrison and a former Consul General and American ambassador to Egypt.

Regrettably no price records survive for the sale on December 22, 1919, but subsequent reference works record the purchaser as Joseph T. Kinsley of Philadelphia. The portrait is now known as the Kuhl-Thomas Skelton Harrison-Dripps portrait and resides in a private collection.

If this was the essence of "old school" American collecting – it was no accident that autographs and

Edwin Atlee Barber (1851-1916), who became the director of the Pennsylvania Museum and School of Industrial Art in 1907, remains an important figure in the connoisseurship and classification of American ceramics and glass. As the author of a series of books from *The Pottery and Porcelain of the United States* (1893) to *Marks of American Potters* (1904) his energies encouraged the appreciation of American-made pottery, porcelain and glass. In particular, his *Tulip Ware of The Pennsylvanian-German Potters* (1903) played an important role in the rediscovery of the rich potting heritage of the state's largest ethnic group, largely ignored by the city's collecting institutions until the final moments of the 19th century.

His collection – on exhibition at the PMA for many years – was sold at Samuel T. Freeman & Co. in 1917 following the "profound regret ... that the Institute with which Dr. Barber was so long connected did not have the means to acquire it".

imagery of heroic and historical figures were afforded such prominence at the Sanitary fairs – then this period also brings early indications of "modern" collecting impulses.

In Freeman's December 1917 catalogue devoted to the collection of the late Edwin Atlee Barber, Philadelphia witnessed its first major sale devoted to American-made ceramics and glass. In 1907 Barber had assumed the directorship of the Pennsylvania Museum and School of Industrial Art (it only became the Philadelphia Museum of Art in 1938). Through a series of books he had revived the names of lost American artisans and aided a subtle collecting shift that began to see worth in the arts and crafts made by and for the ordinary man. Alongside a scatter-gun assemblage of European pottery and porcelain lay a touchstone collection of homespun products: Tucker porcelain, Bennington stonewares, "crude and grotesque, but historically interesting" South Carolina green-glazed face jugs and the Pennsylvania German slip-decorated redwares that he believed were central to the American folk art tradition.

However, that the city's major museum had failed to raise sufficient monies to save Barber's collecting efforts for posterity is an indication that material relating to the state's largest ethnic group did not yet feature high on the list of priorities in the city's collecting institutions.

It was not until 1926, when duPont money bankrolled the installation of a kitchen and bedroom from a German-American miller's house at the Museum of Art that the public at large had access to the sort of material that is now at the very heart of the collecting field known as Americana.

But, while it was still fashionable for the cognoscenti to furnish with objects made for the elite of American society – its Revere silver, its Stuart portraits, its Affleck mahogany – there were others who believed Barber was on the right track.

Another example of this early collecting impulse was provided by the cache of folksy American antiques assembled in the 1910s and '20s by the architect and celebrated stamp collector Dr. Clarence Wilson Brazer. With an eye to furnishing the Colonial Court House of Chester, built in 1724, Brazer had shown a prescient fondness for homespun coverlets, painted dower chests and iron and brass hearth tools and door furniture. Many pieces had formed part of an exhibition at the Pennsylvania Museum in the fall of 1925.

"Finely decorated Pennsylvania German dower chests" were, Freeman's catalogue said, "becoming exceedingly

Among the collection of American antiques assembled in the 1910s
and '20s by the architect Dr. Clarence Wilson Brazer was this
walnut wainscot armchair with poplar secondary woods dating to
circa 1715-35. In 1926 it was sold by Samuel T. Freeman & Co. to
the Philadelphia Museum of Art. It was purchased with the Joseph
E. Temple Fund

PHOTO BY PHILADELPHIA MUSEUM OF ART

difficult to find and had become more valuable in the
last year or so, particularly when dates and names
appear." The Philadelphia Museum and School
of Industrial Design was among the buyers at the
sale in April 1926, carrying off a walnut wainscot
armchair with poplar secondary woods dating to circa
1715-35.

By the time of the Brazer dispersal, the company coffers
swelled by events in Massachusetts, Samuel T. Freeman
had moved to bespoke premises at 1808 Chestnut.
Under the watchful eyes of George C. and Albert L.
Freeman, and the architects Tilden and Register, a
valuable plot of Center City real estate purchased very
near the peak of real estate prices was transformed into
something that, in 1924, was state of the art. Behind its
handsome stone-and-concrete Beaux Arts facade were
six floors connected by electrical elevators, with two
galleries and a basement for storage and sales of general
merchandise.

Providing continuity with buildings past was the
boardroom hung with dynastic portraits and furnished
with a King of Prussia marble fire surround that had
been removed from the offices in 12th and Walnut. A
boardroom table was a gift from the basement crew, a
silver and ivory presentation gavel from the 100th

anniversary served as the reminder of a long
heritage.

Providing a glimpse of the future was a revolving
partitioned stage that would rotate a quarter turn to
reveal the next lot up for sale. While the very latest in
auction-room trickery, it was as practical as it was
theatrical. Among those who made the journey to
Philadelphia to see the revolving stage in action was
Major Hiram Parke. He had been an early member of
Freeman's fine art team but his familiarity with some of
the company's female staff had proved at odds with the
moral standards of Samuel T. and Addison B. Later, Parke
would would emulate and update the stage in the New
York gallery of his own firm, Parke-Bernet.

If Freeman's needed a great Philadelphian to open their
new galleries, then they found it the Charter of Liberties.
The story rarely told when relating Penn lore of brotherly
love, religious utopia and handshakes with the Lenape at
Shackamaxon begins not with the revolutionary system
of government in place by 1683 but in a document
signed and sealed in the offices of London solicitors
Thomas Rudyard and Harbert Springer on April 25,
1682. It was in the Charter of Liberties that William Penn
would crystalize his ideas for a substantial parcel of New

America's oldest auction building – the Samuel T. Freeman Auction House at 1808-10 Chestnut Street designed by Tilden & Register and completed in 1924.

Established around 1916 by Ecole-trained partners H. Bartol Register and Marmaduke Tilden Jr., Tilden & Register operated from offices in the Franklin Building. The practice endured a brief hiatus when in 1917 its proprietors both received officer's commissions in the U.S. Army but survived to design a number of public buildings in the Philadelphia area including the Abington Memorial Hospital on Old York Road (1920-22) and the U.S. Post Office in Germantown (1922). In 1926, with the addition of the young George Wharton Pepper Jr., Tilden & Register became Tilden, Register & Pepper and entered Philadelphia's skyscraper market.

World woodland granted him by King Charles II in memory of his father.

To Penn, it might have represented the beginning of the Holy Experiment, but his first attempt to draft an acceptable civil system of government in the colony already populated by settlers from Sweden, Finland and Holland would not meet with widespread approval when, in the fall of 1682, he sailed "600 miles nearer the sun" to the place known as "Pennsilvania."

A mere four months after organizing the first legislative assembly under the guidelines he had carefully devised in England, Penn found himself revising his charter of "fair and representative government for all free citizens". There had been complaints that its content gave too much authority to the Governor and Council and too little to the elected assembly.

Although metaphorically torn up by faction and private interest – a revised version was signed and in place on April 2, 1683 – the original Charter survived to return to England with Penn in August 1684. By the mid 18th century, this forgotten two-page parchment of gall ink and sheepskin had fallen into the hands of the great manuscript collector Sir John Fenn. It received periods of 19th century stewardship under William Dalton and his fellow member of the Society of Antiquaries in London, Richard Almack.

However, in 1893, the first Charter of Liberties took the geographic turn that put it back on the path to ownership by the people of Pennsylvania.

In that year Dr. Richard Maris, a Philadelphia Quaker, acquired the Charter from Almack's son through an English Quaker bookseller, Henry T. Wake, for £320. By 1895, and aware that the Assembly's copy presented by William Penn had been lost or destroyed many years prior, Maris was hawking the document around the city in the hope of a State purchase.

Governor Daniel Hartman Hastings was in favor, but partisan squabbles over the proposed purchase, detailed by Stan V. Henkels in a privately printed pamphlet on the document, prevented the idea from moving forward. Instead, Maris sold the Charter to the Episcopal layman and Philadelphia banker George C. Thomas.

A partner for many years in the firms Drexel & Co. and J.P. Morgan & Co., and the philanthropic impulse behind a number of public and parochial facilities, cigar-smoking Thomas was in the happy financial position to lavish large sums of money on rare books, documents and ephemera.

Samuel T. Freeman & Co.
Established November 12, 1805

"To all People…" William Penn's Charter of Liberties dated April 25, 1682 was sold by Freeman's in 1924 on behalf of the Philadelphia banker George C. Thomas. As the *Public Ledger* reported on the front page of its November 19, 1924 issue, the Charter was purchased for $21,500 by New York collector Gabriel Wells but a campaign by the newspaper to keep the document in Pennsylvania had seen the people of the city raise the necessary $25,000 by Christmas Eve.

IMAGE COURTESY OF THE PENNSYLVANIA HISTORICAL AND
MUSEUM COMMISSION BUREAU OF ARCHIVES & HISTORY

There was not another collection like it in the country – a small but select assemblage that ranged from first editions by Dickens and Thackeray to the prayer book Louis XVI had carried to the guillotine and John Hancock's copy of *The Psalms of David*. Upon his death, Thomas's son – for whom designing golf courses was more a passion than historical memory – chose to sell the collection at Freeman's, in an auction held on November 18-19, 1924.

The announcement of the sale to be held at the new gallery had made front-page news in the *Public Ledger*. At the auction it became clear that more headlines lay ahead. A.S.W. Rosenbach, owner of Philadelphia's eminent Rosenbach Galleries, was in attendance and secured several plum lots. He paid $10,000 for Abraham Lincoln's January 26, 1863 letter to Major General Joseph Hooker assigning him command of the Army of the Potomac. He followed this with $4,000 for General Ulysses S. Grant's holographic telegram to Secretary of War E.M. Stanton informing him of General Robert E. Lee's surrender.

The rarest signature of any of the signers of the Declaration of Independence is that of Button Gwinnett who, shortly after his entry into Georgia state government, was killed in a duel with General Lachlan McIntosh on May 27, 1777. George C. Thomas owned one of only a handful of authenticated examples of Gwinnett's signature extant. Edmund Brickley (by this time Stan Henkels had left to set up business with his son on Walnut Street) hammered it down at $14,000.

But it was the future of the Charter of Liberties that had the audience transfixed on November 18. And it would be a day of disappointment for many of those onlookers.

As the *Public Ledger* reported on the front page of the following day, the Charter was purchased for $21,500 by New York collector Gabriel Wells. Once again, it would be leaving Pennsylvania. The newspaper's editor wrote: "When the time-stained parchment finally went under the hammer at the establishment of Samuel T. Freeman & Co., 1808 Chestnut Street, the State was deprived of the greatest single relic of its ancient and honourable past".

As the citizens of Pennsylvania would soon learn, the emotive editorial was more than hollow words intended to boost newspaper sales. By November 23, the *Ledger* was able to report that Wells, who claimed he could have accepted other offers of up to $100,000, was prepared to sell the Charter to the Commonwealth of Pennsylvania for only a modest profit. The newspaper went on to say that it was launching an appeal to reclaim the seminal document for the Commonwealth's archives: "Mr. Wells consented to the proposal of the *Public Ledger* to sell it to the people of Pennsylvania for $25,000, with the understanding all should have an opportunity to share in its purchase." Wells had allowed the newspaper "a reasonable length of time" in which to raise the funds to buy the document.

Each day for the next 25 days the newspaper printed every contributor's name, as donations arrived from all across Pennsylvania – from schoolchildren to the president of the Pennsylvania Railroad. Often the gifts were modest – many were only $1 or 50 cents – but anyone who sent money was listed in the paper. The outpouring culminated on Christmas Eve with the receipt of a $1,000 check from Mr. and Mrs. George H. Earle Jr., of South Rittenhouse Square. As Dr. Leopold Stokowski led the choir and bands in Independence Square, and carolers sang Silent Night, the *Public Ledger* released the news that the $25,000 goal had been met.

The Charter of Liberties now permanently resides in the Pennsylvania State Archives, in Harrisburg.

Freemen...

The 100th anniversary dinner held at 12th and Walnut Streets in December 1905.

100th ANNIVERSARY DINNER
at 12th & Walnut Streets
December, 1905

"Mr. S. T."

ON HIS RIGHT

Mr. Harbeson · Major Parke · Joe Kirby · Harry Deininger · Billy Jann · Bill Wearshing
John Purfield · *Ed Brickley · *Sam Freeman · Roger Langford · Bob Clymer · Miss Hand

ON HIS LEFT

Miss Illy · Charlie Bryde · Walter Sharpless · George Freeman · John McFadden · Dick Thomas(?)
Jimmie Moran · William McLaughlin · Lee Hartz · *Steve Shriner · Leon Wilcocks
Charlie Osborne

* Denotes "Still in Service"

ANNIVERSARIES

Every year since 1899, Freeman's has hosted an annual dinner for its entire business family. In its 100th year, the festivities were kicked up a notch.

On November 12, 1905, 23 gentlemen and just two ladies gathered at a single banquet table at the gallery on 12th and Walnut to dine on raw oysters, cream of celery soup, and roast duck with all the trimmings, followed by fancy cakes and ice cream, and coffee and cigars for the gents. The day had also been marked by an auction, which was publicized by means of an enormous American flag imprinted with the sale details. The oversized banner was brought indoors and included as a backdrop for the official 100th anniversary dinner photo, so emblematic of the overt patriotism of the time.

The 20th century would visit both euphoric highs and devastating lows on the house of Samuel T. Freeman, but the spirit of the Freeman family and its staff proved itself indelible, and the tradition of the annual dinner continued, even in times of war.

At its next major milestone, the company's sesquicentennial on November 12, 1955, a program book was published to document the highlights of a jovial occasion (its contents note that a series of 13 toasts ensued as Freeman's staff supped on snapper soup à l'Anglaise and filet mignon). Unlike the more formal atmosphere of annual dinners held in an earlier era, it was an evening of relaxed conviviality. As the dinner program informed: "Tonight, we gather in a more intimate fashion - no place cards, no menu, no speeches. Sit where you wish; select what you please. Come and get it."

Addison B. Freeman, the family wordsmith who constructed the text for the section of the menu titled *A Bit of History* recounted Freeman's growth, from an auction house that dealt primarily in real estate at the turn of the 20th century to a vendor of munitions after the First World War and a formidable purveyor of art and antiques in the decades to follow.

The booklet's salutation included what could be regarded as an intuitive glimpse into the future: "Be not fearful of competition," it said. "Be fearful of a compromise with the ideals which have allowed us to live for 150 years … we must remember the obligation that is thereby put upon us. This birthday of ours is, of course, a day we may all be proud of, but tomorrow we start another year – the beginning, we hope and believe, of another century and a half of honest, intelligent, industrious and competent service."

FREEMAN'S AT 200

1808 CHESTNUT STREET

SEPTEMBER 2005

FRONT ROW
(LEFT TO RIGHT)
JONATHAN C. FREEMAN, CHAIRMAN SAMUEL M. FREEMAN, II, SAMUEL T. FREEMAN, III

SECOND ROW
MONA LINDSEY, ELIZABETH FIELD, NOEL FAHDEN, NOELLE BURGOYNE, GARY EICHELBERGER, STEPHANIE PARKER, JENNIFER PULLARA

THIRD ROW
HANNA DOUGHER, SHING CHAN, OLIVIA SNYDER, MICHELE KISHITA, STEPHANIE WELCH, JOE HUENKE, JANE EPSTEIN, BRENT LEWIS, ANDREA URBAN

FOURTH ROW
TARA OLDT, GERALD DAVIS, DAVID BLOOM, ERIC SMITH, LYNDA CAIN, DOUGLAS GIRTON, DAVID WEISS, MATTHEW WILCOX

BACK ROW
JAMES BUCKLEY, PAUL ROBERTS, DAVID DONALDSON, ALASDAIR NICHOL, MARCELL ZOMBORI, DON WALTER, RICH HENSEL, LEE YOUNG

Samuel T. Freeman, the grandson of Thomas McLean's appointee, was presented with this suitably inscribed silver-mounted ivory gavel on November 12, 1905.

The palatial 100,000 square foot mansion in Chestnut Hill known as Whitemarsh Hall was commissioned in 1921 by Philadelphia's wealthiest man, Edward T. Stotesbury, a senior partner with both Drexel and Co. and J.P. Morgan. Reportedly, it required a staff of up to 150 servants to maintain the 147-room colossus where movie stars and crowned heads were entertained in lavish style.

Great Estates

"Duveen was just then engaged in some very nice pieces of business. Among them were sales of several paintings to Mr. and Mrs. E.T. Stotesbury of Whitemarsh Hall, Philadelphia, who were picking out the choicest treasures from among the handsome wares on display inside the new Merchant Marine building at 720 Fifth Avenue."

MERYLE SECREST, DUVEEN: A LIFE IN ART

Edward T. Stotesbury, a senior partner of Drexel & Co. and J.P. Morgan, and his wife Eva topped the social ladder not only in Philadelphia, but also in Bar Harbor, Maine and Palm Beach, Florida, where they also maintained extravagant mansions. Photograph reproduced from King's *Philadelphia and Notable Philadelphians*, 1901.

In his prime, during the third and fourth decades of the 20th century, superlatives flowed easily around the name Edward T. Stotesbury: "The richest man in Pennsylvania", "Philadelphia's greatest financier", "Owner of the city's largest and grandest home".

The son of a prosperous Quaker sugar refiner, but a man who knew what it was like to take home 16 bucks a month, Stotesbury earned his personal fortune excelling in the arena of international finance. He was senior partner at Philadelphia's premier banking institution, Drexel & Co., held a similar position at J.P. Morgan, and served on numerous boards, including those of the Reading Railroad, Pennsylvania Steel Co. and Girard Trust Co. The word "millionaire," French in origin, had not entered the English vocabulary until the early years of the 19th century. In 1927, Stotesbury was reportedly worth around $100 million.

The most obvious symbol of this enormous wealth was Whitemarsh Hall, a 147 room, six-story marble and limestone palace designed in the Georgian style by architect Horace Trumbauer for a 300-acre plot in Chestnut Hill. Limestone Ionic columns, manicured gardens, marble and gold-plated bathroom fixtures, a staff of up to 150 gardeners, cooks, chambermaids and

drivers. Henry Ford is reputed to have said after visiting: "It was a great experience to see how the rich live."

It was at Whitemarsh that Edward T. Stotesbury and his wife Eva could indulge their shared passions for thoroughbred trotters and fine art and antiques. To rear horses for the Stotesbury teams, Edward T. kept a farm at Wingo, Chestnut Hill, and assumed the presidency of the National Horse Show. For sumptuous furnishings befitting the home they called America's Versailles, they turned to Duveen Brothers.

By the end of the 19th century most of the top European art dealers had a shop front in New York. There was Knoedler & Company, Durand-Ruel and Gimpel & Wildenstein, but the Stotesburys' favorite dealership could be found on Fifth Avenue, housed in a splendid four-story imitation of Louis XV's Ministry of Marine Building in the Place de la Concorde.

Joseph Duveen had courted the Stotesburys as clients. Like most of the American industrialists who were building themselves palatial homes, they chose to fill Whitemarsh with the kinds of treasures that wealthy Europeans had accumulated for centuries. As Duveen knew all too well, "new money" Americans with no family lineage to speak of were perfectly willing to adopt more illustrious forebears. Likewise he knew economic conditions in the Old World dictated there were plenty of "old money" aristocrats willing to part with a pair of Chinese temple jars or a Lawrence portrait to settle death duties or bridge a shortfall in income from tenant land.

Possessed of considerable means, Edward T. Stotesbury knew few barriers when it came to his quarry. He and Eva were such good customers for French chateau-style furnishings that Duveen commissioned Douglas Chandor, the London society portraitist, to execute by stealth a pastel portrait of Mrs. Stotesbury. He would present it to her as a surprise Christmas gift in 1920.

Edward Stotesbury had gone on record as saying he intended to spend his fortune completely by the time he died. And, withdrawing $55,000,000 from his account at Morgan's between 1933 and 1938, he came very close to achieving that goal.

Upon his death, aged 89, his widow was left with sufficient funds to live out her years very comfortably although not enough to perpetuate the deluxe lifestyle to which she had become accustomed. It had cost around $1 million per year to maintain America's Versailles and more to keep up the splendid properties

in Bar Harbor, Maine and Palm Beach, Florida, where the Stotesburys had migrated with the seasons.

In 1944, the staff dismissed and Whitemarsh for sale (it was finally demolished in 1980), Eva R. Stotesbury summoned executives of Samuel T. Freeman & Co. and instructed them to liquidate many of the spectacular furnishings acquired over the previous four decades.

It was wartime. Almost 246,000 citizens were registered for the draft, and Philadelphia had again assumed her old role as supplier of materials of war to the nation. Some of Whitemarsh's finest and most valuable pieces had been sold privately to dealers after Edward Stotesbury's death, and more were donated to the Philadelphia Museum of Art prior to sale.

Nevertheless, thousands attended a ticket-only preview of remaining Stotesbury treasures held between October 21-24 at Freeman's galleries. For the pleasure of handling the objects on display – a much more tactile and intimate experience than a visit to the local museum – each attendee was asked to pay $1 toward the American Red Cross War Fund.

The sale stretched to three catalogues and four days. Eighteenth century French giltwood furniture, paintings from the Paris salons, tapestries, Chinese Export wares

and Golden Age English portraiture, silver and objets d'art – all provenanced to Philadelphia's finest house or Marly, the Washington D.C. mansion where Mrs. Stotesbury had resided with her first husband, Oliver Eaton Cromwell.

The Stotesburys had a particular passion for the 18th century Chinese porcelain that Duveen Brothers bought and sold in great quantity. Hammered down at $4,000 was a pair of 2ft. 4in. (70cm) high Qianlong period (1736-1795) temple jars with covers, while a pair of 4ft. 6in. (135cm) Yongzheng (1723-1736) Mandarin jars and covers, formerly of Acton Reynolds Hall in Shropshire, England, attained $6,200. Several paintings sold in the $2,000-$5,000 range, but it is indicative of the fashion of the times that a complete set of *The Cries of London* – 13 engravings after the paintings of Francis Wheatley – would trump all other entries at $8,000. They would scarcely bring more today.

On May 31, 1946, Eva Stotesbury passed away at the age of 81. In August of that year, the contents of Wingwood, the neo-Colonial seaside estate at Bar Harbor, were auctioned on site by order of the Provident Trust Co. of Philadelphia. Three months later, more French chattels were offered in a three-day sale at Freeman's galleries. And in February and March of 1947,

This 7ft. 10in. (2.35m.) Louis XV acajou and bronze doré mounted regulator clock was sold for $3,000 in the Whitemarsh auction held October 25-28, 1944. Originally purchased from Duveen Brothers, the 18th century timepiece features a lyre-shape trunk embellished by chased bronze doré shells, morning glories and acanthus-leaf scrolls.

The Stotesburys were social luminaries in south Florida, as they were in Philadelphia. Edward T. Stotesbury is shown here enjoying Palm Beach with the cotton magnate George McFadden in the winter of 1921.

THE LIBRARY COMPANY OF PHILADELPHIA

El Mirasol (The Sunflower) in West Palm Beach, Florida is where Eva Stotesbury spent her last years. At El Mirasol she is credited with having introduced the "relaxed villa" interior decoration style to Palm Beach-area mansions, incorporating Mediterranean and Moorish styles. Shown here is the home's south loggia.

Freeman's headed to Palm Beach to conduct an on-site sale of the complete furnishings of El Mirasol, a trend-setting Spanish-style oceanside villa designed by Addison Mizner for the Stotesburys in 1927. There were 37 rooms and a 40-car garage to clear. Admission to either the sale or preview was $2.

Monied Philadelphians' penchant for town-and-country living had begun in the late 18th century. Then the true mark of having arrived was to own not only a white marble and red brick house in the city but also a sprawling European-style estate within an hour's ride of Market Street. Here, away from the hustle, bustle and filth, a gentleman and his family could enjoy the delights (but none of the hardships) of rural life and find sanctuary at the first signs of fever should it strike the city during summer months.

The migration of Philadelphia's wealthy continued with the pace of railroad construction. By the beginning of the second decade of the 20th century, a full 25 percent of Philadelphia's population was living the life of the Main Liner, cosseted in the verdant western suburbs beyond the Schuylkill River. In the years before some of the great American fortunes were lost in the

stock market crash of 1929, Philadelphia's business giants elevated the town and country lifestyle to a virtual art form. Accumulating wealth during the week and retreating to their opulent estates on weekends to ride, shoot, play golf and entertain on a lavish scale. Often it was through the medium of collecting or through choice of architectural style that the arriviste might reveal their true cultural identity.

The pride of Main Line Philadelphia was Penshurst. Lower Merion's largest and most lavish country manor was owned by Percival Roberts Jr., a descendant of one of America's first Welsh settlers, the president of Pencoyd Iron Works and a future director of U.S. Steel. Sitting on land that had remained in his family since first settled by John and Gainor Roberts in 1683, his 75-room home and its spectacular water gardens had been built in 1903 at a cost of $3 million. The style was Jacobean (it incorporated ornamental hardware and timbers taken from centuries-old properties in Europe), and the furnishings indicated a strong adherence to the eclectic English country house style that has so rarely fallen out of fashion. Roberts and his wife, the former Betsy Wolcott Frothingham of Boston, employed a staff of 50 to maintain both Penshurst and its working-farm where the industrialist could indulge a keen interest in

pedigree hogs and Ayrshire cattle imported from Scotland. It is said that Penshurst's barns and dairy stalls were impeccably spotless.

But this rural idyll – supplemented by pumped water and electricity – would survive less than a single lifetime. Struggling under the burden of huge fixed costs, dwindling income and increased taxation, by 1939 the eighth-generation heir made plans to leave the family estate when informed he had lost his fight to stop Lower Merion Township from building an incinerator nearby. Unwilling to accept the intrusion, Roberts made the decision to sell off Penshurst's contents, down to the last Jacobean coffer and Chippendale chair, in preparation for the mansion's demolition.

In a landmark sale held February 7-9, 1939, the "Rare American and English Furniture of the XVII and XVIII Centuries" as well as Chinese and European porcelains, rugs, books, silver, pottery and glass were auctioned from Freeman's galleries. Among the offerings were two 16th century French tapestries, bronzes by Antoine Louis Barye, original etchings, woodcuts and engravings by Dürer, Rembrandt and Whistler; and paintings by eminent European artists. Eight months later, Percival Roberts signed a check for $1,000 to engage the

The 75-room Jacobean-style mansion known as Penshurst was built in 1903 by Percival Roberts Jr., a direct descendant of one of America's first Welsh settlers. The centerpiece of a thriving farm known for its use of the latest technological advancements, Penshurst – with its spectacular setting and fountained gardens – was the jewel of Philadelphia's Penn Valley. Roberts demolished Penshurst when Lower Merion Township refused to acquiesce to his pleas not to build an incinerator near his home. When he died in 1943, at the age of 86, the original homestead land was purchased by the Home Life Insurance Co. and subdivided for new-home construction. .

services of a demolition crew. He and his wife would spend their remaining years living in smart hotels.

Once a business associated with misfortune and the sometimes crude redistribution of used personal belongings, the auction process had assumed a new respectability in the United States, just as it had in the carpeted rooms of Sotheby's and Christie's in London a century earlier. By the outset of the 20th century it had become both fashionable to buy, and socially acceptable to sell, at auction in America.

Samuel T. Freeman & Co.'s first major estate sale had been conducted in New England for a long-standing client. The year was 1937, and Freeman's had been contacted by The Pennsylvania Company, executors handling the estate of Marie Louise LeBel Knight, recently deceased. Mrs. Knight and her husband, Edward Collings Knight Jr., had been longtime residents of Philadelphia but in later years had divided their time between a 15-bedroom winter lodge on North Carolina's Outer Banks and their principal residence, a Tudor-style waterfront home in Middletown, Rhode Island, known as Stonybrook. Per an agreement between the executors and Freeman's, the entire contents of Stonybrook were to be auctioned on site – scarcely a challenge for a company with a designated "outside

Stonybrook, the Tudor-style home in Middletown, Rhode Island, that served as the principal residence of Mr. and Mrs. Edward Collings Knight Jr. was divested of its elegant contents August. 16-20, 1937, in an on-site auction conducted by Freeman's.

Edward C. and Marie Louise LeBel had lived in Philadelphia for many years and owned fine examples of early Philadelphia furniture. Among the top-selling lots in Freeman's 1937 auction at the Knights' Rhode Island home, Stonybrook, was a set of five (two shown here) Queen Anne fiddleback side chairs. The quintet of black leather slip-seated chairs with shell-carved cabriole legs terminating in modified web feet brought $1,050.

Admission to the preview and on-site auction at Stonybrook was by card of admittance only. Freeman's printed 2,000 such cards to "eliminate most of those who might otherwise attend purely out of idle curiosity." More than 175 individual buyers left the auction with furniture or decorative art objects from the Knight estate.

division" capable of clearing an entire town. In all there were 1,000 lots.

Apparently keen to ensure the August 16-20 event did not become a spectacle for curiosity seekers, company president George C. Freeman chose to regulate attendence. Potential buyers needed to apply in advance for a "card of admittance." In all, 2,000 of the printed cards were presented at the preview by bidders from as far west as Missouri, as far north as Canada, and as far south as the Carolinas. Among those permitted to purchase a catalog at 50 cents was the wife of former Kansas governor and presidential candidate Alfred M. Landon.

Stonybrook's furnishings, a fashionable mix of English and American chattels in the 18th century style, had comfortably exceeded expectations. Men outfitted Newport-style in summer suits and ties, and women in silks and straw hats gathered in a cavernous marquee on the grounds to watch and participate as, room by room, the house was cleared. More than 175 individual buyers left the auction with furniture or decorative art objects from the Knight estate. A set of five Philadelphia Queen Anne fiddleback side chairs were among the highest-achieving lots at $1,050.

★   ★   ★

CARD OF ADMITTANCE

Exhibition and Auction
At "STONYBROOK"
The Residence of the late
MARIE LOUISE LE BEL KNIGHT
MIDDLETOWN, R. I.

EXHIBITION   SALE

August 14th and 15th   August 16th to 20th
                    1937

One of Philadelphia's legendary philanthropists, George W. Childs Drexel, inherited Wootton, a circa 1880, 40-room Main Line mansion in Bryn Mawr, from his father's best friend, *Philadelphia Ledger* publisher George W. Childs. When Drexel's widow, Mary Irick Drexel, died in 1948, Freeman's was appointed to auction Wootton's furnishings, as well as Mrs. Drexel's jewelry.

THE LIBRARY COMPANY OF PHILADELPHIA

When delving into the life-cycle of a community, marking the ebb and flow of its assets, the auction house is the place to be. It is here, in the archives of the bought and the sold, that we encounter the estranged relationships, the waxing and waning of economic fortune, the debtors, the creditors, the personalities and the changing faces of taste and fashion.

With the support of leading trusts and estates attorneys Ballard Spahr Andrews & Ingersoll, Freeman's would continue to help dismantle the final vestiges of Philadelphia's original millionaire class in the "fresh-start" years of the late 1940s and early '50s.

Wootton in Bryn Mawr had been the home of another financial titan of the Gilded Age. George W. Childs Drexel – he took his first three names from the newspaper publisher who was his father's best friend – was the youngest son of the 19th century financier and university benefactor Anthony J. Drexel. The apple had not fallen far from the tree. Drexel Jr. had excelled in banking and, with his brothers, had co-founded a private bank in Philadelphia with branches in New York and Paris that would generate enormous wealth.

In 1891, George W. Childs Drexel had married Mary S. Irick, the well-bred daughter of an army general from Vincentown, New Jersey. For three years they had lived in the heart of Philadelphia, enjoying and patronizing the cultural and artistic delights of the city from a custom-built three-story, marble-fronted pile at the northeast corner of South 39th and Locust Streets. The house – it now serves as a fraternity house on the University of Pennsylvania campus – had been a gift to the newlyweds from Anthony J. Drexel.

However, upon the death in 1894 of his namesake, Drexel would embrace the town and country lifestyle as the beneficiary of a 40-room mansion in suburban Bryn Mawr. In this mock castle situated in 168 verdant acres, the Drexels spent the remainder of their lives in quiet luxury.

In 1948, Mary Irick Drexel, who had outlived her husband by four years, died at the age of 80. Freeman's took the call to sell not only the contents of Wootton but also Mrs. Drexel's magnificent jewelry collection.

Two separate auction events were organized for May of that year, each with its own auction catalog emblazoned with the Drexel family crest. The beneficiaries would be the Drexel Institute of Technology. It took five full days of selling, from May

3-7, to clear Wootton of its illustrious interior and garden furnishings, books, statuary and sporting paraphernalia.

The day after Tuesday's opening session, the *Philadelphia Inquirer* reported "several hundred stylishly dressed women, many of them from New York, Baltimore, Pittsburgh and other Eastern cities" had packed the vast library of the Drexel estate to dodge the rain, and "bid prices up sharply," for 100-lots of European porcelain and glassware.

As the skies cleared, the afternoon session had moved to the garden. By the close of Monday, May 9 (no session was scheduled for the Sunday), Wootton had been emptied, with Edmund Brickley crowing the sale's gross had exceeded presale expectations by 25 percent. The house was sold and in due course would provide handsome lodgings for boarders at a private Catholic school for boys.

Freeman's auctioned Mary Irick Drexel's "Valuable Precious-Stone Jewelry" on May 19-20 in a 254-lot sale at the Chestnut Street gallery. Tiffany, Cartier and Charlton of New York. Caldwell and Bailey, Banks & Biddle of Philadelphia. Such conspicuous signs of wealth, so willfully embraced by the Drexels as proof of

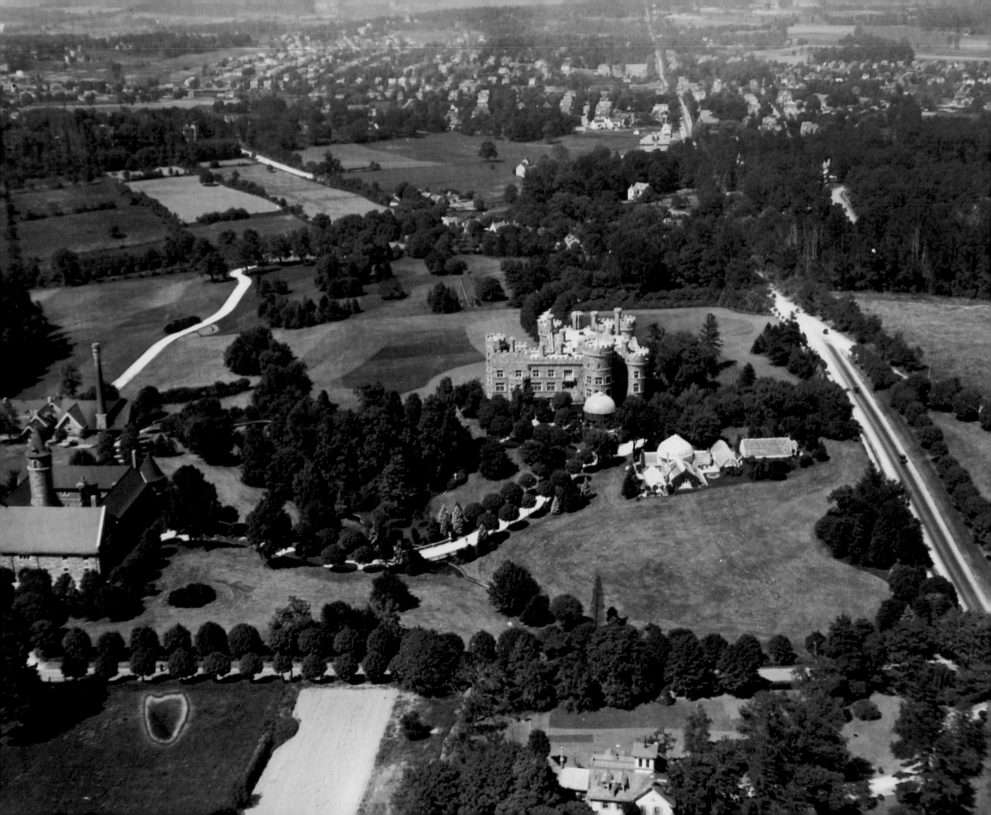

This artist's copy of Gilbert Stuart's Athenaeum portrait was sold by Samuel T. Freeman & Co., in 1933 for $11,200.

THE THREE FACES OF GILBERT STUART

It is estimated that, in his lifetime, Gilbert Stuart (1755-1828) painted no fewer than 100 Washington portraits, most of them versions of his three primary compositions now referred to as the Vaughan, Lansdowne and Athenaeum types. In each case, the name refers to the original commissioner or original owner of the portrait. The differentiation is the sitter's pose.

The Athenaeum portrait, known in Stuart's lifetime as the Mount Vernon portrait, was commissioned around 1796 by Martha Washington for the family home in Virginia. The President had grown weary of posing for portraits and had decreed there would be no more, but his wife persuaded him to sit one last time for Stuart who chose an intimate bust format with the left side of the face to the fore. The challenging commission, made more difficult by Washington's ill-fitting false teeth, was never completed, and the paintings remained in Stuart's possession until his death in 1828, after which they were acquired by the Boston Athenaeum. The artist did however, receive commissions for a number of copies. In 1933, fourteen years after the sale of a Lansdowne George Washington portrait at 1519-21 Chestnut Street, one of

these Athenaeum-type portraits passed through the doors of number 1808.

Freeman's consignor was Elizabeth M. Smith of Huntingdon, West Virginia, with provenance through Mary C. Smith of Keyport, New Jersey, and the estate of her uncle, the late Henry N. Cook of Philadelphia. Two letters of authentication supported the painting's claim to being a genuine Stuart. One of the letters, written by Philadelphia expert Charles Henry Hart, stated the portrait had been secured by Henry Cook "in Virginia shortly before the War of Secession." On May 17, bidding for the canvas started at $5,000, with more than half a dozen prominent collectors keen to acquire it. Bidding, wrote the *Philadelphia Inquirer* the following day, rose in increments of $1,000 up to $9,000 at which point the competition slowed to increments of $200. The painting was sold to Henry W. Breyer of Jenkintown, Pa., for $11,200.

John Singer Sargent's 1904 full-length, oil-on-canvas *Portrait of Lady Millicent Hawes, Duchess of Sutherland* was among the pictures deaccessioned from the William P. Wilstach Collection and sold at Freeman's in 1954. At the time, swagger portraiture was deeply unfashionable, and the painting sold for $1,400.

WILSTACH DEACCESSIONED

"Over four days last week an estimated 2,500 persons viewed the antique silver, porcelain, china, glassware and paintings in Memorial Hall … which Samuel T. Freeman & Co. is auctioning off for the city". So wrote *The Evening Bulletin* dated October 26, 1954, as the William P. Wilstach Collection came under the hammer.

Museum deaccessioning was then, as now, a controversial issue. In 1876, the country's centennial year, the City of Philadelphia had received a monumental gift of paintings from Wilstach who had amassed great wealth as the supplier of tack to the Union Army. On permanent display at Memorial Hall in Fairmount Park for 78 years, the collection had become a source of pride to Philadelphians, but in 1954 the park's commissioners deemed the building where it resided better suited to other purposes. They voted to move the most valuable pictures and objects to the Philadelphia Museum of Art and to auction off the remaining works. Freeman's was called in to handle the sale: 239 of the collection's 360 pictures as well as a sizable additional selection of decorative art, silver, porcelains, arms and armor.

According to the house-published *Freeman's Monthly News,* the silver and objets d'art offered over three days from October 26-28 brought in $56,000, with $440 paid for an English copper luster jug printed with a portrait of Lafayette and the surrender of Cornwallis at Yorktown. The paintings, primarily minor or *outré* Continental works, made $118,000, with a swagger portrait by John Singer Sargent selling for $1,400.

In the May 19-20 Freeman's sale of "Valuable Precious-Stone Jewelry" from the Estates of the Late Mary S. Irick Drexel and George W. Childs Drexel, this important diamond necklace of 46 graduated round diamonds of fine color, weighing approximately 80 carats and mounted in platinum, was purchased for $38,000. Most of Mrs. Drexel's jewelry came from Tiffany, Cartier and other prestige firms.

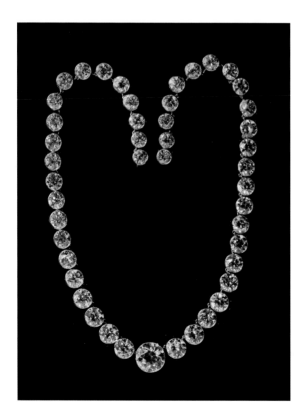

their success in the early years of the 20th century, had become more challenging to the palate after the Second World War. But diamonds rarely fall out of fashion.

On the first day, a Tiffany brooch, set with diamonds around an oval cabochon sapphire, had glittered at $2,600. But it was during the second session that the highest prices were paid. A pendant containing a 25-carat oblong emerald and 16 high-grade diamonds weighing 8 carats was purchased for $30,000, topped only by an 80-carat diamond and platinum necklace, which was hammered down at $38,000. Handwritten notes in the margins of the only remaining in-house copy of Freeman's catalog for this sale indicate the two-day total for Mary Drexel's jewels was a massive $304,491.

If the Drexel name has become synonymous with international finance and local philanthropy then Samuel D. Riddle's place in history comes with his reluctant purchase of a horse. It was 1918 when Riddle, the son of an Irish immigrant and second-generation owner of the Riddle woolen mills, had attended a bloodstock auction in New York. Only because his wife had cajoled him did Riddle raise his hand as the bidding

reached $5,000 to purchase a thoroughbred yearling known only as "Mahubah's colt." That horse became the most successful and famous equine of the 20th century: Man O' War.

Between June 1919 and October 1920, Man O' War would demolish longstanding records at dozens of races. At the Preakness and Belmont Stakes he would come home 20 lengths ahead of the competition. His owner, the dapper country squire who *Seabiscuit* author Laura Hillenbrand said bore a startling resemblance to the mustachioed tycoon on the *Monopoly* board, saw his wealth increase many times over. Not only was Man O' War a platinum investment on the track, he also commanded record-setting stud fees. In his lifetime, the stallion nicknamed "Big Red" reportedly sired 64 stakes winners and a succession of fine brood mares who, themselves, foaled 124 track titans.

Samuel Riddle lived in a genteel fashion on a 6,000-acre country estate in suburban Philadelphia known as Glen Riddle. He also owned the sprawling Glen Riddle Farms in Berlin, Maryland, and other horse properties in Saratoga Springs, New York, and Lexington, Kentucky, where Man O' War and his two most famous sons, War Admiral and War Relic, were eventually laid to rest. While some described Riddle as a curmudgeon, those

Through this doorway, the entrance to the home on Samuel D. Riddle's country estate, Glen Riddle, antique buyers flocked to bid on early British and American furniture, decorative objects and horseracing mementos belonging to Man O' War's owner, Samuel D. Riddle. The sale was one of three conducted by Freeman's in 1951 to settle the Riddle estate.

with a more intimate insight knew his dislike for intrusion was based solely on a desire to protect his prized racehorses. Riddle's true nature and generous spirit became far more widely known after his death, in 1951.

The 90-year-old multimillionaire's will bequeathed $2.5 million and 72 prime acres of Glen Riddle to the people of Media, Pennsylvania, for the construction of a hospital in the local community he loved. It took five years for the battle over Riddle's estate to be resolved and a charter to be granted for ground to be broken for Riddle Memorial Hospital. The institution opened its doors on February 18, 1963.

While the hospital bequest inflamed passions within the Riddle family, there was less opposition to the decision to break up the furnishings from Riddle's various estates. Everything was to be sold in a series of auctions conducted by Samuel T. Freeman & Co. The first and most important of the sales was held on May 1-5 and May 7-10, 1951, on the premises of Glen Riddle. Freeman's 2,100-lot catalogue described the offering as "The most remarkable sale of its kind ever held in or near Philadelphia," and noted: "The proceeds to be devoted to the charitable purposes expressed in the will of Mr. Riddle."

With its eight leaves installed, this circa 1800 mahogany and brass-inlaid dining table attributed to Philadelphia furniture maker Henry Connelly (1770-1826) reaches a length of 17ft (5.2m). The table sold in Freeman's May 1-10, 1951, on-site sale at Samuel D. Riddle's Glen Riddle estate. Purchased by one of Riddle's relatives, the table reappeared at auction in 2004, bringing $254,400.

The contents were a wealth of American- and British-made riches: an 18th century Hepplewhite inlaid mahogany sideboard ($175), a circa 1790 bird's-eye and curly maple candlestand ($95), an 18th century Chippendale mahogany and haircloth sofa ($925). Outstanding was a 17ft. (5.2m) circa 1800 carved mahogany and brass-inlaid "accordion" dining table attributed to the workshop of New Yorker Duncan Phyfe. It brought $7,000, one of the highest prices in the sale, and was purchased by Sarah Jeffords, Samuel Riddle's niece.

SHAKESPEARE'S FIRST FOLIO

It has been called the most important book in English literature, the first undertaking to bring together in a single 900-page volume thirty-six of Shakespeare's plays. Perhaps 600 or so copies of the so-called First Folio of Mr William Shakespeare's *Comedies, Histories & Tragedies* were printed seven years after the playwright's death in 1623. Of those, fewer than half have survived, with only a handful in private hands. The appearance of a copy at auction has always represented a momentous event.

Freeman's had launched headlong into the booming post-War business arena with a series of three auctions to disperse the celebrated collection of antiquarian books and historical autographs acquired by Rhode Islander, Frederick Stanhope Peck (1868-1947). It was the largest sale of its type held at Chestnut since the George C. Thomas sale in 1924 and perhaps the last time a collection of such importance would be disassembled outside the modern collecting environment.

Freeman's had secured the consignment while Peck, a ninth-generation member of a Mayflower family, was still alive; but his death as the catalogue went to press necessitated the involvement of fiduciaries in a supervisory capacity. Trustee involvement would see the withdrawal of the first session's showpiece – a superb 1855 first edition, first issue copy of Walt Whitman's *Leaves of Grass* but it did not halt the sale

of the four 17th century printings of Shakespeare's plays that had belonged to the Shakespeare historian Lord Sidney Lee.

In his *Life of Shakespeare*, Sidney Lee details the evolution of these important posthumous printings. For the First Folio a syndicate of five men was formed, headed by Edward Blount and William Jaggard. The actors John Heminge and Henry Condell undertook to edit the plays – they chose to exclude *Pericles, Prince of Athens* and *The Two Noble Kinsmen* (now thought to have been a collaboration with John Fletcher) – while copies were printed, none too well, by Jaggard's son, Isaac. In 1632 a second folio was issued and in 1663 a third. The second printing included both the missing plays and several others of more dubious attribution, including *Cardenio, The London Prodigal* and *The History of Thomas Lord Cromwell*. In 1685 the fourth and final folio was published.

Freeman's annotated house copy of the February 1947 catalogue indicates Peck's First Folio sold for $17,500; his Second Folio for $3,500; the Third Folio for $325 and the fourth for $275.

Only sporadically do they appear on the market today. Most copies have some defects – rarely do they include the famous portrait engraving of Shakespeare by Martin Droeshout – but complete copies of the first three folios were sold by Christie's New York in October 2001 as part of the Abel E. Berland Library.

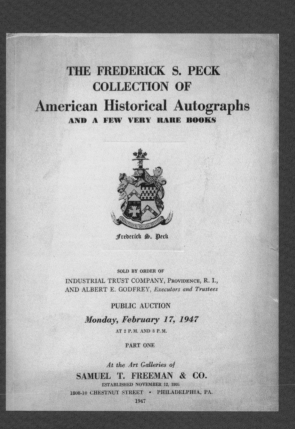

THE FREDERICK S. PECK
COLLECTION OF
American Historical Autographs
AND A FEW VERY RARE BOOKS

Frederick S. Peck

SOLD BY ORDER OF
INDUSTRIAL TRUST COMPANY, PROVIDENCE, R. I.,
AND ALBERT E. GODFREY, *Executors and Trustees*

PUBLIC AUCTION
Monday, February 17, 1947
AT 2 P.M. AND 8 P.M.

PART ONE

At the Art Galleries of
SAMUEL T. FREEMAN & CO.
ESTABLISHED NOVEMBER 12, 1805
1808-10 CHESTNUT STREET • PHILADELPHIA, PA.
1947

THE MULLEN COLLECTION

It was in their place of work, a pharmaceuticals plant, that Nelle Mullen (1884-1967) and her elder sister Mary (1875-1957) first developed their aesthetic sensibilities. An unlikely environment, perhaps, but as senior employees of the patent medicine millionaire Dr. Albert C. Barnes they were exposed daily to a remarkable collection of 19th and 20th century masterworks that inspired the spinster sisters to first appreciate, then study and ultimately collect art.

Barnes would encourage their interest, enjoy their friendship and come to value their judgment. When in 1922 he established The Barnes Foundation, a school for the study of fine art and horticulture in Philadelphia's Lower Merion Township, he appointed his company general manager (Nelle) and the head of his publicity department (Mary) as two of the institution's five original trustees. During their many trips to Europe, the Mullen siblings manufactured wonderful purchasing opportunities as the personal acquaintances of art dealers, museum curators and some of the artists themselves, Matisse among them. And this before 20th century pictures had made their mark with "serious" collectors of Western art.

Barnes would perish in an automobile accident in 1951, Mary Mullen would die in 1957 and Nelle in

The Mullen Collection

The Mullen sisters – Nelle and Mary – benefited greatly from the astute guidance and financial backing of their mentor, pharmaceuticals millionaire Dr. Albert C. Barnes. The November 15, 1967, sale of the cream of their collection grossed more than $1 million. This Paul Cézanne's landscape titled *Le Mas Provençal* opened reticently at $25,000 but quickly shot to $110,000.

1967. After Nelle Mullen passed away, the sisters' art collection from the walls of their Merion home was sent to auction. A frenzy of interest followed Freeman's announcement that the 78 paintings plus early Meissen, French and English porcelain would be sold on the evening of November 15, 1967. A six-day public preview was organized due to overwhelming demand, with the admission to the auction itself by invitation only. Six hundred approved attendees culled from a pool of 2,000 applicants packed the gallery, while others watched via closed-circuit television from Freeman's other floors. It was the time of the first great art boom and the emergence of the Moderns. Paul Mellon had started the ball rolling when he paid $220,000 for Cezanne's *Le Garçon au Gilet Rouge,* from the collection of New York banker Erwin Goldschmidt at Sotheby's in London in 1958. But, still two decades before the Impressionists would attract Wall Street and Japanese money as the most vibrant and identifiable of art with which to communicate success, those who were there remember this as a typically Philadelphian and typically Freeman's affair: shirt and tie rather than tuxedo and a fair pace that saw the spectacular contents dispersed in less than two hours.

The auction did nonetheless gross $1,079,200, the first $1m fine art sale conducted by the company, with the top seller, Paul Cézanne's circa1885 landscape *Le Mas Provençal* taking in $110,000. While Freeman's maintained a dignified silence about the buyer's identity, the *Philadelphia Inquirer* reported the next day that the purchaser had been Henry Pearlman, a private collector from New York City regarded as one of the world's "largest owners of Cézanne originals."

Renoir
Matisse
Pascin
Soutine
Prendergast
Cézanne
Demuth
Glackens
Utrillo
Degas

1808-10 CHESTNUT STREET, PHILADELPHIA, PENNSYLVANIA

Exhibition
November 8th-9th-10th-11th-13th-14th
Daily 9 A.M.- 5 P.M.

Sale
November 15th
Commencing at 8 P.M.

1967

The Leary copy of the Declaration of Independence broadside printed by John Dunlap

"When in the course of human events, it becomes necessary for one people to dissolve the political bands which have connected them with another, and to assume among the powers of the earth, the separate and equal station to which the Laws of Nature and of Nature's God entitle them, a decent respect to the opinions of mankind requires that they should declare the causes which impel them to the separation."

Declaration

"Leary's Book Store, Ninth Street below Market, opposite the Post Office is known from the Atlantic to the Pacific. Every school child, every student and every bookworm in Philadelphia knows how to reach No. 9 South Nine Street. In fact, every stranger who arrives in town, with a literary turn of mind, is not slow to learning the location of this wonderful store. There is nothing like it in the country outside of the Congressional Library in Washington. It is an institution of our Quaker City and has reached its vast proportions after more than one hundred years of continuous prosperity. Book hunters who visit Leary's never go away unsatisfied."

PHILADELPHIA NORTH AMERICAN

Two 19th century views of the Leary's Book Store situated on the
corner of Market and South Ninth Street, since 1837.

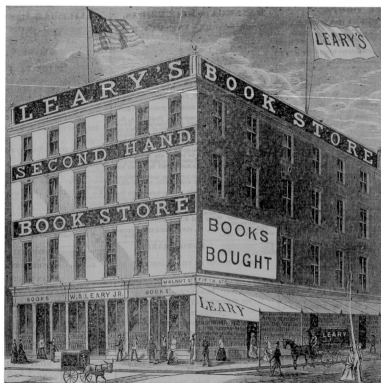

In the 1930s, when this eulogy was written by the *Philadelphia North American*, Leary's Book Store was the largest and most venerable antiquarian and rare bookstore in America. Since 1837 the company had hung out its shingle at the corner of Market and South Ninth Street, welcoming generations of Philadelphians. But toward the end of 1968 – caught up in the ambitious urban renewal projects of the postwar years – this Philadelphia institution was preparing to close its doors permanently.

Leary's employees had been given the opportunity to buy out the business and keep it going, perhaps at a new location. But, lacking the funds to undertake such a venture, they declined. The company would simply wind down, and the new tenants, next-door neighbors Gimbel's department store, would absorb Leary's floor space into its own.

At the time of Leary's dissolution, its compact premises still bulged at the seams with books and other printed matter. Some of it had languished in storage areas and obscure corners for many decades.

As employees set about the task of conducting a final inventory and clearing out the shop's contents during the first few months of 1969, they kept in mind their employer's promise: that they could have "anything in the building" as a retirement bonus. The magnitude of owner W. Stuart Emmons' parting gift was not fully realized, however, until Freeman's book expert, Joseph Molloy, was called in to catalogue the contents for auction.

He made an astonishing discovery. While sorting through some wooden crates stashed on the sixth floor and largely forgotten since 1911, Molloy stumbled onto a scrapbook containing early currency, letters and other historical documents kept over a 70-year period by the Dixon family of Marshall Street, Philadelphia. Tucked in one of the leaves, and folded several times, was what appeared to be a first printing of the Declaration of Independence.

After conducting a cursory examination of the $19^9/_{16}$ by $15^{11}/_{16}$in. (50.75 x 40cm) document, Molloy rushed to the American Philosophical Society where he could compare his exciting find with one of the two authenticated copies of the Declaration residing in Philadelphia (the other is in Independence National Historical Park).

There, laid side-by-side with the society's own copy, the Leary broadside was assessed by three experts – Dr. Whitfield J. Bell, Dr. Murphy Smith and Willman Spawn. All enthusiastically declared this to be an authentic first printing. On February 4, 1969, Frederick R. Goff, head of the Rare Book Division of the Library of Congress, issued an additional, and definitive, written opinion: "There is no question in my mind that the 'Leary' copy of the John Dunlap broadside of the Declaration of Independence, which I examined yesterday, belongs to the original edition printed in Philadelphia during the evening of July 4 or early on July 5, 1776."

With only 15 copies of an unknown print run known to have survived, the presence of a sixteenth copy in private hands was greeted with amazement. Unlike the collecting of ephemera germane to the freedom fight of enslaved Africans or labor history, important broadsides, pamphlets and prints associated with the flux of the Revolutionary period, and the moment of colonial independence in particular, had been valued since the event itself. Established in 1731, the Library Company of Philadelphia, for example, had made its first secessionist acquisitions in 1777 and had been the highest bidder at an auction in 1784 to acquire a cache of War of Independence material assembled by one of its members, Pierre-Eugène Du Simitière.

In the years that followed, all known surviving copies of the Dunlap broadside, in varying degrees of completion and condition, had made their way into libraries and historical societies up and down the East Coast, while two had traveled to the Public Record Office in London. Not so far flung, this new discovery had been found just two blocks from the bricklayer's house at 230 High Street where Thomas Jefferson had worked in the hot summer of 1776 and a stone's throw from 48 High Street where John Dunlap, the official printer to the Continental Congress, entered the history books on the night of July 4.

News of the presence of a first printing of the Declaration put an entirely different spin on the sale scheduled to take place at Samuel T. Freeman's on May 6-7, 1969. Suddenly, the event morphed from an interesting assemblage of literature, color plates, and historic and holographic documents obtained from a landmark Philadelphia bookstore to a moment in American history that would attract global media coverage. The Declaration broadside, lot 440A of a 556-lot inventory was featured in its own voluminously descriptive booklet that had been published as an accompaniment to the main catalog.

The presale publicity surrounding the Declaration and two other historic documents found in that same scrapbook – resolutions pertaining to the impending British invasion of Pennsylvania, and an attendant call to arms – had drawn a crush of curious spectators to the preview. On auction day, during the final session of the sale, the Declaration broadside dominated proceedings from its easel on Freeman's velvet-draped stage.

"It was a blustery day," recalls Beau Freeman. "The room was crowded, and the windows had been opened by one of our employees to let some air in. Then the most incredible thing happened. A gust of wind entered the room and sent the Declaration crashing down onto the marble floor. In one motion, everyone in the audience leaned forward with their arms outstretched to try to catch it, but it fell face down onto the floor."

To everyone's relief, the precious document – which had earlier been framed and placed beneath unbreakable glass – escaped its fall from grace unharmed. It was lifted off the floor by Freeman's staff members and carefully set back into place on its stand, this time with all of the room's windows firmly shut.

With that moment of drama over, and amid a flurry of crowd chatter and a hail of flashbulbs, auctioneer John M. Freeman got on with the business at hand. Competition for the lot opened with a $100,000 absentee bid lodged by the House of L. Dieff, New York. From there, bids jumped in increments of $25,000, until the contest for ownership narrowed down to two suitors: legendary New York rare book dealer Hans P. Kraus and Texas millionaire industrialist Ira G. Corn Jr. The two men

parried aggressively to $403,000, with Kraus holding the advantage at that point. A pause ensued, Corn upped the ante by another $1,000 and, after a shake of the head from Kraus, the Texan secured the document for $404,000. It was one of the great American auction prices of the Swinging Sixties. It would also remain a house record at 1808 Chestnut Street for another generation.

Asked later why he had dropped out of the bidding, Hans Kraus – who only one week earlier had paid $155,000 for a first printing of the Constitution – told reporters, "I've got five children, and they have to eat."

Immediately after the auction, the victorious Texan, who had made his headline-grabbing purchase in partnership with his corporate associate, Joseph P. Driscoll, cheerfully obliged spectators by autographing auction catalogs held out to him. That day he did not leave the building with the Declaration in tow, but, rather, advised Freeman's he would be back soon to consummate the purchase.

The next day, Corn returned to the gallery. As his auction transaction was being finalized, the subject of sales tax arose. Corn was not a Pennsylvania resident and wanted the Declaration to be shipped to Texas, his state of legal residence. If shipped out of state, the document would not be subject to Pennsylvania state sales tax. "But he first wanted to take it to New York to show to some friends," Beau Freeman said, "so we suggested that he hire a limo and accompany the broadside to New York. A licensed limo is considered a legal transportation agent, so it was a perfectly lawful and legitimate method for him to use in transporting the document out of state before flying home."

Corn thought it was a fine idea and immediately organized for a limo to pick him up and carry him, and the precious cargo, to Manhattan. A few days later, the Declaration broadside was at its final destination, Dallas. Eventually, the Leary Declaration became the property of a cartel of Dallas civic leaders, including Corn and Driscoll, who collectively paid off the bank note that had financed its auction purchase. On July 4, 1978, the co-owners officially donated the Declaration broadside to the City of Dallas, for display in its newly dedicated City Hall. Four years later, the document was moved to Dallas' J. Erik Jonsson Central Library where it remains on display on the library's seventh floor. Today, with subsequent discoveries taken into account, it is one of 25 known copies of Dunlap's first printing of the Declaration broadside, but it remains one of the finest extant examples and the only one housed west of the Mississippi.

A WONDERFUL BOOK STORE

LEARY'S BOOK STORE, Ninth Street below Market, opposite the Post Office is known from the Atlantic to the Pacific. Every school child, every student and every book-worm in Philadelphia knows how to reach No. 9 South Ninth Street. In fact, every stranger who arrives in town, with a literary turn of mind, is not slow in learning the location of this wonderful store. There is nothing like it in the country outside of the Congressional Library in Washington. It is an institution of our Quaker City and has reached its vast proportions after more than one hundred years of continuous prosperity. It has shipped books to every part of the world, and from every part of the world it has gathered to its shelves the old, rare, curious and interesting works of the master minds of all ages and all climes Book hunters who visit Leary's never go away unsatisfied. The store was founded upon the principle of supplying what was wanted, and no matter where or when published, if the book is not upon the shelves and is still extant somewhere, its resting place can be told. Order, the first law of heaven, is apparent the moment a person enters the seven story and basement building, in which are stored twenty thousand square feet of books, representing nearly five hundred thousand volumes.

"Whole libraries of choice books, which the owners have perhaps spent years in collecting, are upon Leary's shelves. The places where to find them and the classification of the books are plainly marked with signs hung upon the shelves, so that a purchaser can act as his own librarian. The stockroom and distributing department is on the sixth and seventh floors, where duplicates and remainders of editions are kept, and the shipping department is on the fifth floor. A large business is done in new books as well as old, rare and curious works. A wonderful place is Leary's Old Book Store."—*Philadelphia North American*

Leary's Book Store
Ninth Street below Market
Opposite Post Office   PHILADELPHIA, PA.

MORE THAN A FINE PHILADELPHIA DESK?

Deep into the second day of the Seabrease estate sale, a 26-year-old Beau Freeman scanned the audience. Before the days of computer registration and paddle bidding, it was his job to approach successful bidders to secure their names, contact details and a deposit. He recognized most in attendance as being local dealers, members of the American antique furniture trade from Boston and New York, and monied city residents from the good parts of town. But one gentleman seated at the rear of the room stood out as unfamiliar. Conspicuous for his formal attire – shirt, tie, gold-rimmed spectacles – and his apparent disinterest in the proceedings of the sale, he nevertheless began to bid steadily when lot 394 was brought before the audience on that now-famous revolving stage.

Opening slowly at $3,500, bidding ensued between two protagonists, escalating in $1,000 increments to $10,000, then $20,000 and finally to a massive $40,000.

Few of those who have admired a handsome Philadelphia slope-front mahogany desk at Franklin Court and pondered on the identity of its first owner are aware of this dramatic event that took place at 1808 Chestnut Street on October 23, 1962. Freeman's had been asked to sell "Franklin's desk" as part of the collection of Germantown resident Mrs. N. McLean Seabrease. Armed with relatively modest resources but a good eye, she had acquired the desk from the Philadelphia dealer Thomas Curran as a Franklin heirloom that had been among the estate goods of one Samuel Henderson.

Freeman's had chosen to make fewer claims for the desk, and conservatively described it as a fine example of a distinctive form popular in America's first capital city during the 1750s, with five shell-carved interior drawers, a double-pedestal base of five drawers and four quarter-round fluted pilasters, and a slope resting on pen box drawers. But a potentially magical association had provided the "X" factor.

The $40,000 was the highest price for a piece of American furniture since 1929 when Henry Francis duPont had paid an unprecedented $44,000 for a Philadelphia highboy that now resides at Winterthur. It was also a lot of money to accept from a new client.

When Beau asked him for his details, he simply handed over a business card. He was David Wallace, a State Department representative of the Independence National Historical Park; his competitor, Benjamin Franklin Cotes, a direct descendent of the great man. The desk, the *Inquirer* announced the following day, was the first major purchase for a planned Benjamin Franklin museum, a striking steel "ghost house" that would outline the site of Franklin's home demolished in 1812. It is still there today.

So is this Franklin's desk? Scholars still aren't sure. Its construction fits the vague description of a desk Franklin mentions in a letter to his wife Deborah dated April 29, 1757, in which he said she would find what she needed in "the little right hand drawer under my desk." And recent genealogical research suggests the Henderson surname appears in the Franklin family tree. Ben Franklin's great-great-granddaughter, Esther Ann, had a grandson called Samuel Henderson, whose estate was dispersed in 1909. However, Independence National Historical Park is today reluctant to call this anything more than a fine Philadelphia desk from the 1750s with an intriguing Franklin association.

Edward Hicks' *A Peaceable Kingdom* sold by Freeman's in 1980 for $210,000, the most expensive painting ever sold in Philadelphia at that time.

Hicks used the Biblical theme of the lion lying down with the lamb to illustrate the schism that by the 1830s had developed between two schools of Quaker ideology. The factions were the Orthodox Quakers who accepted the emergence of the industrial city, and the Hicksites, followers of the fervent abolitionist Elias Hicks (the artist's cousin), who hoped for a return to the spirituality of George Fox and William Penn. The theme of this painting, drawn from chapter 11 of the Book of Isaiah, was undoubtedly attractive for its message of peace: "The wolf also shall dwell with the lamb, and the leopard shall lie down with the kid, and the calf and the young lion and fatling together; and a little child shall lead them."

Competition

CHAPTER TEN

"Be not fearful of competition. Be fearful of a compromise with the ideals which have allowed us to live for 150 years ... we must remember the obligation that is thereby put upon us."

ADDISON B. FREEMAN, 1955

Samuel M. (Beau) Freeman: Born

The heir to an auctioneering heritage that goes back 175 years has decided "we're going to somewhat change our ways."

Photograph by Gerard C. Benene

If you're a boy and your name is Freeman, you become an auctioneer. Royalty has hemophilia, Freeman's has antiques — it's in the blood. "I ain't never had no other job," cracks Samuel (Beau) Freeman, 43, convivial vice president of the 175-year-old family firm on Chestnut Street. Right out of college he started "the way everybody starts here: doing anything you're told to do, moving furniture, setting up sales, sweeping the floor, delivering appraisals to banks and lawyers' offices."

They call Freeman's the first auction firm in America, even the oldest in the world under continuous management by one family. "I guess because I was a Freeman the people here were kindly and helpful to me. Sometimes it has been known they haven't been, maybe, as kindly and helpful to outsiders who have wanted to come work here," admits the blond, balding, blue-eyed fellow in shirtsleeves and seersucker slacks against the gentle thud-and-hum of an ancient air conditioner. By Philadelphia standards, he says, the family is "not that old. Well, late 18th century. Tristram Banfield Freeman, a printer and engraver, came here from England. He was appointed official auctioneer for the City of Philadelphia in 1805. That was super. *He* didn't have any competition."

Every generation had its Samuel. "There's a quirk in the family — what shall I say? — concerning feelings about being Junior. There never was a Samuel Freeman Jr. There was Samuel T., and he named one of his five sons Samuel M., and *his* son was Samuel T. 2d, and *his* son was Samuel M. 2d, and there's a Samuel T. 3d — instead of Samuel T. Freeman V," he explains, stroking his chin. (Beau is Samuel M. 2d, and his son is Samuel T. 3d.) How'd he get his nickname? "Well, I was a Samuel along with two living Samuels and one was called Sam, the other Sammy, and there was not too much else you could do with Samuel. My father was reading that wonderful syrupy novel *Beau Geste*, ergo, Beau." He has an older sister, but girls have no place in the business. "When I was

"The heir to an auctioneering heritage that goes back 175 years..." A youthful Beau Freeman gives an interview for the *Philadelphia Inquirer* as his company marked another anniversary in 1980.

With the Dunlap Declaration in 1969 and the $1m Mullen collection two years before it, Samuel T. Freeman & Co., had been on the verge of greatness. The industrial sales that had placed the firm among the biggest auctioneers in the country were ebbing away but as a meeting place for buyers and sellers of fine art and antiques this family-owned firm were proving a formidable opposite number to any rival on the East Coast.

Increasingly the company had a new figurehead. John Freeman (1910-1985), son of George Clendenin Freeman (1875-1955) remained the president. His only child George C. Freeman Jr. would work alongside him. But, as the company moved into the lively market of the 1970s, it was Samuel M. Freeman II who emerged as the dynamic figure of his generation and a man with a natural affinity with the business of his forebears.

Joining the company in 1958, Samuel M. Freeman II – since childhood he had been simply "Beau" – had learned the business from the ground up. Raised with the scent of attic dust in his nostrils and bedtime stories of Stotesbury, Childs Drexel and Riddle, he learned to appreciate Philadelphian furniture and American clockmaking while setting up sales, making deliveries and sweeping the floor. Gracious humility and courteous

In November 1974 Freeman's sold furniture and furnishings from the personal collection and private residence at Winterthur of the late Henry Francis duPont. It was a relatively modest dispersal by the standards of the celebrated Delaware collection but nonetheless including fine objects such as this New England Queen Anne striped maple slant front desk circa 1760-70. With a particularly fine serpentine and fan carved interior, it was sold at $9,500, the highest price of the sale.

mannerisms were both vestiges of the old school into which he was born. An effusive charm and a dry wit an asset to client management.

If the estate clearances upon the scale of those that followed the Second World War were now evaporating in the face of historical conservation, then on a smaller scale Freeman's relationship with the great surnames of Pennsylvania continued. For the heirs of the late Henry Francis duPont the company sold furniture and furnishings from his private residence at Winterthur in November 1974. For the descendents of William Logan, a Thomas Affleck chest-on-chest was sold to the Metropolitan Museum of Art at $92,000. An American bicentennial sale in November 1976 included the Sprague set of all 56 signers of the Declaration of Independence sold at $180,000; while in October 1979 Charles Willson Peale's self portrait from the estate of Julia Rush Biddle Henry was sold to the Independence National Historical Park for $67,500.

The following year Beau Freeman met with one of the Henry heirs in the first class lounge at Philadelphia Airport to appraise "a painting of animals" presented to him wrapped in brown paper. It was later authenticated by experts as *A Peaceable Kingdom* by folk art master Edward Hicks. This so-called middle-period work,

among the finest of the surviving versions of the Quaker allegory, would provide the centerpiece to the Freeman's 175th anniversary sale conducted in the fall of 1980. When local Pontiac dealer and art collector Robert Lee bought it for $210,000, it became the most expensive painting ever sold in Philadelphia.

★   ★   ★

And yet these years were not kind to Freeman's traditional way of doing business. Just as Philadelphia of the 1960s and '70s witnessed a population implosion and the drain of intellectual talent, then so it was with the city's fine art and antiques. As 400,000 fled the ageing row house fabric between 1950 and the 1970s (Philadelphia was the fourth-largest city in the United States in the census of 1960, losing third place to Los Angeles), consignments from once-great collecting families that might previously have gone to 1808 Chestnut Street were packed and shipped to Manhattan.

New Yorkers had first been offered the transatlantic equivalent of London's great auction houses with the establishment of the American Art Association in 1883. One of its earliest projects had been a much-derided exhibition of *Works in Oil and Pastel by the Impressionists of Paris* and in various guises the company would be part

This Philadelphia Chippendale mahogany chest-on-chest was probably part of a group of furniture bought by William Logan (son of James) from Thomas Affleck in 1772-3 on the marriage of his daughter Sarah to the Quaker merchant Thomas Fisher. Consigned to Freeman's by a Logan descendent, on March 24-25, 1975 it would sell at $92,000. It was bought by New York dealer Albert Sack of Israel Sack Inc. on behalf of the Metropolitan Museum of Art. The underbidder sitting on the front row was George Broadhead, a Philadelphia lawyer acting for the legendary collector Robert McNeil who had declared his intention to donate the piece to the Philadelphia Museum of Art.

of the Big Apple's artistic and collecting scene for half a century. However, as it foundered during the Depression, it had been bought out by two of its principals, a Swiss German G.T. Otto Bernet and a Philadelphia gentleman and former Freeman's hand, Major Hiram Hanley Parke.

By the mid 1950s, the Parke-Bernet Gallery was operating from purpose-built premises on Madison Avenue, its star rising in 1958 following the trio of showpiece sales of the collection of the late Arthur Sussel who had died earlier in that year. The heirs of the legendary dealer who had learned the ropes of the antiques trade at 1808 Chestnut Street, chose New York over Philadelphia as the "best" place to sell his inventory of Pennsylvania pottery, fraktur and folk art. "Even a pewter bedpan he had bought for 50 cents early in his career ended up selling for $1,200," remembers his daughter-in-law, Sonnie Sussel.

In 1961 Parke-Bernet had won a fierce three-way battle with representatives of the London auction houses Sotheby's and Christie's to sell an extraordinary collection of Old Master paintings belonging to the advertising agency founder Alfred W. Erickson. The jewel in the collection was Rembrandt's *Aristotle Contemplating the Bust of Homer* that would sell to the Metropolitan Museum of Art for $2.3m.

Charles Willson Peale's bust-length self portrait, circa 1795, sold by Freeman's on October 30, 1979 for $67,500. The oil on canvas came from the estate of Julia Rush Biddle Henry (Mrs. T. Charleston Henry), a descendent of Benjamin Rush and a grande dame of old Philadelphia society. It is possible that it was once on view in Peale's Philadelphia Museum, although no connection with two self portraits sold in the famous sale of 1854 has been found. At 1808 Chestnut Street, it was sold to the Independence National Historical Park and is on display in the State House.

However, soon after Parke-Bernet would lose the war to control the New York marketplace. In 1964, as the company searched for a way out of a debilitating leasehold agreement, America's largest fine art auction house was bought by Sotheby's for $1m.

✶   ✶   ✶

Sotheby's foothold in an American market that was just waiting to be sold the full razzmatazz of the upscale auction experience was the beginning of the end for London as the traditional center of the art market, a role it had filled since the days of the French Revolution. It was also a threat to a family-owned company for whom hardball business getting, lines of credit and global marketing strategies were alien. "My grandfather believed your name should appear in the paper probably once, maybe twice in your lifetime," Beau Freeman mused. "Definitely when you died and maybe when you're born".

Sotheby's had opened a walk-in branch office in Philadelphia in 1978. At 1630 Locust Street, it was practically around the corner from Freeman's. Christie's had followed suit in 1979. At the same time, J.B. Lippincott and Company, a one-time auction business turned the last of the city's major independent publishing houses, was sold to New York's Harper & Row. Would another venerable family-owned Philadelphia institution follow?

Unlike its counterparts in London and New York by the mid 1970s, Freeman's did not have specialized departments or specialized sales in now distinct market categories such as Americana, Russian, Japanese or Chinese works of art. More often than not, auctions at Chestnut Street were a potpourri of furniture, ceramics, glass, paintings, silver and textiles and really as much a social event as a collecting opportunity for the residents of Rittenhouse Square and its environs. There was still a laid-back Philadelphia quality about Samuel T. Freeman & Co. that some locals really liked but now New York was no longer an hour and a half away. And money talked.

Christie's, which had previously operated only consignment offices in America for goods to be shipped and sold in London, had opened an auction gallery in Manhattan in 1977. The company brought to these shores European practices of reserves and 'chandelier' bidding, department specialists and a curious method of billing clients, known as the ten and ten premium structure.

The "ten and ten" turned the American fine art auction business on its head. For centuries previous, it had been commonplace for the auctioneer to generate income through the charge levied upon the consignor. Typically, although the terms of a contract could be reviewed in the case of an exceptional consignment, the charge for an auctioneer's service would be 20 per cent of the value of the items sold. Christie's was proposing something quite different. They would charge the vendor just 10 per cent of the "hammer" price achieved at auction but would glean a further 10 per cent from the buyer of the lot sold. The so-called buyer's premium was highly controversial. Dealers threatened to boycott sales and John Marion, the chairman of Sotheby's Parke Bernet, likened it to the Stamp Tax. But the new levy had undeniable appeal to the consignor. After Christie's secured a plum consignment of Impressionist paintings from Henry Ford II, Sotheby's had fallen into line by October 1978, and in time, America's longer-established auctioneers would follow suit. It was these charges that were the subject of the Sotheby's and Christie's price-fixing scandal that rocked the auction world in 2000.

Freeman's would not offer the advantageous consignment rates allowed by adopting the buyer's premium until the fall of 1980. "We're an old firm and we're slow to react," Beau Freeman admitted in an interview that September.

Concerned at this attempt to cut smaller the small slice of cake that Sotheby's and Christie's were leaving America's regional auctioneers, Beau Freeman was looking for new direction as the global art market first dipped and then surged in the 1980s. He found it in an alliance with a local rival.

The number of Philadelphia auctioneers had shrunk dramatically since the days of the Civil War. Twenty-five downtown firms in the 1870s had become half-a-dozen by the 1970s, with Freeman's the sole fine art and estate specialists. A recent closure had been the business of William Morley, an old-school gent with a fresh cut bloom in his lapel and a kiss for the hand of a lady, who had started in Sansom Street in 1925. On occasion he had given Freeman's a run for its money in competition for the big sales – he had sold the estate of the Dodge family in Florida – so when problems with his landlord became too much, John Freeman went down personally and thanked him for closing.

There were, however, new kids on the block. William Bragdon, a New Jersey auctioneer, had opened on Broad Street with the help of Freeman's long-term specialist in paintings and European decorative arts, William Bratten.

He was not the only one to strike out from the nest of 1808 Chestnut Street.

Former broadcaster James E. Buckley, had moved to Philadelphia in 1972 with his new wife Sheila – she is from Amersham, the Buckinghamshire town where William Penn was born. He had been introduced to John Freeman following a chance visit to an antiques shop in North Carolina and quickly become acquainted with the rhythms and character of life on the auction room floor as a member of Freeman's basement crew. The hustlers, they called them.

Hustlers, or teamsters, are the bedrock of any salesroom, responsible for the physical moving of pictures and objects throughout their auction life. They oversee the logistics as a sideboard leaves its private residence, arrives at the auction store, is catalogued, photographed, placed into temporary storage and then prepared for exhibition and sale. Finally, the hustler may be called upon to deliver the merchandise to its new home.

Buckley worked alongside two old hands: Robert Johnson whose encyclopedic knowledge of the Oriental rug trade had been learned under William Morley; and Bill Kissane, an Irishman with a genial podium manner

A former automobile showroom, the saleroom of The Fine Arts Company of Philadelphia at 2317 Chestnut Street as it looked shortly after opening in 1981.

who had started at 1808 Chestnut way back in the '20s and now bossed the lower floor. He was no academic – his skills at timber analysis stretched no further than "tree wood" – but after half a century watching and learning he knew within a nickel what a lot would bring. Everybody in the business is a teamster at some time, but Kissane said Buckley was the first guy to threaten to leave after three years of learning the ropes and actually follow through.

Jim Buckley left to start The Fine Arts Company of Philadelphia with another former Freeman's employee, John H. Frisk, in 1976. They opened a consignment gallery on Walnut Street to collect merchandise for semiannual auctions at the Historical Society of Pennsylvania on Locust.

The two men parted company in 1981 as Frisk sold his shares and Buckley entered into a partnership with Alexis C. Manice, a Long Islander and a veteran of Sotheby's New York. Together they eschewed the prestigious but high-maintenance walls of the Historical Society for a favorable five-year lease with three-year option on a permanent salesroom in an up-and-coming part of town. The Vincent Kling building, a former automobile showroom with an urbane and

James E, Buckley conducts a sale for The Fine Arts Company of
Philadelphia in 1981.

contemporary feel at 2317 Chestnut, was five blocks
west of Freeman's.

A confident Daniel Freeman, son of John Freeman who
at 34 was the youngest member of the family firm, had
shown little concern for the competition when he was
interviewed for the local press that year as part of the
approaching Philadelphia Century IV celebrations. "Of
course it would be nice if it wasn't there but we're not
really worried about it" he said. But the first jolts arrived
three years later when, shortly after a $750,000 sale at
Freeman's that included a Queen Anne cherry side chair
that sold for $121,000, Fine Arts enjoyed record
business with a sale grossing close to $400,000. A local
competitive situation had arisen for the first time in
years.

Young, energetic and enthusiastic, Buckley and Manice
believed their venerable neighbor was complacent and
too used to the merchandise arriving on the doorstep.
The newcomers harried trust departments, pushed
glossy catalogues through mailboxes, attended social
functions, took advertising space in places where the
competition did not advertise, undercut on prices, used
computers, employed a certified appraiser with a forte
for marketing and hired a company to come up with a
contemporary logo.

A novelty was the decision to place alongside every
catalogue entry a price estimate – the inexact but often
informed guideline that suggests the sort of money a
potential buyer might have to bid to make a successful
purchase. Dealers did not like it as it removed one of
their principal advantages over the general public and
the auction novices who were often a little coy about
asking the value of an object. But putting a price on
things in the catalogue proved an irresistible hook for the
private buyer when first tried in Great Britain with the
opening of a new Sotheby's saleroom in the Belgravia
district of London. It would be a hook for American
buyers, too, and Freeman's would choose to introduce
printed price estimates in the fall of 1982.

"People who did business with us did business with us
because they didn't like Freeman's and their attitude,"
recalls Buckley. Freeman's still had the loyalty of the
antiques trade. Fine Arts cultivated a different crowd of
collectors, homeowners and yuppies.

Beau Freeman described the union of the two companies
that occurred in 1988 as "a merger between someone
who needed a manager and someone who needed
space." Philadelphia's oldest auctioneer – its gross sales
totaling short of $4.5m in the year Van Gogh's *Irises* had

This highly sophisticated Queen Anne cherrywood side chair, a masterpiece of the Philadelphia style circa 1750-60, sold to New York dealer Albert Sack of Israel Sack Inc., for $121,000, at Freeman's on April 16-18, 1984. It was the highest price a piece of furniture had realized at a Philadelphia auction. The chair – from the same set as a pair that had sold for a record $140,000 at Sotheby's New York in 1977 – was among a cache of Philadelphian furniture consigned by the second husband of Mrs. Thomas Curran, the late wife of a legendary Philadelphia antiques dealer. Famously, Curran had bought a number of pieces of the celebrated General John Cadwalader furniture – including lot 168, "a handsome antique console table," for $450, that now resides in the Metropolitan Museum of Art – when it was sold at auction at Davis and Harvey's Art Gallery on Walnut Street on November 3-4, 1904.

sold at Sotheby's New York for $53.9m – sought a new direction when appraiser and auctioneer George Freeman Jr. announced his intention to leave after 20 years of shouldering the burden of family responsibility. "I hate this business", he had told employees. On his own, Beau was aware that he had competition.

Philadelphia's newest auctioneer – knocking on the door with a turnover of $3m after a decade of sales – was looking for new premises as the eight-year lease expired on a building that, in five years of center city redevelopment, had become desirable real estate.

Seated in the Freeman's boardroom, watched over by those portraits of five generations of Freeman family businessmen, nine months of negotiations were concluded on June 29, 1988. A merger was proposed and a ten-year agreement signed between the partners of a new company to be called Freeman\Fine Arts. Chairman Beau Freeman would have the largest interest, but no major decisions or changes in the business would be made without the agreement of president Alexis Manice, who assumed close to a 30 percent stake. The two men provided a study in contrasts: Freeman, the bow-tied Chestnut Hill gent, diligent, conservative, and restrained; Manice, the flamboyant Long Islander. A decade later when philosophical disagreements led to

a parting of ways, Manice would describe their differences simply in those terms: "Beau and I have totally different ideas of how to run a business, he said. "We never had any major problems. It's just that I'm a New Yorker and he's a Philadelphian."

Some changes were immediate with the injection of new blood – a total of nine new members of staff. The computers arrived, the gallery previously closed on weekends opened for Saturday sales while the Sansom Street loading dock was made off limits to purchasers in favor of a receptionist on Chestnut Street who – in the modern way of doing things – asked that bidders register officially and use a numbered paddle to make a bid. The stylish FA logo was adopted (it worked for both Freeman's Auctions and Fine Arts and thus was acceptable to both parties), but added to it was the slogan *A Tradition With New Ideas*.

But to most Philadelphians it was still Freeman's, the oldest, best-established regional full-service auction house in the country. And with that came good and bad.

Long-standing relationships with old Freeman's customers had left them struggling to say no to consignments of little value. In theory the minimum consignment level was set at $250. In reality the company was selling 50,000 lots a year with an

Book specialist David Bloom, who joined Freemans in 1983.

average lot value of under $100. Ambitious urban renewal projects of the post-War decades contributed to the culture of high volume sales of low value material at the decaying floors of 1808 Chestnut Street.

An art market crash in 1990 that saw many prices tumble did not help. Equally problematic and much closer to home was the unwanted perception cultivated in the previous decade of a loosely run family business with ebbing expertise and a complacent attitude. *A Tradition With New Ideas* perhaps. But, recalls Buckley, "the clients did not follow."

Applying a makeshift Band-aid across the wounds was the occasional magnificent discovery. Memories of great book sales past had been revived on December 16, 1993 with the sale of a 1792 hand-written communiqué from George Washington to planning commissioner David Stuart. In the letter Washington expressed his private concerns over the unfolding physical layout of the District of Columbia. Major Pierre L'Enfant, he suggests, might be better fit for the job of superintendent. Estimated at $25,000-50,000, it would be hammered down at $170,500. The winning bidder, who participated by phone, was Beverly Hills, California, dealer Joseph Maddalena, owner of Profiles in History.

The letter was part of an 88-lot haul from a previously unknown collection amassed, thought specialist David Bloom, sometime in the first two decades of the 20th century through the London antiquarian booksellers Maggs Bros.

Maddalena prevailed on several other lots, including a July 15, 1864, letter written by Abraham Lincoln on Executive Mansion stationery to S.J. Seberman in Philadelphia, thanking him for sending a suit of clothes ($29,700) and a July 29, 1747, letter written by Ben Franklin on matters dealing with the printing trade, which sold for $20,900.

Among the wealth of other historical treasures scooped up on auction day were Thomas Jefferson's February 14, 1806, letter to the Marquis de Lafayette – "Your presence at New Orleans would give security to our government there" – ($46,200); Lord Byron's original manuscript of the poem *To Florence,* ($16,500); and a 1784 Samuel Johnson letter in which the English essayist and lexicographer discusses a recent bloodletting ($10,450). Perhaps the most curiously Victorian lot sold was a letter written by Charles Dickens to his publishers in which the author writes that "Mr. Browne" will be coming to inspect his pet raven, Grip. The letter was acquired for the Free Library of

Philadelphia where Grip, mounted in a glass and mahogany case, also resides.

At the end of the day, the sale had rung up a remarkable $583,000, prompting auctioneer Beau Freeman to comment, "We can do it here; you don't have to go to New York."

When the consignments arrived, there was no problem selling them for landmark prices in Philadelphia.

In the spring of 1997 Beau Freeman had been on a call to a modest house in Willow Grove. Through a trust officer, the father of a boy who played on the soccer team of his second son, William, he had been introduced to a client interested in selling a pair of vases in his possession before a move to Florida. He was told they had been a gift from a descendent of John Wanamaker but was not expecting to encounter two superb vases from the Tucker China Manufactory.

Not forgetting the forlorn two-year experiment of Gousse Bonnin and George Anthony Morris at the American China Manufactory in Southwark from 1770-72, it is to William Ellis Tucker that we must turn for the first commercially successful American porcelain factory. Tucker, the second of 12 children from a line of prolific New England Quakers, had taken his first steps in the ceramic arts as a backyard decorator of vases,

pitchers and tea wares imported "in the white" from Europe. But his ambition soon turned to American soil – blue kaolin clay from Middlesex County, New Jersey, and a lode of feldspar discovered on a farm in New Castle County, Delaware. His so-called secret formula (the Philadelphia Museum of Art has a copy in his hand dated October 30, 1830) yielded commendable hard paste porcelain distinctive for its green translucence. Between 1825 and 1838, the Tucker China Manufactory, located first at the Old Water Works on Schuylkill Front Street and later on Chestnut and Schuylkill Sixth (now 17th Street) would rival the factories of Europe for product and price.

When the company finally gave way to competition younger brother Thomas Tucker had opened a retail store at 100 Chestnut Street but three years later put everything up for sale – at auction, of course. A Philadelphia auctioneer Charles C. Mackey conducted a series of 'closing down' sales in November 1841.

The vases that captivated Beau Freeman one-and-a-half centuries later were among the most ambitious conceits of the Tucker enterprise. They stood 21 in. (53cm) high, were modeled in several parts loosely bolted together and employed the talents of metalworker Friedrich Sache (who worked in the shop of Christian Cornelius), to model and cast the gilt bronze griffin handles. There

are two similar pairs in the Philadelphia Museum of Art, one decorated with bouquets of garden flowers, the onother with views of the Tucker China factory at the Old Water Works.

As Beau Freeman studied the decoration of the vases he had been asked to appraise closely, he noticed subtle variations to the gilded border patterns and two central vignettes that were quite different in both subject and mood.

One depicted a view of *Sedgley, seat of James Fisher* titled just below the scene, and to the reverse, a view of *The Schuylkill River from Sedgley Park*. The other, more dramatic, was decorated with a shipwreck scene and a man and a woman fleeing Native Americans on horseback, perhaps scenes from the life of the Jamaican-born Quaker merchant Jonathan Dickinson.

To great excitement in the collecting community, the vases returned close to their place of manufacture on April 17, 1997. Auctioneer Beau Freeman, the vases he discovered placed on a pedestal beside him, opened the bidding at $30,000 and took bids at $5,000 advances from New York dealer Gary Stradling seated in the room with his bidding number held high. At $115,000, Stradling (it later emerged he was bidding on behalf of the Metropolitan Museum of Art) had successfully seen off competition from the telephone manned by Lex Manice, but another phone bidder entered the competition and stayed with the $5,000 advances until Stradling shook his head at $265,000. With the 10 per cent commission they brought $291,500, a record for American porcelain and the highest price for a lot sold at a Philadelphia auction house since the Dunlap Declaration had raised $404,000 back in 1969. The buyer on the phone was Stuart Feld, president of New York dealers Hirschl and Adler. He would keep the Sedgley vase for his personal collection.

★   ★   ★

It was a positive memory to take from a troubled period. The following year a talented accounts and office manager Hanna Dougher, who had joined the company in 1990, handed in her notice. She cited as her reasons the culture of low pay, a failure to invest in the technology that was changing the auction business, crumbling infrastructure and the alienation of clients through poor customer service.

David Bloom, the solitary specialist in the building, was also questioning if his encyclopedic knowledge of Pennsylvania printed matter might be better served elsewhere.

So when the partners' agreement that had bound together Manice and the Freeman family quietly ran out after its 10 years, it was at least an opportunity for change. At a price that valued the 194-year-old company at just $380,000, Beau Freeman bought out the interest of his president. Manice left the auction business after 30 years to pursue real estate investment in Florida. Samuel T. Freeman III, the great-great-great-great-grandson of the founder was named to the board, and the name on the letterhead again was Samuel T. Freeman and Co.

Freeman's was back in family control, but with turnover in freefall at just $4m, in serious trouble. The company would have to reinvent itself to survive.

The celebrated Tucker vases sold by Freeman\Fine Arts for $291,500 in 1997. The vase to the left is decorated with a scene titled *Sedgley, seat of James Fisher* and to the reverse, a view of the Schuylkill River from Sedgley Park.

Sedgley, erected sometime between 1799 and 1803 on the grounds that now form the northern part of Fairmont Park, was designed in the gothic style by Benjamin Henry Latrobe for William Cramond, a successful Philadelphia merchant who just happened to be a client of T.B. Freeman. The house was later owned by the banker James Fisher who used Sedgley as his country retreat from 1812 to 1836.

The dramatic shipwreck scenes to the companion vase remained unidentified at the time of sale although they are likely taken from prints and might represent scenes from the life of Jonathan Dickinson, the Jamaican-born Quaker merchant whose dominance of the sugar trade would guarantee him a place among the elite of early 18th century Philadelphia. Dickinson, who would assume a political career in the city, was best known for his published diary *God's Protecting Providence* that chronicled an encounter with a hostile tribe of Native Americans after his three-masted barkentine *The Reformation* ran aground off the coast of eastern Florida in the fall of 1696. Along with his wife, an infant son and a party of 20 men, he was held captive by the Ais for several weeks before completing the odyssey in the spring of 1697. His best-selling story was doubtless a suitable subject for the home of a Quaker grandee.

Rebirth

CHAPTER ELEVEN

"Until one is committed there is a hesitancy, the chance to draw back, always ineffectiveness. Concerning all acts of initiative (and creation) there is one elementary truth, the ignorance of which kills countless ideas and splendid plans; that the moment one definitely commits oneself, then providence moves too. All sorts of things occur to help one that would never otherwise have occurred. A whole stream of events issues from the decision, raising in one's favour all manner of unforeseen incidents and meetings and material assistance which no man could have dreamed would have come his way. I have learned deep respect for one of Goethe's couplets: 'Whatever you can do or dream you can, begin it. Boldness has genius, power, and magic in it'."

W. H. MURRAY, THE SCOTTISH HIMALAYAN EXPEDITION
AND **JOHANN WOLFGANG VON GOETHE,** 1749-1832

"Consignors will bring you what they feel you sell. If they see you
selling general estate merchandise then they will consign estate
merchandise. If they see you selling valuable works of art then they
will bring you the same." Paul Roberts, president of Freeman's since
1999.

Englishman Paul Roberts had first encountered
Freeman's in 1996. At the time, he was the newly-
appointed president of the North American division of
Phillips, then the world's third-largest and third-oldest
fine art auction house. The company harbored ambitions
to expand beyond its network of more than 20 British
regional salerooms into the international market. Turning
a profit in a New York office hemorrhaging money at a
rate of $2 million a year in the early 1990s had been his
first priority, but part of phase two was the addition to
the franchise of Selkirk's, a venerable auction business
established in St Louis, Missouri, around 1830. More
North American acquisitions were in the business plan
and Roberts thought a fading but still nationally
recognized name like Freeman\Fine Arts might fit the
Phillips model. He rode the Amtrak from Penn Station,
New York City to 30th Street Station, Philadelphia to
take a look.

★   ★   ★

Beau Freeman remembers it well. A sale was in process
– at Freeman's there was always a sale of something –
and he had allowed his guest the opportunity to see him
in action on the auction floor before any more formal
introductions. Interest from a multi-national company in
the family business was not something he would have

entertained in his earlier years, but times had certainly
changed. He was happy to show this Englishman around
1808 Chestnut Street and would at least hear what he
had to say.

"The Freeman's boardroom," he announced ushering his
guest into that small room on the fifth floor of the
building. He proceeded to point out the portraits of his
direct ancestors – "Tristram Bampfylde, the company
founder, his son Tristram William Lockyer, Samuel T" and
so on. He had watched this Manhattan executive
experience a moment of wonderment. He liked that.
Nevertheless, he sensed the imminent conversation was
not one the gentlemen who looked down upon them
would likely have enjoyed.

Freeman's in its 191st year, argued Roberts, had confused
feverish activity and a busy saleroom with profitability.
The venerable tradition of selling anything and
everything, one that went back to the days of Center
City factory dispersals was late 20th century folly. His
immediate analysis suggested Freeman's was making a
profit on just 20 per cent of the lots they sold, and those
lots were all of a higher value.

Outright purchase of the business was clearly not on the
agenda for the great-great-great grandson of the
company founder. Instead, Roberts' offer to Beau

Freeman as discussions continued, had possessed more subtlety. In exchange for a minority shareholding in the company, Phillips would work with Freeman's, offering America's oldest auctioneer business expertise and economies of scale as part of a larger network. Overall ownership and control of the company need not change hands.

It was, as Beau Freeman now reflects, a decision he fortunately never had the chance to make. The Phillips-Freeman deal had only been on the plate for a matter of weeks when Roberts' own career took a dramatic turn. Christopher Weston, the grand old man of Phillips who had overseen the growth of his company from Jersey to Glasgow and from Geneva to New York, took this moment to bow out and sell to a firm of venture capitalists. Unhappy with the direction the company would take under its new owners, and with the inevitable souring of relationships, Roberts' head had been turned by an alternative challenge emerging in Scotland presented to him by the merchant banker and arts patron Sir Angus Grossart.

Resurrecting Lyon & Turnbull, Scotland's oldest auction house established in 1826, would reunite him with former colleague Nick Curnow and bring them alongside a young and talented team of directors they had helped build during their time at Phillips. Paul Roberts and his family left their riverside house in Greenwich, Connecticut for Edinburgh, and a diaspora of talent risked their careers to join the project. By the fall of 1999 Lyon and Turnbull had re-emerged, in a fine neoclassical Georgian temple in Edinburgh's New Town, as an immediate force in the Scottish auction market. Freeman's "white knight" was appointed deputy chairman. There would be no more talk of an American branch network at Phillips.

Roberts, however, did not forget what he had seen in Philadelphia or his plans for the sleeping giant of the American auction business. He continued, as can be his nature, to interfere, and when in September 1998 Freeman's announced a new-look board of directors, the Press reported both a seventh generation Freeman (Beau's eldest son Samuel T. Freeman III) and a new face as president that was helping to reacquaint the firm with its British roots.

Taking inspiration from a passage in a book by Scotsman-mountaineer, W. H. Murray – surely a first for a fine art auction business – Paul Roberts harbored ambitions to hoist Edinburgh and Philadelphia out of the shadows of London and New York. He would work double duty as vice chairman of Lyon & Turnbull and president of Samuel T. Freeman & Co.

The question, however, for his more conservative chairman Beau Freeman was this. Did he want to buy into Roberts' radical vision for the company and risk both his own money and the 200 years of company and family history he carried so obviously on his shoulders? Freeman's, said Roberts, could no longer be the place to buy a second-hand piano for $50 or a $25 box of kitchenalia. "Consignors will bring you what they believe you sell. If they see you selling general estate merchandise then they will consign estate merchandise. If they see you selling valuable works of art then that's what they will bring you."

Survival demanded the firm eschew the *vin ordinaire* of the typical house clearance that had seen Freeman's process 50,000 lots in 1998 for a turnover under $5m and instead pursue again the serious collections and estates. There would be heavy investment in the building, implementation of more modern marketing techniques and more emphasis upon customer service. Crucial, however, was the recruitment of respected business winning departmental specialists.

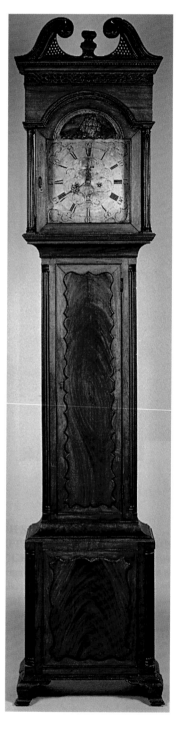

Establishing a new auction record for an American clock when it sold at Freeman's for $452,000 on April 15-17, 1999 was this 8ft 1in (2.46m) high Delaware Chippendale tall case with works by Duncan Beard and an outstanding mahogany case by John Janvier Sr. During cataloguing, a chalk inscription was discovered to the pendulum door reading: "Made at Cantwell's Bridge, Delaware, 1779".

This Philadelphia compass seat side chair adorned with a shell and volute carving has on the inside of the back rail the initials *SM* in chalk. The so-called Transitional period chair circa 1750-60 is thought to be from a set of 12 owned by the ardent patriot Samuel Morris. He was one of the founders of the First City Troop of Light Horse, who served with Washington at the Battles of Princeton and Trenton. Estimated to bring $80,000-120,000, at Freeman's sale on April 15-17, 1999, it sold for $331,000.

The prime objective of any new business plan as dictated by Beau Freeman was more simplistic. It was to ensure the survival of the company in family ownership to its bicentennial birthday. He was well aware that the company had been experiencing a trough and was conscious that the auction market at the end of the 20th century was offering fresh opportunities. He harbored grave reservations as to the merits of marketing but found reassurance from his long-term vice president Jim Buckley, who espoused the principles put forward in the new business plan from the outset. "The only reason I am doing this is because you want it," he told Buckley before he gave his consent and unwavering support to the new plan.

It was a relatively bloodless coup. Some employees took early retirement, while some of the more unsavory aspects of the company's backroom culture ebbed away when a handful of "hustlers" quit when a new dress code of chinos and polo shirts was introduced as company policy.

Meanwhile, Roberts had joined forces with Eric Smith, a former Phillips finance and operations manager who would put financial flesh on the skeletal plan as Freeman's chief financial officer. The pair had already turned, at Beau Freeman's suggestion, to former

David Donaldson, who joined Freeman's in 1999 to set up the first designated marketing department.

employee, Hanna Dougher, to gain a deeper financial understanding of the company. She was eventually persuaded to rejoin the firm she had left two years previously as the first appointment in the "renaissance plan," arriving just prior to a large fair-haired Scotsman and paintings specialist by the name of Alasdair Nichol. Financial targets and budgets were established, and plans were put in place to overhaul the customer service. David Donaldson, a former marketing man at the Yale Repertory Theater, gave the long-standing firm its first designated marketing department.

The new team had hit the ground running with a morale-boosting sale on April 15-17, 1999. An exceptional Delaware tall case clock had been found by Jim Buckley during the valuation of the estate of a long-standing Freeman's client Letitia Martin Pittman, of Phoenixville, Pennsylvania. An appraisal conducted in a dark stairway had suggested a finely engraved dial signed *Duncan Beard, Appoquinimink* and an outstanding Chippendale case of a type associated with the workshop of Odessa cabinetmaker John Janvier Sr. A wonderful discovery made during cataloguing was a chalk inscription to the pendulum door, sealed from view behind a board for over two centuries. It read: "Made at Cantwell's Bridge, Delaware, 1779."

This, the very best of the clocks from the Janvier and Beard workshops, might have cost a year's wages of a yeoman farmer in late 18th century Delaware. It sparked interest well above its $40,000-60,000 estimate. Sticking to bidding increments of $10,000, auctioneer Beau Freeman traded bids between two Pennsylvania dealers, Philip W. Bradley of Philip H. Bradley, Downingtown, and Todd Prickett of C.L. Prickett of Yardley. When Prickett finally shook his head, Freeman dropped his hammer at $410,000, selling the clock to Bradley for a total of $452,000, a record for an American clock at auction.

In a runaway Americana market, the "Franklin" Queen Anne curly maple dressing table from the estate of the late George Vaux that had been sold at the Sanitary Fair was hammered down for $386,000, and a Philadelphia compass seat side chair from a set once owned by the patriot Samuel Morris for $331,000.

But the feel-good factor that accompanied the good fortune of three blue-chip pieces of American furniture could not hide the anxieties the company would experience as it began to break out of the shell it had inhabited for a generation. The creation and execution of the so-called "renaissance plan" and the radical changes that followed by no means constituted a smooth

A page from the archive that proved too good to be true. This musical score titled *The March of Washington at the Battle of Trenton composed by Francis Hopkinson Esq. In the cause of American Freedom* included a portrait of George Washington on horseback together with a number of previously unrecorded 'Hopkinson' verses.

A FORGERY UNCOVERED

A page from the archive that proved too good to be true. At the eleventh hour, manuscripts that purported to be undiscovered music and poems of the 18th century poet and songwriter Francis Hopkinson (1731-1819) were withdrawn from sale at Freeman's on May 16, 2002. The reason? After consulting with specialists in 18th century printing and music, book specialist of 20 years David Bloom had become convinced that the collection of notebooks, lyrics and pen and ink drawings was an elaborate early 20th century forgery.

What seemed to be a lavishly illustrated manuscript for "the first American opera," the Revolutionary War oratorio *The Temple of Minerva* by America's first composer, is now thought to be the work of an infamous Philadelphia forger, Charles Bates Weisberg who died in prison in 1945. It had been Weisberg's genius not to attempt to recreate Hopkinson's handwriting but instead to suggest his work was a contemporary copy written in an anonymous hand. What falsely convinced Bloom of its authenticity was a letter found among the papers to the late 18th century publisher Benjamin Carr that suggested the poems were being prepared for publication only a few years after Hopkinson's death. "That was a trap that was set for me, just as it was set for whomever was shown this when it was first created."

Weisberg probably created and sold the documents at least a decade before he achieved notoriety in the 1940s, perhaps sometime around 1926 when a Hopkinson biography was published bringing the Revolutionary figure into the public eye once more. The buyer at the time for $500 was the grandfather of the consignor Charles Nagy, an antiques dealer whose Philadelphia store went under during the Depression. Whether or not Nagy knew of their suspicious nature remains unknown, but he never sold them. Instead the box of papers was stored in a basement where they were discovered by his granddaughter Anne Marie Connolly of Brookhaven, Delaware, early in 2002.

The global audience. At a time when communications are expanding exponentially, new opportunities abound in the art, antiques and collectors' market. Internet bidding is one of the more recent innovations embraced.

transition. The heavy re-investment in staff, marketing and the fabric of the building dramatically increased costs at a moment when the company was rejecting 70 per cent of the lots it had previously sold.

Saying no was difficult. Screams of anguish both inside and outside the company reverberated around the antique trade. No longer was Freeman's the source of vast quantities of low-end merchandise hiding the occasional poorly catalogued treasure. The turnover figures during reconstruction were of equal concern to the new management team during 2001-2002 – a cause not helped in the following spring when, the day before a sale of books and manuscripts, a much-vaunted John Hopkinson archive was withdrawn after David Bloom was persuaded it was an elaborate forgery.

By their own admission Roberts and Smith had significantly underestimated the time it would take to reap the benefits of radical restructuring, but while everything around him was changing, there was no recrimination from the chairman as his company's fate hung in the balance. "Beau's steadfast support for, and faith in, the new plan which he had been so slow to embrace was as courageous as it was extraordinary," remembers Paul Roberts.

However, as W.H. Murray predicted the "unforeseen incidents and material assistance which no man could have dreamed" did come to their aid.

＊　　　＊　　　＊

Indeed, while Freeman's battled to right itself in choppy waters, seismic changes were occurring in the international marketplace that, if used to advantage, might ease the voyage. First, the introduction of effective new technology began to bear fruit.

If the essence of the auctioneer's craft had changed little in two millennia, then the tools available to bring buyers and sellers together were ever more sophisticated. Online auction technology had certainly moved on since those days in the 1990s when the "live link up" was little more than a gimmick – at best slow and at worst torturous. Participants in the modern auction room can hardly fail to be impressed by a slick operation now scarcely more obtrusive to the rhythm of a sale than the increasingly standard bank of telephone bidders.

Sotheby's had shown what could be done with the new medium when it chose to offer a Dunlap printing of the Declaration of Independence at an online auction in July 2000, a marketing opportunity bar none. This printing –

legend has it that it was discovered in the back of a picture frame bought for $4 at a Pennsylvania flea market – represented the 25th copy of the Declaration extant when it had first appeared at Sotheby's in 1991 selling for $2.42m. Only a decade later online bidders exchanged blows up to $8.14m.

The largest financial transaction struck across cyberspace was great publicity for Sotheby's pioneering, if ultimately over-ambitious, online auction website. It would, however, prove a portent for the progress of America's regional auctions where today internet bidders, connected to the salesroom through eBay's global marketplace, are regular participants. No longer did you have to be in London or New York to access the international market.

It is unlikely that online bidding will ever successfully replace a live auction. The live show is important and in a market where subtleties of color, condition and quality are paramount to value, there will scarcely be a substitute for seeing and bidding in the flesh. However, at Freeman's that rotating metal platform that stands at the far end of the stage on the third floor gallery, has gradually became redundant as a large screen flashes up digital images of the lots being sold.

With bidders able to participate as the action unfolds from their armchair at home, the world's regional auctioneers were now armed with a credible weapon with which to compete against the London-New York hegemony that existed in the fine art auction market. And, when two hammer blows connected to test Sotheby's and Christie's credibility and dominance of that market, the regional auctioneers were also given an area of moral high ground from which to fight the battle.

By 2000, as Freeman's experienced its growing pains, Phillips, the auction company Roberts had left for his dual role in Edinburgh and Philadelphia, was experiencing its own remarkable transformation. The new owner was the extraordinarily well-resourced French businessman and LVMH grandee Bernard Arnault.

Rejected as a suitor by Sotheby's, but keen to out-maneuver Francois Pinault, his business rival in the luxury goods market who had bought Christie's in 1998, Arnault chose instead to make Phillips a credible third player at the very top end of the fine art market. He was armed with a war chest of more than $500m.

In the long term, the massive pre-sale guarantees that Phillips could promise to consignors of blue-chip works would prove their undoing. In the short term, the previously lucrative upper end of the picture market was wrested away from the market leaders at a time when their finances were about to unravel.

Scandal was around the corner. *The New York Times* had been the first to break the news of price-fixing on the Upper East Side on September 22, 2000. As evidence emerged of a bungled attempt to agree on the rates of commission they charged consignors, Sotheby's and Christie's agreed to share a bill for $512m to settle price-fixing allegations from a class action of 120,000 clients. Additional punishments would follow. Sotheby's owner, Detroit shopping mall tycoon A. Alfred Taubman, would pay a $7.5 million fine and spend a year and a day behind bars. Sotheby's chief, Diana "Dede" Brooks, would avoid jail time but pay a $350,000 fine, perform 1,000 hours of community service and spend six months in home detention.

For both companies courtroom drama would leave a lasting stain on polished reputations, while savage cost-cutting deemed necessary for survival radically reduced their ability to serve the day-to-day needs of all but their most important clients. There were opportunities for those smaller houses that could demonstrate their ability to fill the gaps. No company was longer established in North America and few better placed to exploit this opportunity than Samuel T. Freeman & Co.

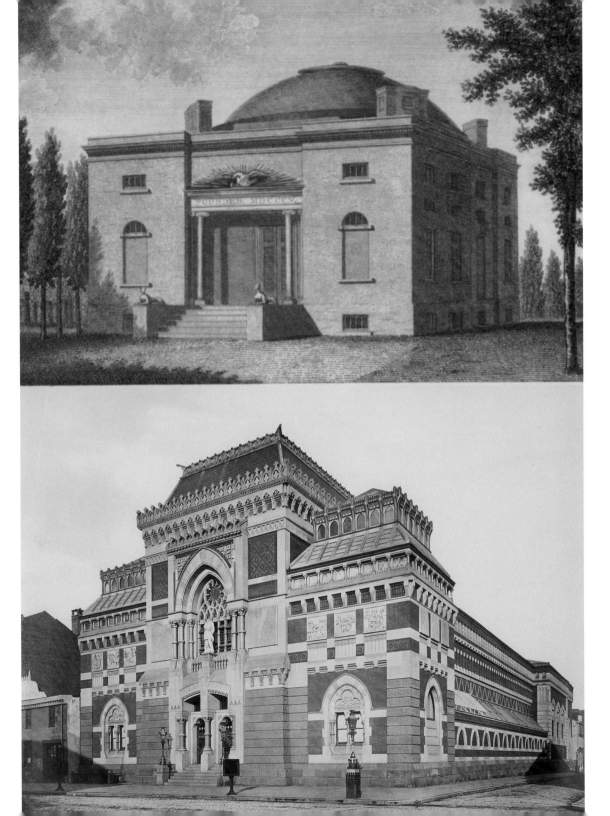

The first building of the Pennsylvania Academy of the Fine Arts, situated on Chestnut Street, was designed by amateur architect and professional auctioneer John Dorsey. This engraving by Benjamin Tanner (1775-1848) after a 1809 drawing by John James Barralet (1747-1815) that appeared in *The Port Folio* magazine of June 1809, shows the building (which was remodeled after a fire in 1845) in its Federal glory, with a low skylit rotunda and a carved wooden eagle above the doorway.

The Academy, founded by painter and scientist Charles Willson Peale, sculptor William Rush and other artists and business leaders in 1805, made possible the notion of professionalism for American artists and provided a showcase for their work. The institution moved to its current home, the remarkable Frank Furness and George Hewitt building on North Broad Street, in the centennial year of 1876 around when this photograph was taken by the Philadelphian photographer Robert Newell.

The dawning of the new era on Chestnut Street arrived with the first sale of paintings dedicated to the alumnae of North America's longest established academy of art, Pennsylvania Academy of the Fine Arts.

For over a century America has been the great engine room driving the international art trade. Most of this demand used to be focused on buying works by the great names of 18th century painting and sculpture and the great names of European furniture and decorative arts. Gainsborough, Reynolds, Boucher, Chippendale, Reisner, Sèvres, Meissen: these were the interior currency of Frick, Vanderbilt, Morgan and Stotesbury.

However, the story of the last century was one of a declining supply of 18th century masterpieces from the Old World to be replaced in large measure by a growing pride and chauvinism in indigenous works. Coached by pioneering dealers, more and more affluent Americans spent more and more money on homegrown products, paying sums that have come to dwarf what they would be prepared to give for similar works by equivalent British or European artists.

As recently as a decade ago, the Pennsylvania Impressionists, or New Hope School – perhaps the most recognizable group of painters to emerge from the

"So far as we can foresee in the future, it must be many years before we can be persuaded to leave our present home which has come as the logical result of the labors of all of us."

Paul Freeman, from the dedication ceremonies for 1808 Chestnut Street, June 28, 1924

When, in 1998 Freeman's increased their buyer's premium from 10 to 12 per cent – it currently stands at 19.5 per cent – the promise was made to put the money into the decaying fabric of a once-great building. That included the repair and redecoration of both galleries including – perhaps the most poignant moment for chairman Beau Freeman – the tearing down of the once magnificent red velvet drapes from the walls of the premier gallery early in 2003. The curtains had been an extravagant finishing touch to the newly completed building in the 1920s and had been a constant in Beau's life since he started work at Freeman's – including that day in 1969 when a rare Dunlap printing of the Declaration of Independence was sent crashing to the marble floor.

While the building is of considerable interest to architectural historians – partly as it remains almost unchanged from 1924 – elements of its layout and design are not conducive to running a modern auction house, and plans to introduce sympathetic changes to some of its upper floor office space are currently in the pipeline. New exhibition space for forthcoming sale highlights, client entertainment areas and an open-plan working environment for department

specialists are all part of putting the contemporary spin on a very old business.

Number 1808 is receiving a face-lift at a time when the street on which it stands shows similar signs of gentrification, 30 years after the character of the street was radically changed by well-meaning urban planners and the proposed (but never realized) Chestnut Street Transitway. Cars were back on Chestnut by 2000 and helping claw back the street's retail reputation, at a time when many storefronts were vacant or leased by low-rent "turnstile tenants," was the arrival at 19th and Chestnut of deluxe department store Boyd's. Although, citywide, Philadelphia has lost four percent of it population since 1990, the population in the Center City area has grown by almost ten percent, attracting a high proportion of twenty- and thirty-somethings with disposable income that Freeman's are looking to attract as future clients.

Alasdair Nichol, a leading authority in the specialist field of
Pennsylvania Impressionists.

Pennsylvania Academy of the Fine Arts (PAFA) –
remained a relatively untapped seam for "serious"
auctioneers of the Mid-Atlantic States. Fast-forward ten
years and this once dealer-led market is currently among
the hottest areas from the "traditional" end of the
American picture business.

Ironically, it was a Scotsman who became the first
auctioneer to showcase works by PAFA as a cohesive
artistic group. A struggling artist-turned furniture porter
living and working in Edinburgh, Alasdair Nichol had
discovered a talent sourcing pictures for auction first in
Glasgow, then in London and then alongside Roberts in
Manhattan. Joining Freeman's in 1999, he was the first
of a number of highly qualified specialists on the payroll
attracted by the new, more realistic wage structure and
the smell of unfulfilled potential.

Both established in 1805, there is an obvious link
between Freeman's, America's oldest auction company
and PAFA, an indispensable element in the flourishing of
high culture in 19th and early 20th century Philadelphia.
Less commonly acknowledged has been the role an
auctioneer played in the establishment of PAFA two
centuries ago. T.B. Freeman's peers upon his
appointment to the office of auctioneer included John
Dorsey, a founding member of the board at the

Academy and indeed the architect of its first building. In
2000, Freeman's cemented the relationship with the
institution with the creation of the Samuel T. Freeman
Memorial Scholarship. This award, presented annually
to a graduate at the Academy, is funded by a cut of the
hammer price generated from the sale of works by PAFA
artists. Significantly the original guarantee of $10,000
has been dwarfed by contributions doubling and tripling
that figure.

Since December 2000, the PAFA artists' sale has
become a fixture on the American auction calendar. The
New Hope School in particular remains very much an
East Coast affair, but one sensed that this Americanized
approach to the Impressionism movement had arrived
with the sale at Freeman's in 2003 of *The Old Mill,
Washington's Crossing*, a trademark plein air winter
landscape by Edward Willis Redfield (1869-1965). It sold
for $691,250. The Dunlap Declaration sold for
$404,000 in 1969 had been beaten in 1999 by a
Duncan Beard tall case clock, but now had finally (on
paper at least) been battered.

Along with Daniel Garber, Redfield has emerged as the
ace in the New Hope pack, but Nichol – who has worked
hard to cultivate interest in the Academy beyond its

The highlight of the December 2004 fine art sale was this stunning 24 1/2 in. (63cm) high bronze *Danseuse* by the grand old man of Cubist sculpture, Jacques Lipchitz (1891-1973).

Inscribed and dated J. Lipchitz 1913, the bronze was conceived four years after the artist left Lithuania for the Parisian artistic communities of Montmartre and Montparnasse. It is one of an edition of seven lost-wax casts made at the Valsuani Foundry, Paris, some time before 1940 when Lipchitz fled Hitler's troops and moved to America. Another cast is in the Barnes Foundation in Merion, Pennsylvania (the State has long been a destination of admirers of the artist's work), while in 2003 Sotheby's sold another as part of the celebrated Meyer and Vivian Potamkin collection of Philadelphia.

This example had a provenance by descent from the artist's studio and had entered the collection of Philadelphian lawyer Philip F. Newman in 1962 via the New York dealers Bernard Reis and Company at a cost of $8000. At Freeman's it carried an estimate of $400,000-600,000 – that was necessary to pull the consignment away from the admiring eyes of Sotheby's and Christie's – and it got away at $465,750, the winning bid was tendered over the phone by New York agents/dealers Mitchell-Innes Nash against London trade underbidding.

back yard – has also seen Freeman's establish artist records from the Academy's second string.

The rise of the Pennsylvania Impressionists as a force to be reckoned with in the American art market was one of two pillars upon which a remarkable sale in December 2004 was built. The culmination of four years of development, this welcome early gate-crasher to the Freeman's 200th anniversary party posted close to $5m total that was close to the annual turnover of the company as a whole just five years previously and the highest-grossing sale since Addison B. Freeman knocked down $17m of Great War surplus in two hours in 1919. It was also the sale that coined the phrase "more world records than unsold lots," of which the marketing department at Freeman's is proud.

Records aside, for a winter nocturne by Redfield pupil George William Sotter ($223,750) and *The Delaware, Reflections* by Fern Isabel Coppedge ($201,750), the third floor gallery also played host to a consignment from the family of Philadelphia lawyer Philip F. Newman. This included the 1913 bronze *Danseuse* by Jacques Lipchitz. It was promoted on the international market through the ever-deepening relationship with Scottish strategic partner Lyon & Turnbull. At the sale the bronze was subject to competition from leading London and

New York dealers before selling at $465,750. In 2004, with the input of David Weiss (who joined Freeman's as a second picture specialist following the financial capitulation of Sloan's auction house of Washington, D.C.) the sales total for the paintings department was more than $9.3 million. The total turnover for the year rose to more than $16m and the first significant profit of the new era was returned.

It is often said that the auction business prospers due to one of the three "Ds": death, divorce and debt. In the modern auction environment "department" can be equally important. As Freeman's sales calendar, previously dominated by three major gallery sales a year, evolves towards a series of semiannual specialist sales, so recognized departments have emerged in other disciplines catering to well defined areas of the market. In 2005 the much-loved but resource-sapping mixed-discipline estate sales that were once a weekly occurrence in the Freeman's basement numbered just four. Providing better service to a smaller number of clients buying and selling higher value objects is the impetus behind the new philosophy.

To that effect, Freeman's first 20th Century Design sale was launched in May 2000, boasting exceptional works by New Hope architect and designer George Nakashima

GEISTWEITE'S MASTERPIECE

"I would rather have this than all the frakturs I have ever owned," Westborough, Massachusetts, dealer David Wheatcroft told the *Maine Antique Digest* shortly after he bought it for a record $366,750 at Freeman's in 2004.

A masterpiece of this Pennsylvania German art form, the ink and watercolor document measuring 16 by 19in. (40 x 57cm) was inscribed with a verse from a *Hymn to the Nightingale* and illuminated in quasi medieval style with a deep border populated by stylized flora and enchanting fauna. To the back of the frame was a written history of the piece detailing its creation on June 5, 1801, for "Grampa Bower" by his day school teacher George Geistweite, whose signature could be found in the lower right hand corner.

The Reverend George Geistweite (c.1761-1831), licensed as a minister at the German Reformed Synod held in Reading in 1794, lived in Centre County, Pennsylvania, from circa 1792 to 1804. He preached in Shamokin, Selinsgrove, Sunbury, and occasionally to the populace of the embryonic settlement of New Berlin in the Buffalo Valley. In 1804 he was called to York where he would tend to his flock until he died in 1831. He is buried in the Reformed graveyard.

Geistweite's masterwork, deemed better than the only other work by his hand extant that survives in the Geesey collection at the Philadelphia Museum of Art, had last appeared on the market in wartime New York when it sold at the George Horace Lorimer sale at Parke-Bernet for $190. It had been bought by a Pennsylvania dealer who had sold it a few months later for $225 to the Freeman's consignor who, on April 24, 2004, was approaching her 96th birthday. The $366,750 paid by Wheatcroft was twice the previous auction record for a fraktur.

This exquisite George Nakashima coffee table made in English burl oak signed and dated November 1969 sold for $35, 050 at Freeman's 20th Century Design sale of November 16, 2003. It had been estimated at $8,000-$12,000.

INTO THE 20TH CENTURY

Exceptional works by two of Pennsylvania's modern masters.

Furniture from the New Hope workshop of architect and designer George Nakashima (1905-1990) has become as important to the history of Pennsylvania arts and crafts as German fraktur and rococo mahogany. Among furniture from the estate of Tom Takubo, a New York City jeweler and Nakashima patron, offered at a Freeman's 20th Century Design sale of November 17, 2002, was this superb cabinet of well-figured Persian walnut and rosewood signed in black marker and dated April 1984. The so-called Kornblut cabinet (the design is named after the client who first commissioned the form) had first been seen at 1808 Chestnut Street a year earlier when, alongside other Takubo consignments, it had been knocked down to a persistent and free-spending bidder at $21,850. The 'buyer' had then failed to pay his bill. However, reoffered only 12 months later as prices for Nakashima continued to strengthen, the cabinet sold sucessfully for $35,250. The following lot, George Nakashima's original sketch and his bill to

Tom Takubo for $1900, sold for an additional $705 to the same buyer. In total the 19 pieces of Nakashima furniture brought in $235,000.

The exquisite George Nakashima coffee table made in English burl oak signed and dated November 1969 sold for $35,050 at Freeman's 20th Century Design sale of November 16, 2003. It had been estimated at $8,000-12,000.

Setting a new financial benchmark for the Polish-born and trained metalworker Samuel Yellin, this early 20th century neo-Gothic writing table sold to a collector from Detroit for $57,500 on May 20, 2000. It was estimated at $15,000-25,000 as part of the largest and best-quality group of wares by the craft revivalist to come up for auction in several decades. The cache of work was once owned by the family of Samuel Goldberg, a craftsman and designer in Yellin's shop for many years. This wrought-iron and slate table, and a similar torchere sold for the same sum, was probably a gift to Goldberg in recognition of his loyalty.

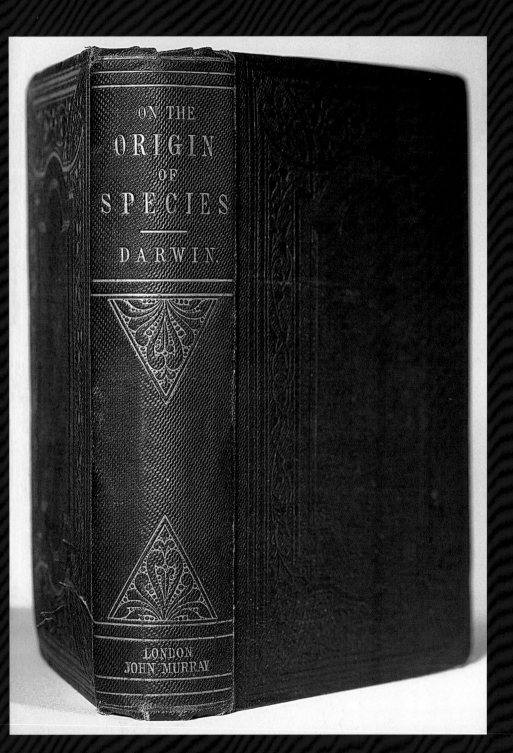

AN EVOLUTION IN BOOK PRICES

The most influential book in the history of natural science. Twelve phone bidders were among those pursuing this well-preserved first-edition copy of Charles Darwin's *On the Origin of Species*, which appeared at Freeman's sale of Rare Books & Ephemera on September 19, 2002. The controversial 1859 treatise linking evolution to natural selection was one of just 1,250 copies printed in the first edition and most of those had gone straight into institutional libraries. David Bloom, director of Freeman's rare book department, remembers meeting the consignor at one of the firm's regular appraisal days. She had brought in a selection of prints to be valued and, in passing, mentioned a few books at home that "might be worth something, including an 1859 Darwin." A brown paper bag containing an assortment of books arrived at Chestnut Street. "First out of the bag was a Darwin reprint," recalls Bloom, "but as soon as I saw the beautiful green cloth of the book underneath it, I knew she had a first edition." The price achieved was $86,250, among the highest ever paid at auction for this iconic title.

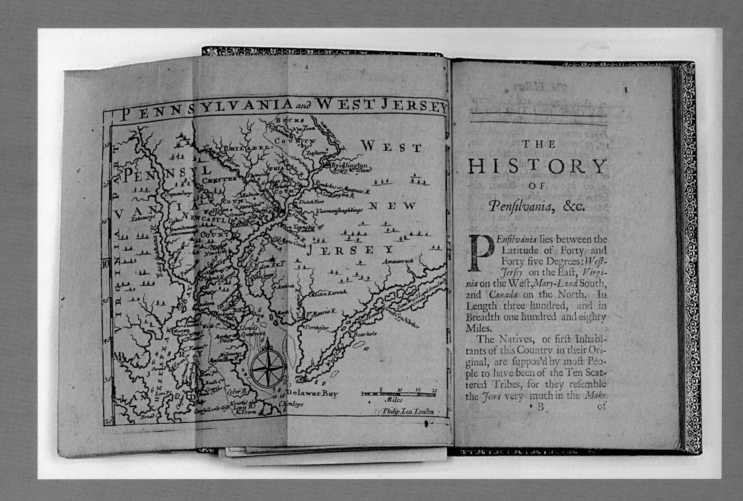

Hanna Dougher, a recent addition to the board at Freeman's.

and the Philadelphia craft revivalist Samuel Yellin, while a recent addition are sales devoted to couture – a market previously dominated by Doyle's in New York. The department, which had its first sale in December 2004, received some welcome publicity when a keen-eyed staff writer at the *Philadelphia Inquirer* discovered that an "anonymous" consignment of almost 550 lots of clothes, handbags and shoes were in fact from Main Line socialite Hilary Grinker Musser. Why was she selling her designer wardrobe at prices that sometimes represented a fraction of their original cost? Simple. She had dropped several dress sizes and no longer needed all those size twelves.

Respectful of company history and the melting pot that is America's East Coast, the British and European Furniture and Decorative Arts department has gathered pace under Lee Young, another Englishman and former employee of Sotheby's.

But here in the cradle of the nation's artistic heritage, clawing back a reputation as a repository for the very best in Pennsylvania craftsmanship is among the challenges for Freeman's Americana department as the company enters its third century. Its finest hour to date under the direction of Lynda Cain, was the discovery of a masterpiece of Pennsylvania German folk art, an ink and

watercolor fraktur created on 5 June 1801 for "Grampa Bower" by his day school teacher the Reverend George Geistweite. Bought in wartime New York for $190, it was sold in April, 2004 for $366,750 twice the previous auction record for a fraktur.

Exceptional results such as this have given life to the launch of the Pennsylvania sale in the bicentenary year, an event dedicated to the history and artifacts of the state to which the auction house is so intricately linked. Tying the venerable company to its locality while repositioning itself in a potentially lucrative national marketplace, it is an idea in which Addison "Battleship" Freeman himself would have taken great pride.

Key to the future of Freeman's is this renewal of the company's 200-year-old commitment to embrace and exploit change, to study the shifting market and take advantage of the opportunities that may come along. As competition for quality consignments becomes national; as the buying audience becomes global; as the market becomes ever polarized between the best and the rest, this commitment becomes ever more important.

If the thrust of the "five year plan" implemented in 1999 was to see the Freeman's brand survive and return to the

Lyon and Turnbull of Edinburgh, Scotland's oldest auction house. Between 2000 and 2005 Lyon and Turnbull in the Scottish capital and Freeman's in Philadelphia experienced parallel years of change and renaissance. As well as having a number of staff members in common, a transatlantic marketing alliance represents an important tool in today's international market.

LYON & TURNBULL

Staff at Lyon & Turnbull man the telephones during the company's landmark sale of metalwork by the Victorian industrial designer Dr. Christopher Dresser held in April 2005. The unrivaled collection formed by the London dealer Andrew McIntosh Patrick, was promoted extensively in the United States through Samuel T. Freeman & Co. Freeman's clients were among the buyers at the Edinburgh sale.

LYON & TURNBULL

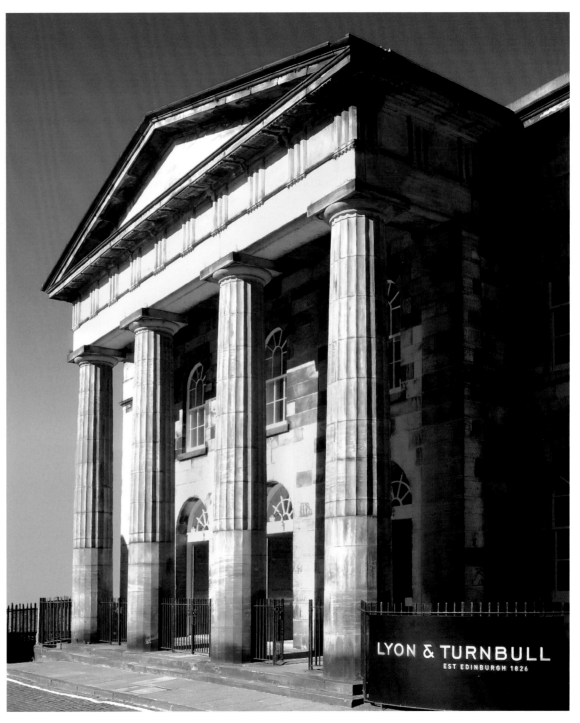

The first, the sixth and the seventh generation. Beau Freeman and his son Jonathan, relax in the company boardroom where a portrait of T.B. Freeman hangs. Jonathan Freeman, who joined the company in 1998, currently works in the Trust and Estates department. His elder brother Samuel T. Freeman III returned to the auction business in July 2005 to focus his efforts on the estate community in Berks, Lancaster and Chester Counties and the State of Delaware.

national and the international stage "then," says president Paul Roberts, "the challenge now is to turn America's oldest auction house into America's best auction house."

Accepting that challenge will involve further investment in America's oldest auction building, in satellite offices and in further department expertise. It has recently proved the catalyst to a widening of the share ownership to include key members of staff who now have a vested interest in the future excellence and success of the company. Representing another small milestone for a company, where for almost two centuries women had counted for nought in the boardroom, Hanna Dougher has recently become a member of the board.

But whatever its aspirations, the signs are that this will remain a family business. When Beau Freeman's portrait finally hangs in the gallery of former chairmen his wish is to see his share in the company established by his great-great-great-grandfather divided equally among his four children. He will find comfort in the knowledge that in the newly opened Trusts & Estates department there are two future vendue masters that carry his name – his sons Jonathan C. and Samuel T. Freeman III. And, with five grandchildren, an eighth generation already looms...

Freeman's - The Years at a Glance

1789

Tristram B. Freeman is working as a printer in Covent Garden region of London. He is bankrupt twice.

1795

Tristram B. Freeman arrives in Philadelphia.
Revolutionary War financier John Nicholson becomes a partner in Freeman & Co.

1797

Tristram B. Freeman employs engraver David Edwin in his printing business.

1797

The first American incarnation of Freeman & Co. folds. Unsold stock is sold in a series of bankruptcy auctions.

1800

Tristram B. Freeman commences retailing and wholesaling from 136 Market Street.

1801

Tristram B. Freeman becomes citizen of United States.

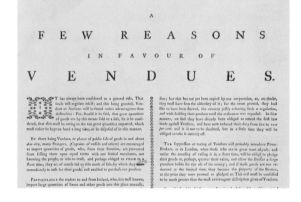

1805

November 12, Thomas McKean, Governor of the State of Pennsylvania, appoints Tristram B. Freeman to the office of auctioneer in Philadelphia.

1808

Freeman's sells estate of Capt. Stephen Decatur.

1809

Amidst an economic depression, Freeman loses his auctioneer's license and is succeeded to the position of auctioneer by Peter Kuhn.

1813

Tristram William Lockyer Freeman, first son and heir, joins Washington Guards under command of Colonel Lewis Rush during War of 1812.

1817

In the wake of the War of 1812 importer-friendly auction legislation is effected in New York. British manufacturers offload huge quantities of goods at advantageous tariffs.

1819

T.B. Freeman successfully reapplies for his auctioneer's license.

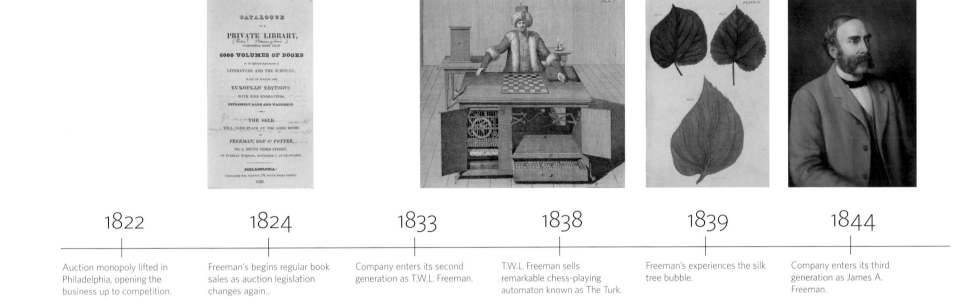

1822
Auction monopoly lifted in Philadelphia, opening the business up to competition.

1824
Freeman's begins regular book sales as auction legislation changes again..

1833
Company enters its second generation as T.W.L. Freeman.

1838
T.W.L. Freeman sells remarkable chess-playing automaton known as The Turk.

1839
Freeman's experiences the silk tree bubble.

1844
Company enters its third generation as James A. Freeman.

1854
269 portraits by Charles Willson Peale from the Philadelphia Museum are sold at auction by rival Philadelphia auctioneer Moses Thomas.

1858
Freeman's moves to 422 Walnut Street.

1876
Rival Philadelphia auctioneer M. Thomas & Son conducts auctions in the wake of Centennial Exposition.

1880s
Among many major real estate transactions, Freeman's sells Philadelphia's Post Office building for $425,000, a record for a single piece of real estate sold at auction.

1898
Company is renamed Samuel T. Freeman & Co.

1903
Edmund B. Brickley joins company from department store John Wanamaker, introducing new style and fine art to Freeman's galleries.

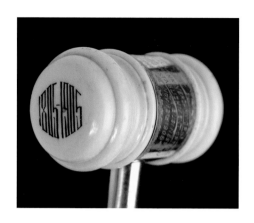

1905
Freeman's celebrates 100th anniversary.

1908
Freeman's acquires business of M. Thomas & Son and moves to 1519-21 Chestnut Street.

Stan V. Henkels, a specialist in historical autographs and portraiture, joins the firm.

1913
Freeman's sells autographs gathered by the late John Mills Hale. A two-page letter written by the Martyr Spy Nathan Hale sells for $1500.

1917
Freeman's sells collection of Pennsylvania Museum director Edwin Atlee Barber.

1919
Freeman's sells celebrated Gilbert Stuart full-length portrait of George Washington.

1920
Under Addison B. Freeman, Freeman's purchases the name and goodwill of J.E. Conant Co., Lowell, Massachusetts.

1922
Freeman's conducts the Nitro, West Virginia sale - the largest sale to date in the company's history.

1924
Auction house moves to its present location at 1808 Chestnut Street. First major sale includes Penn's Charter of Liberties.

1924
Freeman's sells U.S. Navy battleships.

1927
Freeman's sells remnants of Philadelphia's Sesquicentennial exhibition.

1937
Freeman's sells the mill village of Cheney Brothers for $831,215, the highest-grossing New England real estate auction on record.

1944
Freeman's sells the contents of the Stotesburys' Chestnut Hill mansion Whitemarsh Hall.

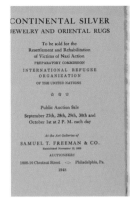

1947

Freeman's sells literary collection of Frederick Stanhope Peck including a First Folio of Mr. William Shakespeare's Comedies, Histories & Tragedies for $17,500.

1948

Freeman's sells Nazi war loot on behalf of the Preparatory Commission of the International Refugee Organization.

1948

Freeman's sells contents of Wootton, the Bryn Mawr estate of George W. Childs Drexel.

1955

The last of the great mill sales in the north is conducted by Freeman's for the textile conglomerate Lockwood Dutchess Inc. of Waterville, Maine.

1960

Addison B. Freeman Jr. dies in the Boston Harbor Air Crash.

1961

Addison B. Freeman announces the closure of the Boston office after 40 years of operation.

1962

Freeman's sells desk reputed to be Benjamin Franklin's to Independence National Park.

1967

Freeman's sells the Mary and Nelle Mullen collection of Impressionist paintings for $1m.

1969

Freeman's discovers Dunlap copy of Declaration of Independence at Leary's Book Store. It sells for $404,000.

1975

Freeman's sells a Thomas Affleck chest-on-chest to the Metropolitan Museum of Art for $92,000.

1976

James Buckley leaves Freeman's to start The Fine Arts Company of Philadelphia with another former Freeman's employee John H. Frisk.

1977

Christie's opens in Manhattan introducing American auctioneers to the buyer's premium. Freeman's introduces the premium in 1980.

1978

Sotheby's opens a walk-in branch office in Philadelphia at 1630 Locust Street.

1980

Freeman's celebrates 175 years in business with the sale of Edward Hicks' *Peaceable Kingdom* for $210,000.

1981

Under James Buckley and new partner Alexis C. Manice, The Fine Arts Company of Philadelphia moves to 2317 Chestnut, five blocks west of Freeman's.

1988

Freeman's merges with Fine Arts of Philadelphia and becomes Freeman\Fine Arts of Philadelphia, Inc..

1997

Freeman's sells Tucker porcelain urns for record $291,500.

1998

Freeman's reverts to name of Samuel T. Freeman & Co.

1999

Paul Roberts of Lyon & Turnbull in Edinburgh appointed president of Freeman's and implements rebuilding plan.

2000

The Scottish connection: marketing alliance formed with Scottish firm Lyon & Turnbull.

2001

Alasdair Nichol, head of fine art department, initiates the PAFA sales and student scholarship.

2003

The Old Mill, Washington Crossing, a winter landscape by Edward Willis Redfield sells for $691,250.

2004

Freeman's couture department holds its first sale.

Freeman's posts $4.82 million for single sale including Jacques Lipchitz bronze sold for $465,750.

2005

Freeman's celebrates 200th Anniversary with the first Pennsylvania sale.

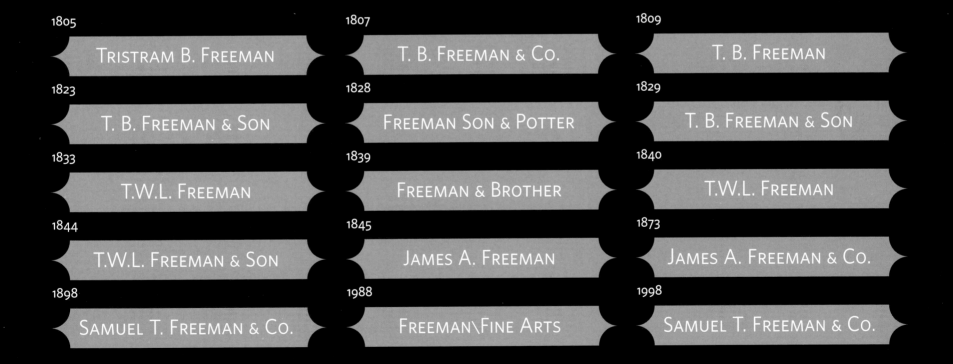

1805 Tristram B. Freeman	**1807** T. B. Freeman & Co.	**1809** T. B. Freeman
1823 T. B. Freeman & Son	**1828** Freeman Son & Potter	**1829** T. B. Freeman & Son
1833 T.W.L. Freeman	**1839** Freeman & Brother	**1840** T.W.L. Freeman
1844 T.W.L. Freeman & Son	**1845** James A. Freeman	**1873** James A. Freeman & Co.
1898 Samuel T. Freeman & Co.	**1988** Freeman\Fine Arts	**1998** Samuel T. Freeman & Co.

Freeman's – The Line of Succession

Tristram Bampfylde Freeman (circa 1767-1842)

Tristram William Lockyer Freeman (1790-1849)

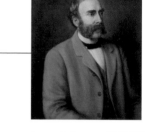

James A. Freeman (1821-1896)

Samuel Thomas Freeman (1839-1913)

George Clendenin Freeman (1875-1955)

John Miller Freeman (1910-1985)

Samuel Thomas Freeman III (b. 1960)

Samuel Miller Freeman (1879-1958)

Samuel Thomas Freeman II (1907-1954)

Samuel Miller Freeman II (b. 1936)

Addison Bampfylde Freeman (1885-1962)

Addison Bampfylde Freeman Jr (1920-1960)

Jonathan Collier Freeman (b. 1975)

Albert Lockyer Freeman (1893-1941)

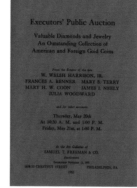

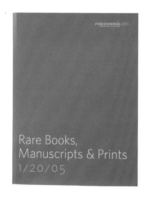

The changing faces of Freeman's catalogues. Today's stylish,
minimalist approach to catalogue cover design – part of the process
of redefining the company brand – contrasts sharply with the rich
use of color photography inside.

Online resources

Alexandria Archaeological Museum
Antiques Trade Gazette
Boston Museum of Fine Art
Connecticut History Online
Exeter Working Papers on British Book Trade History
Franklin Legacy Society
The Historical Society of Pennsylvania
The Library Company of Pennsylvania
Library of Congress
Maine Antique Digest
Manchester (Connecticut) Historical Society
National Gallery of Art
Pennsylvania Historical and Museum Commission
Philadelphia Architects and Buildings Project
State of Pennsylvania General Assembly
Stephen Decatur House Museum
Rhode Island USGenWeb Project
Rutgers University Library
Virtual American Biographies
White House Historical Association

Periodicals

Antiques Trade Gazette
Antique Week
The Aurora
City Bulletin
Columbian Advertiser
The Democratic Press
The Evening Bulletin
The Girard Letter, Volume VIII, November 1928
The Magazine Antiques, February 1974
Maine Antique Digest
The North American
The Philadelphia Inquirer
Philadelphia Mercantile Advertiser
The Philadelphia Public Ledger
Poulson's American Daily Advertiser
Pennsylvania Magazine of History & Biography, Volume XCVIII April 1974, Vol. 84, 1960
United States Gazette

Barber, Edwin A., *Tulip Ware of The Pennsylvanian-German Potters*, 1903
Barratt, Carrie Rebora & Miles, Ellen G., *Gilbert Stuart*, Metropolitan Museum of Art, New York, Yale University Press
Behrman, S.N., *Duveen*, The Little Bookroom, New York, 2003
Brewster, Sir David, *Letters on Natural Magic addressed to Sir Walter Scott*, 1842
Brown, Herbert C, et al, *Memoirs of Lodge No. 51*, F.&A.M of Pennsylvania
Brown, H. Glenn & Brown, Maude O., *A Directory of the Book-Arts and Book Trade in Philadelphia to 1820*, Bulletin of the New York Public Library, May 1949, March 1950
Burrowes, Thomas H., *Butler County in 1847*, State-Book of Pennsylvania, 1847
Crook, J. Mordaunt, *The Rise of the Nouveaux Riches*, John Murray, London, 1999
Deming Jr., John H., *Homes and the Eras in Which They Lived*, by Thompson Printing Co.
Dickson, Harold E., *John Wesley Jarvis, American Painter, 1780-1840 with a checklist of his works*, New York, The New-York Historical Society, 1949
Di Giacomo, Robert, *Missing Mansions of the Main Line*, University of Delaware Messenger
Dunlap, William, *History of the Rise and Progress of the Arts of Design in the United States*, 1834
Fanelli, Doris Devine, *History of the Portrait Collection, Independence National Park*, American Philosophical Society, Philadelphia, 2001
Hazard, *Hazard's United States Statistical Register*, 1839
Hillenbrand, Laura, *Seabiscuit: An American Legend*, Ballantine Publishing Group (Random House), 2001
Huss, Wayne A., *The Master Builders: A History of the Grand Lodge of Free and Accepted Masons of Pennsylvania. Volume II: Grand Master Biographies*, Philadelphia. The Grand Lodge, 1986
Jackson, Joseph, *Encyclopedia of Philadelphia*, Philadelphia, 193

Lacey, Robert, *Sotheby's – Bidding for Class*, Little Brown & Co., London, 1998
Leepson, Marc, *Saving Monticello*, The Free Press (Simon & Schuster), 2001
Leslie, Frank, *Frank Leslie's Historical Register of the United States Exposition, 1876*, Frank Leslie's Publishing House, New York, 1877
Lossing, Benson J., *Lossing's Pictorial Field Book of the War of 1812*, 1869
Mason, Christopher, *The Art of the Steal*, G.P. Putnam, New York, 2004
Mease, James, *The Picture of Philadelphia, giving an account of its origin, increase and improvements in arts, sciences manufactures, commerce and revenue ...*, Philadelphia, B.&T. Kite, 181
Maier, Phyllis, Lower Merion Historical Society, *Rich Men and Their Castles, Montgomery County: The Second Hundred Years*, chapter 109, Vol. II, 1983
Montgomery, Thomas Lynch (edited), *Pennsylvania Archives*, Sixth Series, Volume VIII, Harrisburg Publishing Co., Harrisburg
Morgan, John Hill & Fielding, Mantle, *The Life Portraits of Washington and their replicas*, Philadelphia, 1993
Nash, Gary B., First City, *Philadelphia and the Forging of Historical Memory*, University of Pennsylvania Press, Philadelphia, 2002
Mott, Frank Luther, *A History of American Magazines 1741-1850*, Harvard University Press, 1938
Myers, Albert Cook, *William Penn's First Charter To The People of Pennsylvania, April 25, 1682*, William Moland's Sons Inc., 1925
Pennsylvania Society for Promoting the Culture of the Mulberry, and the Raising of Silk Worms, Clark & Raser, Philadelphia, 1828
Prime, Alfred Coxe, *The Arts & Crafts in Philadelphia, Maryland and South Carolina 1786-1800, Series Two Gleanings from Newspapers ...*, The Walpole Society, 1932
Rottenberg, Dan, *The Man Who Made Wall Street: Anthony J. Drexel and the Rise of Modern Finance*, University of Pennsylvania Press, Philadelphia, 2002

Scarf, J. Thomas & Westcott, Thompson, *History of Philadelphia, 1609-1884*, L.H. Everts & Co., Philadelphia 1884

Secrest, Meryle, Duveen, *A Life in Art*, Alfred A. Knopf, New York, 2004

Standage, Tom, *The Turk – The Life and Times of the Famous Eighteenth-Century Chess-Playing Machine*, Walker & Co., 2002

Stauffers, David McNeely, *American Engravers Upon Copper and Steel, Sims Reed Ltd.*, The Grolier Club of the City of New York. 1907

Wainwright, Nicholas B., *Colonial Grandeur in Philadelphia, The House and Furniture of General John Cadwalader*, The Historical Society of Pennsylvania, 1964

Watson, John F. with revisions by Willis P. Hazard, *Annals of Philadelphia and Pennsylvania in the Olden Time; being a collection of memoirs, anecdotes and incidents of the city and its inhabitants ...*, Vol. I., J.M. Stoddart & Co., Philadelphia, 1877

Watson, John F. with revisions by Willis P. Hazard, *Annals of Philadelphia and Pennsylvania in the Olden Time; being a collection of memoirs, anecdotes and incidents of the city and its inhabitants ...*, Vol. III. J.M. Stoddart & Co., Philadelphia, 1879

Weigley, Russell F., edited, *Philadelphia – A 300-Year History*, W.W. Norton & Co., 1982

Wentz, William D., Nitro, *The World War I Boom Town: An Illustrated History of Nitro, West Virginia and The Land It Stands On*. Jalamap Publications, South Charleston, 1983.

Wood, Mary, edited, *Biographies*, Lower Merion Historical Society, 1988

Woolley, Robert, *Going Once: A Memoir of Art, Society and Charity*, Simon & Schuster, New York, 1995

Archival Resources

James Hamilton Papers, Historical Society of Pennsylvania, Letters in the hand of T.B. Freeman to James Hamilton, Carlisle, Pennsylvania

Unpublished biography of Tristram B. Freeman, Masonic Temple, Philadelphia

Unpublished memoirs of Arthur J. Sussel, Winterthur, Delaware, The Joseph Downs Collection of Manuscripts and Printed Ephemera

Freeman and Frost family papers, 1809-1929, Tristram William L. Freeman, auctioneer, is represented by business correspondence and a few miscellaneous business records, 1835-1848, Historical Society of Pennsylvania

John Nicholson Papers: General Correspondence Series: Nicholson from T. B. Freeman, 1795-1800, Division of Archives and Manuscripts (State Archives), Harrisburg

Tristram Freeman, Naturalization Record, 1801, U.S. District Court of Philadelphia, National Archives & Record Administration, Mid-Atlantic Region, Philadelphia

The act of December 2, 1793 entitled "An act laying duties on property sold at auction", Third Congress of the United States: at the first session, begun and held at the city of Philadelphia, in the state of Pennsylvania.

The act of December 9, 1783, entitled "An act to revive and continue in force the acts of Assembly regulating sales by public auction, and for other purposes therein mentioned.

The act of April 2, 1822, entitled "An act relating to auctions and auctioneers.

The act of March 29, 1824, entitled "A further supplement to the several acts of the General Assembly, respecting auctions and auctioneers.

The act of April 1, 1826, entitled "An act relating to auctions."

The act of April 7, 1832, entitled "An act regulating auctions in the city of Lancaster, and other towns in this commonwealth."

The act of April 6, 1833, entitled "A supplement to the act regulating Auctions in the city of Lancaster, and other towns of this commonwealth, passed on the seventh day of April, eighteen hundred and thirty-two."

The act of April 9, 1859, entitled "An act to modify the existing Auction Laws of the Commonwealth, and to provide more effectually for the Collection of the State Tax or Duty on Auction Sales, in the city of Philadelphia and county of Allegheny."

The act of April 12, 1859, entitled "An act to Restrict Sales by Auction in the counties of Northampton, Dauphin and Lehigh.

The act of April 27, 1864, entitled "A supplement to an act to modify the existing auction laws of this Commonwealth, and to provide more effectually for the collection of the state tax, or duty, on auction sales, in the city of Philadelphia, and the county of Allegheny, passed the ninth day of April, eighteen hundred and fifty-nine."

The act of April 14, 1863, entitled "A further supplement to an act supplementary to the acts relating to hawkers and peddlers, and regulating auctions in the County of Schuylkill.

The act of March 25, 1873, entitled "An act relating to auctioneers in the city of Philadelphia."